TRY AGAIN

ENTERING INTO EVERYTHING YOU MISSED THE FIRST TIME

BOB SEE

WESTBOW
PRESS®
A DIVISION OF THOMAS NELSON
& ZONDERVAN

WestBow Press books may be ordered through booksellers or by contacting:

WestBow Press
A Division of Thomas Nelson & Zondervan
1663 Liberty Drive
Bloomington, IN 47403
www.westbowpress.com
844-714-3454

ISBN: 979-8-3850-3474-1 (sc)
ISBN: 979-8-3850-3475-8 (e)

Library of Congress Control Number: 2024920795

Print information available on the last page.

WestBow Press rev. date: 11/18/2024

CONTENTS

DEDICATION

To all the strays and skeptics, the disappointed and disinterested, the wounded and disillusioned, the spiritually stuck and trapped, and the rebels and orphans who once heard His voice—may you have ears to hear again.

And to all the moms, dads, grandparents, friends, family, spouses, and siblings who continue to hope and pray that their friends and loved ones will have a fresh experience of God's love—keep fighting for them as we *"should always pray and never give up"* (Luke 18:1).

May the party committee in Heaven be forced to work overtime because of all the celebrations for those returning to the Father!

ACKNOWLEDGMENTS

I had a lot of help in writing this book:

Thank you to my sister Pat Polley and my friend Janel Janes. They encouraged me along the way while making suggestions on grammar and content. I'm glad it was your voices speaking into this project.

A special thank you to my friend Ann Bare who spent many hours bringing her professional editorial skill to the manuscript. You made me sound way better than I am.

While Ann, Pat, and Janel helped me with grammar and content, I take responsibility for any mistakes in the manuscript. They are 100% mine.

Thank you to all my friends and family who allowed me to share their stories. I'm certain what you wrote will have more impact on readers than the stuff I wrote.

In writing this book, I drew from the friendships and experiences I've been privileged to have over the years. Thank you to my friends at St. Mark Lutheran Church, Lutheran Bible Institute, LIFE Ministries, Seattle Pacific University, New Life Christian Church, Heaven's View Christian Fellowship, Oasis Church, and Agape School of Supernatural Ministry. Just thinking of these places and people fills my heart with warm memories.

I have deep gratitude for Steve Baertschi and his parents, Pastor Walter and Fran Baertschi. If not for them, I don't know where I'd be today. They opened the door for me that changed everything.

I also have deep love and gratitude for Bill and Joan Hartseil. They paid a price in launching and leading the Jesus Barn ministry in the late 1960s and '70s. Though misunderstood and opposed by many, their faithfulness helped hundreds like me learn to be disciples of Jesus.

Most of all, thank you to my dear wife, Harriet, whose encouragement helped me complete this book. ("When are you gonna get that thing done?!") She was present for most of the personal stories recorded here, and she helped me correctly remember details so I could relate accounts accurately. We have over forty years of marriage, and I am thankful for her every day. With her, every year gets better and better.

INTRODUCTION

"Return to the Lord your God, for He is gracious and compassionate, slow to anger and abounding in love..." (Joel 2:13)

"I will arise and return to my Father." (Luke 15:18)

The Bible from cover to cover is the story of God reaching out to people who have walked away from Him. In the opening pages, we find God calling out to Adam and Eve after they had run away from Him. At the close of the Bible, God's Spirit invites everyone to turn around and "Come and receive!" God is passionate about restoring broken relationships. If you find yourself separated from Him, I guarantee you are on His heart and He is calling to you: *"'Return to me,' declares the Lord Almighty, 'and I will return to you'"* (Zechariah 1:3).

This book is written for people who once trusted in Jesus Christ but now no longer follow Him. At one time He was important to you, and you intended to faithfully follow Him. But now those thoughts are behind you. Maybe you look back and think of those early experiences with Jesus as simply a phase you went through. Now you've moved on to a different life, with different priorities, different perspectives, and maybe different gods. Perhaps you had a personal tragedy in which you felt God had let you down, so you stopped trusting Him. Maybe you walked away from God because you experienced pain, rejection, or conflict at church. Or perhaps you heard ideas against Christianity at your university or college, and you were convinced to abandon your faith. Or maybe it was as simple as losing interest and drifting away.

Even if your earlier experiences with Him are only a distant memory, understand this: God never forgets a prayer, especially one made by a child. Maybe you've forgotten Him, but He has never forgotten you. You only need to take one step toward Him, and He will cover the rest of the distance, coming to you.

This book is divided into three sections. The first is intended to help you return to the Father, giving you some guidance for that journey. The next section might be the most important one as it addresses obstacles that can prevent you from moving forward spiritually. The chapters in this section can lead you into healing, freedom, and restoration. The third section summarizes what God had always intended for you, when you first came to Him earlier in your life. Many people have not walked away from God as much as have walked away from bad theology and bad church experiences. This third section compiles truths about what God had in mind for you when He originally called you to Himself.

Some of you reading this book are long-time disciples of Jesus. As a result, you might find the message and advice written here as being too basic. You may wish many of the topics covered were developed in greater detail, but please keep in mind I'm not writing to answer concerns and questions of people who are actively walking with God. I'm writing to the strays, the wounded, the disillusioned, and the disappointed who once followed Him. My goal is to point them back to their Heavenly Father. My writing ain't Shakespeare, but hopefully the stories, explanations, examples, and encouragements will help the reader turn back toward God.

I hope this book will be like a mountain guide for you. When climbing a high mountain, my buddies and I can simply buy a map of the mountain and try to navigate the way to the summit on our own. Instead, we hire a professional guide because it is far better to be led by a living person who knows the route and knows the challenges we will face. That is why throughout this book you will be guided into encounters with God (called Activations) so that you are experiencing Him and hearing from Him directly. You'll find these Activations located at the end of each chapter. Also, it will be beneficial to carefully read the Bible verses written at the beginning of every chapter, as these express core Scriptural truth about that chapter's topic.

Christianity is supposed to be a relationship, not a religion, meaning you are encountering a Person Who will speak to you and interact with you. My prayer is that you experience Him and that this book will serve as a guide on your journey back to the Father, leading you into the life you missed the first time.

"So he got up and went to his father. But while he was still a long way off, his father saw him and was filled with compassion for him; he ran to his son, threw his arms around him and kissed him." (Luke 15:20)

SECTION I
TURNING AROUND

CHAPTER 1

RETURNING TO THE FATHER

"This is what the LORD Almighty says: 'Return to Me,' declares the LORD Almighty, 'and I will return to you,' says the LORD Almighty." (Zechariah 1:3)

"I will give them a heart to know Me, that I am the LORD. They will be My people, and I will be their God, for they will return to Me with all their heart." (Jeremiah 24:7)

"Come near to God and He will come near to you." (James 4:8)

"I will set out and go back to my father." (Luke 15:18)

RYAN'S STORY

Ryan and Mandy Foster are two of my closest friends. Along with my wife, Harriet, we lead Agape School of Supernatural Ministry in Peoria, Illinois. Ryan also founded Budded Mattah, a ministry that creates urban gardens in distressed neighborhoods. Ryan and Mandy run various businesses and homeschool their four kids. They are an amazing family. But you would have never predicted the life they lead today if you had known them a few years back. Here's Ryan's story:

I grew up in the church. Every time the doors to the church were open, my family was there. My mom didn't care what the church was doing, we would attend. That chafed me as I got older. I wanted to make my own choices, so much so that after leaving high school, I chose to attend the state university farthest away from Peoria. Once in college, I felt free to spread my wings. I became a new man. In fact, I became three different people. I was a good church-going young man when I was home with my folks. At school I was an attentive student who never missed a class. But I also had become a serious party man. My mom, knowing me better than I wanted to admit, contacted our pastor's son who lived near the university. She made him bring me to church during my freshman year. The church was small but spiritually powerful, and the pastor had a prophetic gifting. She called me to the front of the church and publicly prophesied over my future (I reeked of alcohol that first time).

After my freshman year, my pastor's son moved away from the town, and I didn't return to the church. But during my undergrad years, it seemed like every time I was about to do something especially stupid, the pastor randomly appeared. One time she saw me walking the streets wearing a helmet with two beers on it and a straw going into my mouth. At another time I had a fifth of Goldschlager Schnapps, which I was drinking while screaming, "I found gold!" Still another time I was in the grocery store buying five hundred red solo cups and disposable shot glasses. She just stared at me with knowing eyes, and I dropped my head.

As I pursued the college party scene, my reputation and popularity at the university grew (which led to constantly evading the police). In my senior year I moved with three other guys into a house with a full basement and a big backyard. That year, I started a party house. These were very large parties, complete with two bars, professional DJs, bouncers, sponsors, and 8-11 kegs on average. Those parties paid our house bills for the school year. We gained a reputation on campus as I saw many basketball and football team recruits come through my doors, and I showed them a good time. Birthday parties were grand events with people traveling from colleges all over the state to attend. When my senior year ended, I was not ready to leave my college lifestyle as "big man on campus" so I entered graduate school. Grad school was a different animal from undergrad, but we continued holding the monthly parties that paid our bills. At this point I did not go to church unless I was back home with my parents. Running the most popular party house in our college town was very lucrative, and I tended to have a great deal of money in my pockets when I was out around the town.

One night while at a bar I heard the last call, and I quickly slammed a $100 bill on the bar and said, "Line up shots." I took five or six of them myself and passed the rest out to the people all around. I then walked out to my Monte Carlo SS and sped out, driving the wrong way on a one-way street. Police promptly pulled me over; being who I was and previously getting away with so much illegal activity over the years, I was arrogant and acted smart toward the police officer. Then the handcuffs went on, I was thrown into the police car, and my car was impounded. Still thinking I was untouchable, I laughed as I called my girlfriend, Mandy, to bail me out of jail, directing her to my money stash. The next morning it all hit me: I had a ticket for a DUI. I could lose my graduate assistantship (which paid my tuition and stipend every month). I could lose my license. It felt like I could lose everything. I told Mandy I had to go to church. I knew she wouldn't want to go with me because in the past she had vehemently argued against Christianity. But to my great surprise, she said she wanted to come too.

I knew I needed to apologize for the way I treated my booking officer, so we dropped off cookies and an apology card at the police station on our way to church. At the church service, I sat there in my alcoholic stench as the pastor preached. When Pastor Holder gave an altar call to surrender your life to Jesus, I got up to go to the front. At this point Mandy was bawling in the pew; though we came to church because I needed to get right with God, she was the one getting all the attention. I thought she was just tagging along, but God had her in His sights. The pastor called her out by name to come forward. All I could think was: I'm desperate for God's help, and now you are taking all the ministry attention! *After the service, the pastor asked to talk with Mandy privately. This was a new experience for her, so I told her to listen to everything the pastor said because it would be important.*

After church that day we were both in a contemplative mood. I knew God was going to take care of everything. Mandy and I both decided to fully turn our lives over to Christ that day. We did a complete 180 in our relationship. I hired a lawyer, and he took care of the DUI, requiring me to take a class and be on probation. Some things were a slow change. As much as I was ready to shut it down, I couldn't just end the parties. My roommates depended on them to pay the bills, but my role within them changed. Mandy and I agreed to practice celibacy until marriage. From that moment, we started attending the church. I first attended as a drunk college freshman, but now I was attending willingly.

Ryan found out that even if we try to keep God out of our lives, His love still pursues us. He is the God Who says, *"I have loved you with an everlasting love; I have drawn you with unfailing kindness"* (Jeremiah 31:3). And, as in Ryan's case, often our behavior brings us to a crisis moment, a turning point in which we must decide which way we will continue to live our life.

"I have set before you life and death, blessings and curses. Now choose life, so that you and your children may live and that you may love the Lord your God, listen to his voice, and hold fast to him. For the Lord is your life..." (Deuteronomy 30:19-20).

MANDY'S STORY

I also grew up in a church. I was devout, but I focused on the religious rules and wasn't really experiencing a relationship with God. In my teen years, though, I saw people who were leaders at the church among my age group breaking all the rules. I discovered they were holding drinking parties, and boyfriends and girlfriends were sleeping over with their parents' approval. Disillusioned with church, I began lying to my parents about attending services. There were several churches of that denomination in the area so I would walk into a service, grab a program, and leave, able to prove to my parents I'd gone to church. My lifestyle in the dark became drinking, smoking, and promiscuity.

In college I was agnostic. I didn't deny God existed; I just wanted nothing to do with Him. I would be quick to argue with dorm buddies about God and religion. It was during this time I met Ryan. He was leading a wild college life, and we started dating. Ryan was leading a double life, the fun college boy at the university and the good church-going guy at home, but deep down his moral compass was set to true north. In spite of his college behavior, he didn't lie or cheat, and girls knew he was safe, not taking advantage of them.

I started to meet Christians in class. One girl in particular was very open and honest. She was my age, and I could ask her the most personal questions and she would answer me honestly, even if it meant she wasn't perfect by the Christian standards I knew from my childhood church. I started to wonder if maybe all Christians weren't as hypocritical as I thought.

Then one night in the fall semester of 2007, an event occurred which caused my boyfriend to want to go to church. Since I had previously told Ryan he could take his Bible and shove it, he did not expect me to attend church with him but said it was something he needed to do. Much to his surprise, I agreed to go with him.

When we went into that small church, it was a whole new world. For the first time in my life, I was in the minority (it was an African American church). I was in awe as people spoke in tongues, women ran up the aisles during the worship, and people fell to the floor "slain in the spirit." It was a world I didn't know existed. And the entire service I was a giant snotty, crying mess while also wondering what was happening. (Now I recognize it was the Holy Spirit convicting me). At the end of the service, they did an altar call, inviting people to walk up to the altar to give their lives to Christ and receive prayer. Ryan wanted to respond and stepped into the aisle to go to the front, but then the pastor called me by my name. I was unknown to her; we had never been introduced, but she called me by my name, inviting me to come forward. I walked to the front; I don't remember what they all prayed, but she did tell me she wanted to talk to me after service in the side room. As I got back to

5

the pew, Ryan leaned over and said, "Remember everything she says to you. It's important."

So I nervously went into that side room to meet with the pastor. She told me, "God loves you. He misses you. He wants you to stop doing what you've been doing and come back home." I shook my head yes, she hugged me, and I walked out. Now, that was my first encounter with a prophetic person, so I thought she knew ALL my dirty laundry.

Ryan and I went out to dinner and just thought over what had happened. That night or the next, I can't remember which, I looked at Ryan and told him I didn't want to have sex anymore. I was nervous because I also held the false belief that if you weren't having sex, you wouldn't keep the man. He agreed way too easily, which also threw me. Then he told me if I could succeed in this endeavor, he would marry me...challenge accepted. And that's the week I did a 180 in my beliefs; life as I knew it started to change.

We started attending that church every Sunday. For the first two months, I cried through the bulk of the service for no apparent reason. I asked my mom for a study Bible and a purity ring. She knew I was not a virgin and questioned me. I told her I wanted her to hold me accountable—that if I ever had sex again before marriage, I would give the ring back. The women in the church took me under their wing and started teaching me things. I went to Bible studies and spent a lot of time praying and asking Ryan questions. We made new, different choices, and some of my friends said I wasn't fun anymore. But others accepted that I was a little different but still me. I was 21 at the time of my conversion. Ryan and I continued to date and grow. When I was 25, we got married. I still have that purity ring in my jewelry box that I wore until my wedding day.

Ryan's and Mandy's stories reveal a God Who *"is patient with us, not wanting anyone to perish but for everyone to come to repentance"* (2 Peter 2:9). No matter who you are or what you've done, He loves you and wants you to return to Him. He doesn't give up on you.

Where are you in this? Maybe when you were younger, your parents made you attend church so you went under protest, and you were happy to leave it behind as you grew older. Maybe you were active in a Sunday school or youth group, but then you went away to college and became disillusioned with the Christian faith. Maybe you were mistreated by other believers and that drove you away. Or perhaps you just lost interest and gradually strayed away from any active pursuit of your faith. Possibly you found Christianity too powerless or too boring or too narrow or too judgmental or too hypocritical or too _____ (you fill in the blank). So, you left to enjoy freedom from God and to explore other ideas. And even though you had made some type of commitment to Jesus earlier, now you are separated and distant from Him. However, regardless of how you have arrived at your current position, He is calling you to return.

THE FATHER IS CALLING YOU HOME

In other religions, man is seeking God, but in Christianity God seeks man. Jesus said, *"I came to seek and save the lost"* (Luke 19:10). The Bible is the story of God calling people back to Himself, longing for their return. Probably the best-known example of this is the story of the prodigal son in Luke 15. A son wanted to leave his home and live his own life so he urged his father to give him a share of his inheritance now (in effect saying, "I wish you were already dead so I could access your money now"). The father grants his request, and the son heads to a far city and squanders the money in wild indulgence. Then troubles come, and the son finds himself penniless and alone. Broken and ashamed, he stumbles home, where *"his father saw him and was filled with compassion for him; he ran to his son, threw his arms around him and kissed him"* (Luke 15:20), and he was restored to his family. Jesus told this story to show us how God feels about us and how He wants us to return to Him. No matter what you've done, He says, "Come home, where you are loved."

7

ABANDONING GOD

Sometimes it's disappointment with God that causes people to walk away from Him. In the Bible, 1 Samuel 14 records a dismal time in the history of Israel. The Philistine nation had gained control over the Jewish nation and was oppressing the people, taking their wealth and property, and controlling their lives. This led many people to question, "Where is God? If He really exists, why doesn't He help us? Why doesn't He do something?" People were so disillusioned with their faith that many abandoned it completely and adopted a new identity. They deconstructed their beliefs and embraced a different culture. They abandoned Judaism and adopted a new identity as Philistines, living by Philistine values, practices, and lifestyle.

Others did not go that far, but they had become so disappointed with God that they dropped out. They didn't abandon their identity as Jews, but they lowered their expectations and stopped participating in worship services. They lived life as if God didn't exist.

But in Chapter 14 we find God intervening and giving a tiny Jewish army a miraculous victory over the Philistines. The impact of seeing God at work turned people around:

"Those Jews who had previously been with the Philistines and had gone up with them to their camp [i.e., had previously rejected the Jewish faith] *went over to the Israelites… When all the Israelites who had hidden in the hill country of Ephraim* [i.e., were no longer openly practicing their faith] *heard that the Philistines were on the run, they joined the battle in hot pursuit."* (1 Samuel 14:21-22)

Both groups of people returned to their true identity.

We live at a time when many people have abandoned the Biblical beliefs they previously held. Others have gone into hiding; they still hold Christian beliefs but have little outward expression of those beliefs. Perhaps to please the people around them they choose to hide their faith. Yet, like the people in 1 Samuel 14, God still works miracles that compel people to openly return to Him. One of the purposes of this book is to help people re-experience God's love, power, and truth in such a manner as to be compelled to return to Jesus.

FINDING YOUR TRUE IDENTITY

A second purpose of this book is to assist you in entering into all the Father has for you. I believe many people who walk away from Christian faith aren't rejecting Jesus but are rejecting a dysfunctional or false or incomplete expression of Christianity. They have never entered into the identity and destiny that their loving Father originally had for them.

"'For I know the plans that I have for you,' declares the Lord, 'plans for welfare and not for calamity, to give you a future and a hope. Then you will call upon Me and come and pray to Me, and I will listen to you. You will seek Me and find Me when you search for Me with all your heart.'" (Jeremiah 29:11-13)

"...To Him who loves us and has freed us from our sins by His blood, and has made us to be a kingdom and priests to serve His God and Father..." (Revelation 1:5-6)

The most important question in life is: Who is God? The second-most important question is: Who does God say I am? If God is our Creator, then He knows the identity, purpose, and destiny for which He created us. And as the two verses above show, He sees us as royalty with an incredible purpose and destiny for our lives.

While writing this book, I had a dream in which I had found someone's wallet, and I searched for the person who had lost it. When

I found the person, I slipped extra money into the wallet, greatly increasing the amount within, and then returned the wallet to the rightful owner. When I awoke, the Lord showed me the dream was about this book. Jesus wants to restore lost identity to people. Wallets contain our identity (driver's license, photo ID, social security card, bank cards, etc.). Losing your wallet represents losing your true identity. God is calling you back to Himself because He wants to restore you to who He truly made you to be and to free you from the false identity you try to maintain. Furthermore, He will greatly increase your worth and value above what it was before, as you enter into everything He originally intended for you (hence, the action of adding cash to the wallet in the dream).

That's what this book can do for you. You can start over and begin to walk in the identity God has always had for you. You can become the person you were created to be.

ACTIVATION

A. Turning to God
I encourage you now to turn directly to God and take a step toward Him. You might doubt if He exists. Maybe you haven't truly prayed in years. Maybe you have zero confidence that God will respond to you. But this moment is just between you and Him. So let me suggest an exercise:

1. Get alone someplace where you won't feel self-conscious and can even speak out loud.
2. Soften your heart to receive. In other words, position yourself to hear, for the moment laying aside any resistance, fear, resentment, or doubts toward God. Believe this verse: *"The Lord is near to all who call on Him, to all who call on Him in truth"* (Psalms 145:18), and thus raise your expectation that God might actually respond to you.

3. God says, *"If you seek Me with all your heart, you will find Me."* So pray: Jesus, if You are there, the best I know how I'm seeking You and I'm asking (try asking God the following):

— What are You saying to me, Jesus?

— What do You think of me, Jesus?

Just linger and listen. Pay attention to what you hear in your heart. Don't assume any words you hear are simply your imagination. Maybe you'll sense a yearning to return to Him and to open your life up to Him again. Don't discount any physical sensations of warmth, tingling, or other feelings, as these can indicate God drawing near to you. Your trust isn't in the feelings but in the promises of Scriptures. However, you can often sense when He does draw near. We are seeking a relationship with a warm, loving, living Savior, not just a rational ascent to truth!

B. Read the Scriptures again

Reread the Bible verses at the start of this chapter. Ask Jesus what He is saying to you in these verses and how He wants you to respond.

C. Experiencing resistance for choosing Jesus

After walking away from the Christian faith, some of you embraced different religions or other forms of spirituality, such as Wicca. If so, you might experience spiritual opposition and turmoil when you begin to move toward the Jesus of the Bible. The Bible says there is more than one Jesus, as men recreate him to fit manmade religions, but these are not the true Jesus from the Scriptures (see 2 Corinthians 11:3-4). There are spiritual forces that will not let go of you easily. They will resist you when you pursue the Jesus of scripture. This resistance might come as distracting thoughts, sudden desires to stop reading, or physical feelings of nausea. In some cases you might hear inner voices warning you or threatening you to stop. Colossians 1:13-20 expresses the power, authority, and deity of the true Jesus, the Son of God. I suggest you read this out loud and declare it as truth:

"For He has rescued us from the dominion of darkness and brought us into the kingdom of the Son He loves, in whom we have redemption, the forgiveness of sins.
The Son is the image of the invisible God,
the firstborn over all creation.
For in Him all things were created:
things in heaven and on earth, visible and invisible,
whether thrones or powers or rulers or authorities;
all things have been created through him and for him.
He is before all things, and in Him all things hold together.
And He is the head of the body, the church;
He is the beginning and the firstborn from among the dead, so that in everything He might have the supremacy.
For God was pleased to have all His fullness dwell in Him, and through Him to reconcile to Himself all things, whether things on earth or things in heaven, by making peace through His blood, shed on the cross."

Declare aloud: "This is the Jesus I am seeking!" and, as you pray, focus on Jesus as He is portrayed in this passage. Ask Him to lead you into the truth and correct any lies you've believed about Him. Every book of the New Testament contains warnings against false teaching and spiritual deception. Satan comes as an angel of light to deceive you in your sincere desire to know truth. Turn to the Jesus of the Bible, Who is the way, the truth, and the life (John 14:6). He is the One Who loved you and gave Himself for you.

D. Wounded by believers

Some people have rejected Jesus because of bad experiences with religious people. But Jesus also had bad experiences with religious people. Lots of them. Just open the New Testament gospels to any page, and you'll soon find conflict between Jesus and religious people. In fact, religious people killed Him. So, if religious people

12

have hurt you, disappointed you, or made you mad, then know you have an ally in Jesus. Instead of rejecting Jesus, turn to Him and ask Him to help you out of the pain from those experiences (We will address matters such as these in Section Two).

Perhaps you are not ready to make any steps toward the Lord. If so, just continue reading and positioning your heart to be receptive to whatever He might say to you. Continue to ask the Lord to speak to you and reveal Himself to you.

CHAPTER 2

REPENTANCE

"Repent, then, and turn to God, so that your sins may be wiped out, that times of refreshing may come from the Lord." (Acts 3:19)

"The Lord is not slow in keeping His promise, as some understand slowness. Instead He is patient with you, not wanting anyone to perish, but everyone to come to repentance." (2 Peter 3:9)

"Return to the Lord your God, for He is gracious and compassionate, slow to anger and abounding in love…" (Joel 2:13)

THE DOOR OF REPENTANCE

If you want to restore your relationship with God, you must go through the door of repentance. Repentance is a change of direction. You've been walking away from God, but now you turn and walk toward Him. You change direction by turning away from things in your life that have replaced God, and you turn back toward Him.

Jesus preached repentance: *"From that time on Jesus began to preach, 'Repent, for the kingdom of heaven has come near.'"* (Matthew 4:17)

So did Peter: *"Peter replied, 'Repent and be baptized, every one of you, in the name of Jesus Christ for the forgiveness of your sins…'"* (Acts 2:38)

Paul also preached repentance: *"I preached that they should repent and turn to God and demonstrate their repentance by their deeds."* (Acts 26:17-18)

Repentance is the response God requires from us. When the prodigal son turned and walked home to his father, he was repenting. In repentance, you change direction and move toward the life God has for you. Repentance does not begin with self-hatred or self-condemnation, but it begins by seeing the truth of who you are and who you aren't.

BRYAN'S STORY

My friend Bryan Blanch's story is about repentance. Though he grew up attending church, in high school he chose to walk away from God. This created a vacuum that he tried to fill with other gods, goals, and values. Here's Bryan's story:

I grew up in church—Sunday morning, Sunday night, Wednesday night, and sometimes Friday night; I did that until I was about 16 years old. I just didn't feel that into church. I didn't have that many friends in church at the time. My brother was four years older, and he had a big youth group. While I had friends at school or in the neighborhood, I just didn't feel that connected at church.

When I was about 16, cars, girls, and peer pressure all made me feel I could not be cool by going to church. So I said to my mom, "I'm not going." She initially put up a fight, insisting I go, but then she allowed me to step back while continuing to pray for me. (She later said she saw our relationship was more important than anything, and she was not going to let the enemy drive a wedge between us.)

My behavior was pretty decent through high school, but by the time I left school and got into the world, I really took a nosedive in life. I got involved in a lot of bad stuff. I got really heavily involved with drugs (many drugs) and alcohol.

BOB SEE

I was in a lot of gangs, and we did things and said things and hated a lot of people. I had nothing to do with following the Lord. At the time I didn't hate God, but I wanted nothing to do with religion. I was against going to church and felt like I had been brainwashed. Other people would say about church, "You're being brainwashed; that's just brainwash material," and I felt that and allowed those thoughts to creep in and keep me away from the Bible.

As I got into my twenties, I began playing music as a drummer, and that had a powerful effect on me. The music I listened to encouraged the drugs, alcohol, and gang activity in my life. I've been in some dark places; I've been up at 4 a.m. with no sleep for two or three days, out of my mind hallucinating because I was tired, on drugs, not knowing what was going on. I can remember being on the southside of town at three in the morning in a drug house with a pocket full of cash, whacked out of my mind, trying to figure out what I was doing. Why was I here? I remember being scared for my life in those places, but the drugs had me. The addiction had me. (Now that I'm free from all that, it's easy for me to talk with high schoolers or those in addictions because I understand it. I was there, and I know the feeling.)

I hurt a lot of people. I was wrong to girls in my life and wrong to my parents. I lost a lot of friends. I got into bands; nothing was good in my life at that time. It was all about me. I never reached the point of saying, "I'll follow satan"; I just wasn't living for God. I just freely chose to live my life that way.

Over the course of about ten years, I met my wife, got married, and we had three kids. She began to say she wanted to start going to church. I was fine with that because I had grown up in church; in the back of my mind, I thought I wanted my kids to know church. But I personally didn't want to go, and on Sunday mornings I was usually out of it. I started to go with them off and on for some time. I remember the times I was in church as a musician, God began to speak to me in a language I could understand. There were times during worship when the music was playing, I would feel the presence of God; I would stand there in worship and just cry. And I would wonder: What is this?! Where's this coming from? What do I do with this?

This continued for about a year, which led me to thinking about my life. In the early stages of being with my wife, there was a lot of turmoil in our house, which mostly was my fault with the way I was living. I thank God that she never left me. But I knew I wasn't being the husband I should be. I knew I wasn't being the father I needed to be. I knew I was wrong in the things I was doing. I was sick often because of drugs and no sleep. And I just got tired of this. I was in bands, and on weekends we'd play and stay up all night, and the next morning I'd come crawling into bed, out of my mind; at some point I knew this wasn't working.

In church, God was talking to me, saying, "You need to make up your mind." I tried to focus on Him, but I found when I tried to do right, the enemy was right there trying to stop me. The minute I started walking toward God, the enemy had his hand on me, trying to pull me back. During the week, I was okay, but by Friday night I was ready to go out and party. I was able to hold down a job, but sometimes I had to call in on Mondays because I was still passed out, needing a day to recover. So, I was looking at God but still living for the world, listening to God, but with the enemy pulling me back. That went on for a year and a half, a year and a half of a battle between good and evil. I was trying to find God, but the devil kept holding on to me.

Finally, one Friday night I got off work and I was drinking at home then decided to go downtown. But I thought, "I don't want to do this"; I was crying and called out, "God, if you don't want me to do this, then do something! Because I'm going if you don't act! I don't want to be this way! I'm talking to you all the time. I'm in church, so if you don't want me to do this, then stop me!"

That night it was raining hard, and I began to drive toward town. In the back of my mind, I was thinking, "I don't want to do this"; I was driving 65 mph in a hard rain when I hit a patch of water. I began to hydroplane, and I spun around until my car was facing the other direction. I knew God was right there. I had asked Him to do something 'cause I was tired of living that way, and that's what he did.

I drove back home, and no one else was there. I went inside and turned on the Christian radio station, WCIC, and cried out, "God, what do you want?" And the song "Mighty to Save" came on. I stood and sang the song, praying, asking God to change me. And as I was standing there (I'll never forget it), it was like his hand was on me, so heavy that it pushed me down on the ground. I remember laying flat, facedown to the ground, and just bawling, not even knowing what was happening, but that was the moment God delivered me from all things. I don't know how long I was on the floor, but I just know that when I was finally able to stand (I know this sounds like a cliché), but I felt this weight lift off me, and I knew at that time something inside of me had changed. For those of you who know the power of addiction, then you'll understand how powerful this was because from that point on, I never had a hunger for drugs and alcohol again. I know a lot of people who have been through programs, step after step, and can't get free. I never did any of those, and the Lord delivered me that day.

All I can say is because of all that happened during that year and a half, and because of what God did for me that night, my faith cannot be shaken. No one can tell me that God isn't real, that God isn't alive. I feel like he is my best friend, and I can't turn my back on him. There's no way for me to go back.

Bryan found that repentance opened the door to a changed life. Repentance addresses three areas. First, it deals with our disobedience for breaking God's commands. Second, it addresses our rebellion as we reject God's right to lead our lives. That rebellion can be blatantly shaking our fists at God saying, "Stay out of my life!" or it can be a polite "No thank you, God; I'm carrying on okay without You." Both responses deny God's rightful place as Lord over our lives. And third, we need to repent of unbelief, of not trusting in Him and not accepting what He says. We can summarize all our disobedience, rebellion, and unbelief as one thing: sin. Jesus came to save us from our sins. We respond to Him through repentance as we turn away from our sins.

Where are you in this? Do you need to change direction? If you are making steps to renew a relationship with God, then understand that repentance is the door you walk through.

HARRIET'S STORY

My wife's life was not outwardly disobedient—no drugs nor blatant immorality—but Harriet had walked away from God and needed to repent for rejecting God's rightful place in her life.

My story falls under the category, "Good People Need Jesus Too." I don't have a dramatic testimony, but I was just as lost as those who go through a lot of bad stuff. I am thankful that I didn't suffer a lot of consequences of unwise decisions or foolish behavior, and I am grateful that my eyes were opened to see my need for a Savior.

I was born in Denver, Colorado, in the mid-1950s. My parents had already lost two prematurely born babies. They didn't think they could have their own child, so they adopted my sister. But then, my dad, through his work with insurance medical claims, found out about a new medical procedure called Shirodkar that helped prevent premature birth. My mother had that procedure done, and I was born! Just the fact that I was born is truly a miracle!

When I was a young child, my family didn't attend church. My parents said we were Buddhists because of our Japanese heritage. We never went to the Buddhist temple, but I do remember going to a neighborhood Christian Bible school for children. One day, my sister and I raised our hands when the teacher asked if we wanted to ask Jesus into our hearts. I didn't really know what that meant, but I did know about "hell," and I knew I didn't want to go there.

When I was eight years old, my family moved from the inner city of Denver to a small town in the foothills of the Rocky Mountains. Some friends invited us to their church where there were a lot of kids. My dad made us go, but I didn't mind because it was fun. I'm glad I went because even though I didn't have a personal relationship with Jesus, I learned about Him and about Christianity.

All through my school years, I grew up relatively carefree. There were parties and lots of peer pressure that every teenager faces. I drank at the parties even though I couldn't stand the taste, but thankfully, I didn't get into a lot of trouble. I really believe that was because of the Lord's grace. At that time, I thought I was a Christian since I was going to church and I was a pretty good kid. However, I had no regard for what the Bible said. I believed that if I wanted to do something, then it didn't matter what anyone else thought; if I thought it was okay, then it was okay. I think a lot of people feel that way.

After graduating from high school, I worked at Coors Brewery in Golden. One of my close friends was a Christian girl my age. She was so cheerful, didn't complain or gossip like so many others. There was something different about her that I noticed immediately. My sister had also become a Christian and had the same cheerful attitude as my coworker. There was something different about them that I didn't understand, but I knew I wanted.

While working at the brewery, I had a life-changing experience. My appendix ruptured, but it went undiagnosed. A month later I had become so sick and full of infection that I could barely walk. I was hospitalized, but the doctors could not determine what was wrong with me. One day, a visiting physician "happened" to hear their discussions, and he immediately knew it was my appendix. He became my doctor, and the day after Christmas, I had the first of two major surgeries.

The night before the first surgery, a nurse came into my room and asked if she could pray for me. She noticed my Bible (that I seldom read) and asked me if I knew Jesus. If I were to die, would I have assurance that I would go to Heaven? I felt a little offended by her questions. Of course, I knew Jesus; I had been going to church. I was basically a good person; I had never done anything really terrible. I told her yes, I would go to Heaven.

But after she left, I thought about our short conversation and honestly could not say for sure that I had that kind of peace. I appreciated her willingness to pray with me. I wasn't very responsive to her; in fact, I was kind of rude. She probably left thinking she didn't do much good, but she actually had a big impact on me.

After the first surgery, I realized it was a miracle I did not die. I had so much infection that the surgeons had to go in and remove it because it was poisoning me. I had a rib removed because they couldn't get to the infection. Even after the surgery was done, I was still very sick, so a second surgery was done to remove the ruptured appendix. I was in intensive care for ten days and so weak I could not walk. But after a long month in the hospital, I began to recover and was able to go home.

It was so good to be alive! I'd take my dog and go for short walks in the beautiful mountains. As I got stronger, I went up the mountainside to sit and enjoy the peaceful view. I had a lot of time to think, and I realized I wasn't living my life the way Jesus wanted me to. I knew a lot about Him, but I didn't know Him as my friend and Savior. I was the one who was basically in control of my life. I had little regard for the way the Bible said I should live. I was on the throne—not Jesus.

As I sat there, I realized my life had been spared for some reason. One day, sitting on my favorite rocks, I told the Lord I was sorry, and starting that day, I wanted to live my life for Him. I prayed and confessed my sin of putting myself first, and I told Him that from that day forward, I would do whatever He wanted me to do and go wherever He wanted me to go. I had a peace and joy and purpose that was never there before. I now had what I had seen in my sister and coworker. And now, I knew for certain I would go to Heaven after I die.

I really believe it was a miracle that I was even born after my mother had two miscarriages before me. It was not a coincidence that my dad found out about the Shirodkar procedure. And I consider every day since surviving a ruptured appendix to be a bonus. I should have died; it is unheard of to go a month with a ruptured appendix and survive! I am thankful for God's hand on my life, even before I asked Him into my heart at that kids' Bible school (see 1 John 4:19). I have lived a full life, and I am thankful I am now in the "fourth quarter" and will serve Him until He takes me home to be with Him in heaven. It is true: "Good people" need Jesus, too!

METANOIA

God calls everyone to repent. Whether you are good, bad, wild, quiet—if you haven't put God first in your life, you need to repent and turn to Him. The Greek word for "repentance" is *metanoia*, which means "a change of mind." True repentance starts in the mind and heart. This speaks to the difference between religion and Jesus. When you turn to Jesus, He begins to work inside you, touching your heart with His love and correcting your thoughts and beliefs. On the other hand, religion works from the outside. Religion starts with our behavior and seeks to impose rules on how we live. The end result of religion is either despair because we aren't strong enough to keep the rules, or it results in pride, causing us to look down on people we judge to be too weak. Jesus addressed this in a parable:

"To some who were confident of their own righteousness and looked down on everyone else, Jesus told this parable: 'Two men went up to the temple to pray, one a Pharisee and the other a tax collector. The Pharisee stood by himself and prayed: "God, I thank you that I am not like other people—robbers, evildoers, adulterers—or even like this tax collector. I fast twice a week and give a tenth of all I get."

'But the tax collector stood at a distance. He would not even look up to heaven, but beat his breast and said, «God, have mercy on me, a sinner."

'I tell you that this man, rather than the other, went home justified before God. For all those who exalt themselves will be humbled, and those who humble themselves will be exalted.'" (Luke 18:9-14)

The tax collector spoke the language of repentance. *"Godly sorrow brings repentance that leads to salvation..."* (2 Corinthians 7:10). So, God is not calling you to a new religion; He's calling you to a new heart.

THE JUDAS SPIRIT

If you are returning to the Lord, as an expression of repentance, you can begin by renouncing the "Judas spirit." Judas was one of the original twelve disciples. He was part of the team, the guys closest to Jesus. Judas traveled with them. He ministered with them. He was one of them.

But then Judas became disillusioned and disappointed in following Jesus. So, on the night before Jesus's death, he abandoned the team and walked away. Later that night Judas returned as part of the mob sent to arrest Jesus. We read in John 18:

"Jesus...asked them, 'Who is it you want?' 'Jesus of Nazareth,' they replied. 'I am He,' Jesus said. And Judas the traitor was standing there with them." (John 18:4–5)

Earlier, Judas stood with Jesus. Now he stands with Jesus's enemies. Earlier, Judas stood with Jesus's disciples. Now he stands with those who reject Jesus. You manifest a Judas spirit when, like Judas, you once stood with Jesus but now you stand with those who oppose Him. Later, speaking of Judas, Peter lamented, *"He was one of our number"* (Acts 1:17). Can that be said of you? "She once was one of us; he once was one of our number"?

Please understand I am not calling you a Judas. What I am saying is there are spiritual forces at work to tempt you away from the Lord, to draw you away so you begin to walk with those who oppose Him. You might not personally be against Jesus, but you have aligned yourself with those who reject Him.

There are millions of people who in a youth ministry or vacation Bible school or at Bible camp or a campus ministry or in Sunday school received Christ and made commitments to follow Him. But today, they are far from Him, believing other things, serving other gods, and living a life that has no room for Jesus. This is the Judas spirit. There are people who were once active in churches, but then things happened. Maybe there was a conflict in the church or perhaps they were wounded by church leaders or perhaps they drifted away during Covid shutdowns and now they find themselves living life apart from Jesus and His followers. This, too, is the Judas spirit.

This is a spiritual issue that you will need to confront. The Bible says satan entered Judas the evening he made his decision to leave Jesus. I'm not saying that satan himself led you away from the Lord, but your shift of allegiance does have a spiritual force behind it. You have an enemy working to separate you from God. This has been his purpose since Adam and Eve. They once walked with God in love and trust. Then the enemy whispered lies to them in order to separate them from God (see Genesis 3). This has been his strategy from the beginning: speak lies to people and gain their agreement. And if you've walked away from God, then no matter how you came to where you are today, somewhere, sometime you believed a lie about God and about your life.

SPIRITUAL DECEPTION

Nobody likes to be deceived. To be lied to. To be tricked. The Bible does not make sense until we recognize that spiritual deception is at the center of the human experience. Whoever has crafted your view of reality has your allegiance. Repentance is recognizing that your view of reality is distorted or false, so you turn from it toward that which is true. 2 Timothy 2 speaks to this:

"Opponents must be gently instructed, in the hope that God will grant them repentance leading them to a knowledge of the truth, and that they will come to their senses and escape from the trap of the devil, who has taken them captive to do his will." (2 Timothy 2:25-26)

As this verse says, God is offering you repentance today, and the moment you turn to Him, you will begin experiencing spiritual clarity, a "coming to your senses." He does this to save us and rescue us from living life in a false reality, trapped by deceptive spiritual forces.

Therefore, as a start, I encourage you to pray something like the following: *Lord Jesus, forgive me for walking away from You and standing with those who oppose You. I renounce my decisions to walk in the way of Judas, and I ask for Your help to follow the truth.*

A simple prayer like this breaks the agreement you made with the Judas spirit.

When you soften your heart toward God and approach Him with a repentant attitude, you will have His attention. He will draw near to you, and you will experience His loving work in your life:

"For this is what the high and exalted One says—He who lives forever, whose name is holy: 'I live in a high and holy place, but also with the one who is contrite and lowly in spirit, to revive the spirit of the lowly and to revive the heart of the contrite.'" (Isaiah 57:15)

YOUR CHILDREN AND YOUR CHILDREN'S CHILDREN

Bryan's story raises the important issue of the spiritual heritage you are passing on to your children and your children's children. Although Bryan personally did not want to return to church, he was concerned for the spiritual development of his kids, and therefore

25

reconnected for their sake. I suspect many of you have felt convicted at some level for the lack of spiritual training or influence you are providing your children. If you have not made God a priority in your life, then your children will follow your example, and their lack of spiritual foundation will be passed on to your grandchildren. If the Bible is false and Christianity is bogus, then this is no big deal—why pass on a superstition? However, if the Judeo-Christian worldview is true, then you and your kids live in a world that is in a spiritual war, and you have given your children no protection. Further, you have not valued the salvation they need from Jesus. At the heart of the human experience is spiritual deception (see Genesis 3 and how Adam and Eve were deceived by satan). Without the truth of God in their hearts, your children are defenseless against the oppressive forces of darkness who come to deceive and enslave with lies and temptations. Without Jesus they are spiritually lost. While some readers might dismiss what's written here, many of you do have these concerns. It's not too late to turn things around. For the sake of your children and your grandchildren, return to the Lord. Write a new legacy for your family.

"But from everlasting to everlasting the Lord's love is with those who fear Him, and His righteousness with their children's children..." (Psalms 103:17)

REPENTANCE BRINGS GOD'S BLESSING

"Repent, then, and turn to God, so that your sins may be wiped out, that times of refreshing may come from the Lord." (Acts 3:19)

Repentance leads to forgiveness of your sins and prompts the Lord to send refreshing into your life. "Refreshing" in the original language has the sense of relief, like air conditioning on a hot day. Repentance releases blessing. Peter said God sent Jesus to you *"...to bless you by turning each of you from your wicked ways"* (Acts 3:26). It's a blessing when someone prevents you from heading into destruction. It's a blessing when someone steps in front of you and says, "Stop! Turn around!" When Jesus began His ministry, His message was: *"Repent, for the kingdom of heaven has come near"* (Matthew 4:17). He is inviting you into His kingdom. Jesus wants you to know the blessing of His kingdom, a kingdom characterized by righteousness, peace, and joy. If your life is running in the other direction, He now lovingly stands before you and says, "Repent, turn around and enter into all I have for you."

ACTIVATION

A. Three activities to do alone with God

1.) Go to a quiet place to be alone with God. Maybe you still have doubts and objections about what is written here. I encourage you to reread the Scriptures in this chapter and ask Jesus to speak to you through them.

2.) Go to YouTube and find a version of the song "Mighty to Save" (the song Bryan mentioned in his story). Listen and say, "Lord if You are there, speak to me in this song."

3.) 2 Timothy 2:25-26 (above) contains many basic truths about what happens in repentance. Read it again and ask Jesus if this verse has a message for you. Listen for what He has to say.

B. Seeking correction
Consider Psalm 25:

"Show me Your ways, Lord, teach me Your paths. Guide me in Your truth and teach me, for You are God my Savior, and my hope is in You all day long...Good and upright is the Lord; therefore He instructs sinners in His ways. He guides the humble in what is right and teaches them His way." (Psalms 25:4-5, 8-9)

Let this passage sink in and ask Jesus to apply it to your life. Ask Him to reveal to you if your thoughts and opinions are in agreement with lies and deceptions. Ask Him to correct your view of reality, your understanding of right and wrong, and how you are living your life.

CHAPTER 3

SALVATION

"She will give birth to a son, and you are to give Him the name Jesus, because He will save His people from their sins." (Matthew 1:21)

"And everyone who calls on the name of the Lord will be saved." (Acts 2:21)

"....God our Savior,...wants all people to be saved and to come to a knowledge of the truth." (1 Timothy 2:3-4)

SAMEED'S STORY

Sameed is a good friend and was one of the original advisors for our Agape ministry school. His story began halfway around the world, and his spiritual journey is a miraculous account of transformation. Here's his story:

I was born in India, but when I was 9 months old my dad moved the family to Saudi Arabia for work. Saudi Arabia is a very strong and radical Muslim nation, where open preaching about Jesus Christ WILL result in your death. Our whole family became more devout Muslims as a result of being around people so radical. So, Dad wanted me to grow up into a man of faith and if possible, even be an Islamic scholar. Muslim parents want righteous children who do the work of Allah because they believe they will continue to be blessed even after their death; they keep earning good deeds through their kids and will inherit a better place in heaven, if Allah allows you into heaven in the first place.

At age 3, I began training in Islam from a teacher who would come to our house for one-on-one tutoring, learning Arabic and the Qur'an. He was a well-respected teacher; he was even recognized by the Shura Council (the council of scholars who make decisions on behalf of the Muslim population) in Saudi Arabia, and they endorsed his books (which is very hard to get an endorsement of). Around fourth grade, I went on the Internet and asked the question: "What is the most common religion in the world?" The answer came back Christianity. That shook my world. Growing up in Saudi Arabia, surrounded by Muslims, I thought, "This can't be true." So, I studied more to understand, and that day I decided I would change that answer; my mission would be to replace Christianity with Islam as the most common religion in the world.

I started studying different religions; I would read books, do research, follow papers and the teachings of Muslim apologists and blindly take whatever they were teaching as the truth, and I would run with it. At the same time, I was also growing in my understanding of Islam, the teachings of Muhammad, and the laws of Islam,

After I graduated from college, I decided to come to America for graduate studies. I wanted to come because I figured all Americans are Christians, and if I could convert Americans to Islam, then the world would follow. So, I came to America initially for a couple of years, I got accepted at Bradley University in Peoria, Illinois, and I came to America on December 23, 2014.

After arriving at Bradley, I met a group of people on campus during the first week when we were discovering on-campus activities. God does have a sense of humor because right next to the Muslim Student Association table was this group who wore shirts saying "Chi Alpha" or "Christ's Ambassadors." I looked at the Christian table, and I remember thinking to myself: "Fresh meat. I'll go talk to them!" I was very confident that I knew everything there was to know about Christianity. I went over to the table and struck up a conversation. *They invited me to their group and explained they do a lot of fun activities AND at the end of every event, there would be a message about Christ. I wasn't too worried and replied, "I'll come only if you let me talk about Islam as well." They said, "Great, come on over!" (I should have been a little worried about how confident they were.)*

I began meeting with Christians holding discussions about faith. I would raise problems with the Bible to which the pastor would reply that my arguments were out of context. These conversations led me to want to read the Bible to sharpen my arguments; I genuinely thought they were lying and using my lack of having read the Bible as a weapon. While reading the Bible, I found myself being confronted with Jesus's deity, His death on the cross, and other Bible doctrines that I was taught weren't true my whole life. I had been taught the Bible had been changed radically throughout history, and I challenged the pastor about this. The pastor said, "Sameed, you love apologetics, so put the Bible to the test. Research its historical reliability." This began a two-year journey of studying the Bible to make sense of its history and of its reliability. Then I compared Islam and Christianity, thinking, "There is no way the Bible can come anywhere close to the Qur'an." To my surprise, I began to find Islam was not all I originally thought. Islam was failing all the tests that the Bible would pass.

After this failure, I turned to the supernatural. The ONLY way that God gives direction in Islam is through a special prayer called Salat-ul-Istikharah, in which you could get a direction through a dream. Dreams are valued, so I prayed, "Allah, would you give me dreams on how to beat this Bible and these Christians?" And God did; not Allah, but Jesus! (Also, it would be interesting to note that I found out after my conversion that many Muslims are becoming Christians these days because of dreams.) Thus, my dreams began. In my first dream after this prayer, I found myself at a funeral, and I realized I was in the casket. Everyone kept saying, "He is dead." I watched as they took the casket to the graveyard, and I found myself crying out, "God (In my dream I said God and not Allah), help me! I don't want to be buried alive!" With that a white light came from the sky, broke open the casket, and I woke up.

A few days later I dreamt again, and I was at a house, a huge house with hundreds of thousands of rooms, and each room was beautiful. I felt like I was there for days checking out rooms; each room had a theme and was more beautiful than the other. I finally reached the top room where there was a long table with plates and names of those who were to be seated there. And the chairs were thrones. I ran around the table searching for my name but could not find it, and I became sad. I fell to my knees and said, "I want to be invited. Why is my name not on the table?!" After I woke up and talked with Muslim friends about it, they said, "You probably ate some bad pizza." But I couldn't shake the dreams; they were very specific. I remember one Imam (pastor), who I knew to know Christianity quite well, got a little upset with me and said, "This is from Satan; I think you should drop it."

A few days later a pastor at Chi Alpha was talking about dreams and how they are significant. I went up to him later and shared my dreams with him, and boy, did he get excited! He said, "Sameed, that is in the Bible! In John 14:1-3 Jesus said in His Father's house there are many rooms, and He was going to prepare a place for us. You are invited, but you haven't accepted the King's invitation, so you weren't there."

I asked, "What does it mean to be invited?" He said, "You have to admit that you are a sinner and invite Jesus into your life." I was very offended when I was told I had to accept that I was a sinner. According to me, I was living a perfect Islamic life. I was praying five times a day, I was leading as an Imam at the mosque, I never smoked, never drank, never did anything that I considered wrong. So, when he said I had to admit I was a sinner, my first thought was, "Yeah, YOU are, but I'm not." He said, "Okay, that's fair, but I'd like you to go home and really think about that."

When all that started happening, I started having so many of these dreams. There were other dreams, like the one when I was at a lake, and I was throwing a net and catching fish. I woke up, and as clear as day I heard a voice that said, "Follow Me and I will make you a fisher of men"—and I remember I threw the Bible I had on the ground and got scared because I thought: I'm reading this book way too much and I need to stop.

As I was going about this with a year and a half of researching Christianity, one day I went out for a jog, on Bradley's campus, at 4:00 in the afternoon, in broad daylight, walking around the campus, I heard someone say, "Hey, buddy" so I turned around and got hit with a metal pipe on my face and I fell. They kicked me and yelled, "Give us your phone and wallet!" Thirty seconds later they ran away. I was taken to the hospital, and they did a lot of immediate help including 11 stitches under my eye, x-rays, and MRIs. After all that, when I was finally not being prodded or stitched up, two men came to my bed. One of them was a priest and the other was either a lawyer or an administrator. They said, "The doctors don't think you're going to live through the night, so if you die, do you have a final will? And how do you want your final rites to be? Do you belong to a particular faith?" I was shocked and all I could tell them was: "I don't have a will and I think I am a Muslim." The priest asked me if he could pray for me, and I declined; he respected me and left me alone.

They took me to my room. The damage was so bad: bones broken in my face, my left eye was damaged as they had kicked me in my face and stomped on it, they bit my hand for some reason, so there was concern about HIV; they stomped on my torso. I couldn't see out of my left eye as some of my nerves had gotten stuck in the fracture. I was told I couldn't eat and drink as they had me scheduled for surgery the next morning. I remember one of my childhood friends who was at Bradley with me at the time came to see me at the hospital, and seeing my face, he passed out and hit the floor. He had to be taken to the ER, and he got stitches on his head! Some friends from the church visited me as well. I remember saying, "I'm really afraid to die." And they said, "Well, Jesus still answers prayers so why don't you ask Him to heal you?" After they left, I was in my room afraid, and I prayed and said, "I don't know if you are Allah or if you are Jesus, but there is one true God. Please show yourself and heal me."

I didn't even finish the prayer when a white light filled my room. I could best describe it as a figure of a man that walked up to my bed, and I looked at Him. All I could say in the moment was "Jesus." That's all that came out of my mouth: "Jesus." Then I passed out. That's all I remember. I saw His face, I said, "Jesus" and then I passed out.

I woke up the next day, and the first thing I realized was I could see out of my left eye! As the nurse came in, I kept saying, "I can see! I can see!" And she called the doctors. I remember that morning two people from the mosque visited me. One of them was in the leadership, and the other was a doctor at this hospital. The doctor said, "Sameed, you need to praise Allah for this miracle! The nerve that was stuck in the fracture came out on its own; that is a miracle, and you can go home!" I was blown away, not only by the miracle, but I knew who had done it! I knew in that moment: "Jesus is Who He says He is! He is GOD!"

That morning it had snowed as well, and the ground was all covered in white. As I was looking from my room pondering what I had just realized, I heard the same voice say, "I will wash your sins as white as snow." So, when I got home, I knew I had to decide. I knew He was God, but was believing it worth losing everything, especially my family who meant everything to me? In Scriptures, Jesus said, "Count the cost." Was I ready to give ALL of it up to follow Jesus? It was a period of about three months where I would go from "No, it is not worth it" to mourning because I knew eternity was bigger than this life, and I would experience the coming loss of my family, friends and even my own identity. I knew the decision in front of me and its consequences. I remember one day I said, "Jesus, it would be for the best if I became a Christian and You take me to Heaven right away." That's how conflicted I was between knowing the right thing to do and not wanting to lose my family. The point where it all shifted was when I was reading through Luke one day, and I came across Luke 14:26: "If anyone comes to me and does not hate father and mother, wife and children, brothers and sisters—yes, even their own life—such a person cannot be my disciple."

On May 12, 2017, I was in a small group meeting with my Christian friends, and as people were talking, I heard the same voice of Jesus say, "Tonight is the night, right here." So, I told the group leader I would like to become a Christian. We prayed, and it was an overwhelming experience. The next morning, I walked out, and I remember the trees were greener, the sky bluer, and everything was joy and peace, more joy than I'd ever experienced before. And it was ok if I lost my family who I love dearly. I was ok if I lost my life because of this Jesus, because He who gave everything up for me was worth me giving up everything for. I have never looked back a day and NEVER regretted my decision for Christ. And if I had to go through all that again for Him, I would do that in a heartbeat because of what He gives us in exchange: His overwhelming presence, peace and joy in this life, and eternal life in the next.

As Sameed's story shows, the love and truth of the living God can break through into anybody's life. Jesus came to seek and to save the lost (Luke 19:10). He did not come as one religious teacher among many but as the One sent on a mission to save all people. He came as *"the atoning sacrifice for our sins, and not only for ours but also for the sins of the whole world"* (1 John 2:2). In history, most kings expect their people to die for them, but Jesus is the King Who came to die for His people. *"The Son of Man did not come to be served, but to serve, and to give his life as a ransom for many"* (Matthew 20:28).

(You can see a video production of Sameed's life on YouTube at Northwoods Community Church/ *Who Do You Say I Am*)

JOHN 3:16

For many of you, John 3:16 was a key verse in your earlier church experience:

"For God so loved the world that He gave His one and only Son, that whoever believes in Him shall not perish but have eternal life."

Many people made decisions to believe in Jesus because of this verse, and maybe that includes you. It summarizes the Christian message: God loves, God gives, and you believe and receive eternal life. So, perhaps this verse crystallized for you the decision to believe and receive Jesus into your life, maybe at Sunday School or a confirmation class or Bible camp or at a youth group or a campus ministry. The truth that God loved you and gave Jesus for you was compelling and convicting. At that time, you knew you needed a Savior, so you asked Jesus into your life.

But today you find yourself in a different place. The God of John 3:16 seems distant. You don't follow Him in your daily life though perhaps you still believe in Him in some fashion, or maybe you've intentionally and consciously rejected that God and have moved on. But here you are reading a book written for the purpose of helping you return to the God Who loves and gives. So, before reading further, I encourage you to stop at this moment and pray something like this: *"God, I'm still not sure if You are there, but if You are, I ask You to speak to me. I have doubts, but I do want to live my life according to what is true. So help me to know what's right. Amen."*

TRANSFORMATION

John 3:3 is another Bible passage that may be familiar to you. Here Jesus declares, *"You must be born again!"* When you believe in Jesus, you experience a new birth and you become a new person. 2 Corinthians 5:17 says: *"Therefore, if anyone is in Christ, he [or she] is a new creation."* In other words, God intends you to experience a transformation. But maybe the way you experienced Christian faith earlier in your life wasn't very transformational. Maybe you received Jesus mainly so you could go to Heaven when you die. But God's purpose in saving you is so much more. In genuine salvation you are transformed; you become a new person. Transformation is the heart of the Christian gospel.

Think how transformation is a central theme in movies and books. It is often the main point in our fairy tales and children's stories. Think about the ugly duckling becoming a swan, Pinocchio becoming a real boy, and how Cinderella changes from a servant to a princess. Even as children we are moved by the idea that we can become more than we are. A frog becomes a prince, the scarecrow gets brains, and

Simba becomes the Lion King. The idea that there is greatness hidden within us tugs at our hearts, and the fascination with transformation continues as adults. Rocky becomes the champion. Luke becomes a Jedi. In *Lord of the Rings* the drifter Aragorn is crowned king, and hobbits become warrior princes. When you think of the books and movies that move you, chances are this theme is present somewhere. Someone is revealed to be far greater than they appeared. Some unlikely person becomes the hero.

Why are we moved by these stories? I think it's because they speak to a deep truth about who we are. In the book of Genesis, God created people to be the pinnacle of His creation. We are the only beings created in His image, so that we might have a relationship with Him and share in His kingdom rule and glory. But we gave that all away through disobedience and deception (see Genesis 3:1–6).

BOTH AN ORPHAN AND A REBEL

Now we are separated from God and have lost the identity and destiny He originally had for us. And now it's as if two people live inside of our hearts: a lonely orphan looking for love and a fist-shaking rebel demanding his or her own way. Look inside yourself; do you see them?

Many years back, Madalyn Murray O'Hair was an atheistic activist who fought in the courts against public expressions of Christianity. She was behind the Supreme Court decision that removed prayer from the schools. Those who debated her found her to be a bitter, angry person who mocked Christians and despised God with an odd *"I don't believe there's a God and I hate Him"* kind of message. After her death, her personal diaries were opened, and while she had written much about her anger at God, there were also passages of personal despair. Numerous times she wrote, "Won't somebody, somewhere love me?" Her writings reflected both a rebel and an orphan.

I think everyone who has walked away from God can look inside themselves and find both an orphan seeking love and a rebel demanding their own way. But through the cross, God offers His love and a purpose for your life far better than you can imagine. Through the cross, orphans and rebels are transformed into royalty, becoming sons and daughters of the King.

UNDERSTANDING THE CROSS

Maybe at one time the meaning of the cross was clear to you. But perhaps now you are not so sure of its significance. Let me explain the primary meaning of the cross. People who are well versed in theology might find my explanation simplistic, but I think it captures the central Bible understanding. The cross will not make any sense unless we understand three things about God: He is a God of holiness, a God of justice, and a God of love.

As you read further, do not skip over the numerous Bible verses, but instead consider them carefully. I encourage you to ask God to help you understand what follows. Ask Him to speak to you through the Scripture passages. Ask Him how these apply to your life.

THREE TRUTHS ABOUT GOD

To understand God's salvation and the cross, we need to understand three truths about God:

A. God is holy.
He is a God of holiness. This means He is separated from all sin. God is completely pure and righteous. He is set apart from all sin, darkness, and evil.

"God is light; in Him there is no darkness at all." (1 John 1:5)

Furthermore, because He is holy, our disobedience, rebellion, and unbelief separate us from Him.

"Your iniquities have separated you from your God; your sins have hidden His face from you, so He will not hear." (Isaiah 59:2)

The Bible says our self-centered behavior has separated us from God. The Bible says ALL of us have fallen short and missed the mark, *"for all have sinned and fall short of the glory of God"* (Romans 3:23). Our sin prevents us from reaching God. When I don't believe what He says, when I break His commands, and when I put myself first—all of these the Bible calls sin, and sin separates me from God.

B. God is just.

He's a God of justice. This means He will hold us accountable for our actions. And He doesn't miss a thing. Our lives are open books before Him. There will be accountability and punishment for every sin, every selfish action, shoddy deal, deceptive act, every instance of violence, cheating, theft, adultery, immorality, every rebellious deed, every lie, every cruel word. We are held responsible for breaking His commands and ignoring His will.

"Nothing in all creation is hidden from God's sight. Everything is uncovered and laid bare before the eyes of Him to whom we must give an account." (Hebrews 4:13)

"…for we all must appear before the judgment seat of Christ." (2 Corinthians 5:10)

"He will punish those who do not know God and who do not obey the gospel of our Lord Jesus. They will be punished with everlasting destruction and shut out from the presence of the Lord." (2 Thessalonians 1:9-10)

"But I will show you whom you should fear: Fear Him who, after your body has been killed, has authority to throw you into hell. Yes, I tell you, fear Him." (Luke 12:5)

C. God is love.

God has a passionate love for His creation, and the Bible says people are the ultimate object of His love. His purpose in creating you was that you might walk with Him in a loving relationship. His desire is for a loving, joyful, intimate relationship between people and Himself.

"But God demonstrates His own love for us in this: While we were still sinners, Christ died for us." (Romans 5:8)

"God is love. Whoever lives in love lives in God, and God in them. We love because He first loved us." (1 John 4:16,19)

"This is love: not that we loved God, but that He loved us and sent his Son as an atoning sacrifice for our sins." (1 John 4:10)

"You make known to me the path of life; You will fill me with joy in Your presence, with eternal pleasures at Your right hand." (Psalms 16:11)

So, the three truths about God are that He is holy, He is just, and He is love.

GOD'S DILEMMA

When we understand these three truths about God—that He is holy, just, and love—then we can begin to understand the impact of our disobedience, rebellion, and unbelief. Because of our sin, God's holiness demands we be separated from His holy presence. God's justice demands we pay for our sins. But God's love longs for relationship and intimacy with us.

If God applies His holiness and justice to our sins, then we are punished and separated from Him. This leaves His love for us unsatisfied because we are removed from His presence. However, if

His love and desire for relationship saves us but our sins are not dealt with, then God's holiness and justice are left unsatisfied.

His holiness requires all sin to be removed from His presence. His justice requires all sin to be punished. But His love desires to be with us and to bless us. Thus, the issue is how does God satisfy all three traits of His nature—His holiness, justice, and love?

GOD'S SOLUTION IN THE CROSS

His solution was the cross of Jesus Christ.

The entire record of the Bible is the story of how God's holiness, justice, and love are all reconciled. In the Old Testament, we find the gradual unfolding of the truth that mankind's sin required sacrifice for there to be reconciliation with God. We find that sacrifices of bulls and lambs in the Jewish temple were required to make payment for sins. These sacrifices were a shadow, a picture of God's ultimate solution for man's sin. This all culminated on the day when John the Baptist pointed at Jesus and shouted, *"Behold the Lamb of God who takes away the sin of the world"* (John 1:29). Jesus understood His life in this way too: *"I didn't come to be served but to serve and give My life as a ransom"* (see Matthew 20:28). Jesus gave His life on the cross in order to satisfy God's holiness, justice, and love.

A. The cross satisfies God's holiness.
"He Himself bore our sins in His body on the cross, so that we might die to sins and live for righteousness; 'by His wounds you have been healed.' For 'you were like sheep going astray,' but now you have returned to the Shepherd and Overseer of your souls." (1 Peter 2:24-25)

He "bore" our sins. He took our sins from us. He freed us from our sins by taking them onto Himself. He is the Lamb Who takes away the sin of the world. The sin that separated us from God is removed.

41

B. The cross satisfies God's justice.

Jesus was punished for our sins:

"But He was pierced for our transgressions, He was crushed for our iniquities; the punishment that brought us peace was on Him, and by His wounds we are healed. We all, like sheep, have gone astray, each of us has turned to our own way; and the Lord has laid on Him the iniquity of us all." (Isaiah 53:5-6)

Jesus took your place and mine. He became our substitute, taking the punishment our sins deserved. He paid the price that we owed. Justice is thus satisfied.

C. The cross satisfies God's love.

Because justice and holiness were satisfied at the cross, we can now freely enter into the relationship God longs to have with us.

"But because of His great love for us, God, who is rich in mercy, made us alive with Christ even when we were dead in transgressions—it is by grace you have been saved." (Ephesians 2:4-5)

"Here I am! I stand at the door and knock. If anyone hears My voice and opens the door, I will come in and eat with that person, and they with Me." (Revelation 3:20)

Maybe all the discussion above about the cross was confusing. If so, all you truly need to know is Jesus died on the cross for your sins, and if you trust Him, your sins are forgiven, and you will enter into a loving relationship with God that will last forever. All of this is due to the amazing love God has for you.

THE UNIQUE LOVE OF GOD

The kind of love God displayed at the cross was unique. First, He took the initiative. While we were still rejecting Him, He acted in our behalf.

"But God demonstrates His own love for us in this: While we were still sinners, Christ died for us." (Romans 5:8)

Second, He is offering His salvation to you as a gift. You do not earn it by being religious enough or good enough or spiritual enough. It is a free gift.

"For the wages of sin is death, but the gift of God is eternal life in Christ Jesus our Lord." (Romans 6:23)

It is a gift He is holding out to you. All that is required of you is to reach out and receive it. You do this by prayer.

Third, the purpose of Jesus's death was to restore the life that sin and satan stole from you. You are now free to enter the life God always intended for you.

"The thief comes only to steal and kill and destroy; I have come that they may have life, and have it to the full." (John 10:10)

"For He has rescued us from the dominion of darkness and brought us into the kingdom of the Son He loves, in Whom we have redemption, the forgiveness of sins." (Colossians 1:13–14)

At the center of this new life is your adoption by God to be His child.

"But when the set time had fully come, God sent His Son…that we might receive adoption to sonship" (Galatians 4:4–5). Sonship means becoming His child and includes men and women.

"Yet to all who did receive Him, to those who believed in His name, He gave the right to become children of God." (John 1:12)

Jesus died so you can become a beloved child of God. The picture is that of the heavenly Father walking into an orphanage, pointing at you and saying, "I want that one to be My child!" Some teaching reduces salvation and the cross to only be payment for sins, but there is far more going on. Your identity is being transformed. You are no longer an orphan or a rebel, but you are now a treasured child, secure in the love of your Father. More about this in a later chapter.

GOD IS CALLING YOU TO RETURN

Now, the question is: What does the cross mean to you at this moment? If you have walked away from God, know that He hasn't walked away from you. He invites you back to Himself. Perhaps you think you've been away too long, ignored Him too long, or sinned too much, and you doubt if He wants you. If you have these doubts, I encourage you to remember Peter, one of Jesus's closest followers. But even Peter had a moment when he denied Jesus and abandoned Him (see John 18:25-27 and 21:15-17). Maybe you feel you've treated Jesus that way too. But the Bible shows how Jesus forgave Peter and restored him. He will forgive and restore you, too, if you will turn back to Him.

MY PERSONAL TURNING POINT

The Scripture passage that helped me see my need for Jesus is 1 John 5:11-12. When I was a senior in high school, I sat in my friend Steve's kitchen, and his dad, Pastor Walter Baertschi, shared this passage with me. It was the turning point for me:

"And this is the testimony: God has given us eternal life, and this life is in His Son. Whoever has the Son has life; whoever does not have the Son of God does not have life." (1 John 5:11-12)

In that moment, Christianity became clear for me. My salvation wasn't based on me being good enough or religious enough, but it was based on whether I had Jesus or not. Since that evening, this Scripture has always had emotional ties for me, sort of like a first crush in grade school. It was a game changer for me as it brought clarity to my need for Jesus and what I had to do. God gives eternal life. We don't earn it or deserve it. It is offered as a gift, wrapped in His Son, Jesus. Eternal life is in Jesus. It's not in another religion or some other spiritual formula. If you have Jesus, you have eternal life, and if you don't have Jesus, you do not have this life. So, the question is, do you have Jesus?

JESUS COMES TO YOU

Jesus said, *"I stand at the door and knock. If anyone hears My voice and opens the door, I will come in and eat with that person, and they with Me."* (Revelation 3:20)

So what will you do with this gift being offered to you? *"If ANYONE opens the door I will come in."* It doesn't matter what you've done, how far away you've drifted, how many promises you've broken, how long you've ignored Him, how many ways you've rebelled, how big of a mess you've made things, or how dark your life has become. Jesus came to seek and save the lost, and that includes you. He loves you. He came for you. Your part is to open the door, responding to His request to enter your life.

RESPONDING TO HIM

Usually Jesus stands at the door knocking, not forcing His way into our life, giving us the choice to keep the door closed or to allow Him in. This leads people to say God is a gentleman; He won't force His way in. Well, that's true until it's not. Sometimes as we go along in our opposition and unbelief, He blocks our path. Instead of knocking on the door, Jesus knocks us down. And as we lie on the ground looking up, He leans over and says "Hi, we're going to become best friends." That's what happened to the apostle Paul. That's what happened to C.S. Lewis. That's what has happened to some of my friends. They weren't looking for God, but He was looking for them. God won't act against your will, but He can make you willing to act. He can be very disruptive. Rescues often are. But every person whose story is in this book will tell you it's worth it.

You can't be nice enough, spiritual or religious enough, sincere or friendly enough, generous or good enough to earn eternal life because eternal life is not found in your behavior. Eternal life is found in Jesus. Eternal life—the life God always intended for you, the destiny His love has designed you for—is found in Jesus. So that is the key spiritual question for your life: Where is Jesus? Have you opened the door? He is knocking now, awaiting your response.

ACTIVATION

A. Decision time

Maybe you once valued salvation, but the idea has become distant and not very relevant to your life. It's time to return to the cross.

Ask Jesus to speak to you. A starting point is to go back through this chapter, read each Scripture verse again and ask, "Jesus, what do You want to say to me in this verse?" Read these, think on them, ask Him to speak to you about His love for you.

The Bible says this is the day of salvation. You are not guaranteed another day, but today the Father is calling you to Himself. Jesus said, *"Repent and believe the good news"* (Mark 1:15). Turn from going your own way and begin to follow Jesus. Believe His Word. Trust in His cross to save you, not in your ability to be good enough, friendly enough, nice enough. Our good behavior doesn't remove sin; only Jesus can take sin away.

Maybe you are ready to return to Him. If so, look to Jesus and pray a prayer like this:

Lord Jesus, I come to You now asking You to forgive my unbelief, rebellion, and disobedience. Forgive me for walking away from You. I turn from my sin, and I commit to obey You. I turn from unbelief, and I commit to believe Your Word. I turn from living for myself, and I commit to follow You. Help me to stay true to these commitments.

I thank you for Your death on the cross for my sins. I put my faith in You to save me, and I ask You to enter my life anew to be my Lord and Savior. Amen.

CHAPTER 4

LOVING THE GOD OF LOVE

"But God demonstrates His own love for us in this: While we were still sinners, Christ died for us." (Romans 5:8)

"This is how God showed His love among us: He sent His one and only Son into the world that we might live through Him. This is love: not that we loved God, but that He loved us and sent His Son as an atoning sacrifice for our sins." (1 John 4:9-10)

"Jesus replied: 'Love the Lord your God with all your heart and with all your soul and with all your mind.' This is the first and greatest commandment.'" (Matthew 22:37-38)

God shows His love for us by sending Jesus. He took the initiative. He loved us even while we rejected Him and ignored Him. No matter how far away you've run, He is seeking you, to rescue you and to give you new life. God loved you so much that He sent Jesus to give you life (see John 3:16).

KATIE'S STORY

Our daughter-in-law Katie is married to our son Jeremy. They both served as missionaries, and their hope is to return to Asia in the future. But now they live close to us, allowing us to be Grandma and Grandpa to their little son, Aidan. We love Katie so much! She shares her story here, saying how much she only wants Jesus to get all glory from what He did for her.

I grew up in Peoria. We attended church on Christmas and Easter, and sometimes my parents read a kids' Bible to us at night, but our spiritual instruction really came from our neighbor Diane across the street. She began inviting us to Vacation Bible School when I was four. (Years later she let me know the Lord told her to pour into my sister and me.). I gave my life to Jesus at VBS at 6 years of age. I received Him maybe 20 times as little kids are apt to do. I loved Jesus when I was young.

We did VBS every summer, and we were at Diane's house a lot. She'd just tell us about Jesus. As we got older, she'd even pay us to memorize Scripture! We got so much Scripture in us from her. Through her influence I really learned a lot about Jesus and really fell in love with Him. As time went on, I attended Young Life and really wanted to follow the Lord and do the right thing.

But also during those years, things were changing, and around age 12 I began experiencing depression. Depression led to cutting and suicidal thoughts. My sister saved my life in one instance at about age 12 as she saw me on the roof ready to jump onto the concrete and kill myself. She was such a Godsend for me growing up. I started having evil dreams. I had dreams of demons choking me, and then I'd wake up with red marks on my neck. A really nightmarish hell came upon me.

During this time I was crying out for Jesus to deliver me. I was in such torment and felt so alone. I'd just be in my room hugging my knees wanting to die, feeling like I had nobody. I didn't know how to make it stop, and I was begging God for help. I clung to God in those years so hard and sought help from Diane and other people but I couldn't get relief; it just got worse. I'd wear long sleeves to school to cover the cutting, but I continued going into a darker and darker place. Before all this, I was confident and had friends and I was a leader, but as this progressed, I felt like I was losing my mind. It was so scary.

As I entered high school, my mom noticed the cuts and made me go to a psychiatrist. I began taking medicines for depression, anxiety, and OCD. But it continued getting worse. And the whole time I was crying out to Jesus, trying to find Him in this hell that I was in, feeling so confused as to why this was happening.

In high school I had a lot of social anxiety; some of that's normal for kids, but mine was off the charts. By my junior year, I felt I'd cried out and cried out to God, and I had not found Him and couldn't understand why He wasn't helping me, so I started turning slowly away from the Lord. I started getting into the wrong crowds. I started smoking cigarettes at age 16, followed by smoking pot. I began being promiscuous, doing things I shouldn't have done with guys. I started partying, drinking, and playing around with guys. I had consensual sex for the first time at age 18 with an older guy who was tattooed with demons, a very dark human being.

I was still calling out to God, but it seemed like He wasn't helping me, so I tried to fix myself. I went off to college and got deeper into drugs, drinking, and fooling around a lot. In my freshman year, I met a girl at a party who was gay. She invited me to a gay bar, and the rest was history. I ended up dating that woman for over a year; we were pretty much living together. I fell head over heels for her and thought we'd be married. I got deep into the drug scene, doing lots of psychedelics, and I really got into the gay world at that point. And I was still completely miserable. I got an STD at that time, which went away (thank you, Lord), but when that happened, I already hated myself so much that I thought I was just going to punish myself and not eat anymore. And that's when I became anorexic and bulimic; I became skeletal, losing my period for nine months. I hated myself so much. I kept looking for love in all the wrong places.

That girl and I broke up, and then I found a group of gay women, and some gay and non-gay men, who were all living together, and I ran to that. It was a hippy lifestyle of sex, drugs, and rock & roll. I was with all the girlfriends sexually, and we were all out of our minds with drugs most of the time. Surprisingly, I was still a nursing school student at Iowa with good grades (that was all the Lord's goodness).

During all of that, I had totally given up on Jesus. I started looking into all the Eastern religions and New Age teachings. I had friends who were witches, and I really got into all that because I'd always been sensitive to spiritual things. I did so many horrible things in various ceremonies. I tried Eastern meditation and Buddhist practices.

During this time, I was still having frightening demonic dreams. I was with a lot of my friends sexually, but I was with one girl in particular for a long time; she wanted to marry, but I didn't want to commit. She was my best friend. I had been so lonely through the years, feeling like I never fit in anywhere. But that group was my people, and that woman was the best friend I'd ever had. So basically I decided I was gay or bisexual; that was my life then.

So in all this, at around age 21 at my lowest low, very suicidal, cutting, anorexic, bulimic, gay, doing more drugs than I could count, drinking, trying to go through school, into weirdo New Age stuff and the most hellish hell in my mind, at that point, my Uncle Jeff called me.

He had just had an encounter with the Lord and had returned to faith in Jesus. My family knew I was in a bad place. My dad called my granny, worried about me, and my granny told Uncle Jeff. She was so worried I would die. So Uncle Jeff, who I had never talked to on the phone, who I only saw at family Christmas gatherings, called me out of the blue. He left a message, and surprisingly I called him back.

He spoke with me and reminded me of the Jesus I knew as a little girl and spoke so much truth into me. I had so many questions about where God was in all my pain. We spoke for hours, and in that time he led me to give my life back to the Lord. I didn't have a relationship with Uncle Jeff aside from seeing him at Christmastime, but he gave hours to speak with me, telling me all about Jesus again. And the Lord just gave me grace to want Him again. It's always the Holy Spirit Who draws us back to Him.

So I gave my life back to the Lord; then on his second phone call I was baptized in the Holy Spirit. I had never had this experience before, nor was

I taught about this growing up. I think this is part of what I was missing. I was saved but never filled with the Holy Spirit. Over the phone, Uncle Jeff just prayed for me, and the Spirit came on me, and my mind felt overwhelmed with Him. Life began to change radically after this.

Within one month after that call, I went off all my psychiatric medication. I had been on them since age 12. I didn't just stop (as that's a bad idea), but I told my psychiatrist I wanted off them, and she tapered me off so that within one month I stopped completely. It was amazing! God completely delivered me. I think that was a fruit of the Holy Spirit's fullness in me. I think these medicines can be really helpful for people, but in my case, God delivered me. It was the beginning of my very long journey out of hell and out of so much torment.

Uncle Jeff was a saint, and he began <u>emailing me every single day for six years</u>, long emails teaching me about Jesus. He was being discipled, and everything he was learning he shared with me. I was ravenous for these truths, and I knew it was God's Grace that I even wanted Jesus. I had been so angry with God, but He gave me the grace to desire Him. I was devouring the Bible and all this teaching. We talked on the phone every week for hours, and he would answer so many of my questions. I just saw my life starting to turn around. But what's important to know is that my journey back took several years.

I talked with Uncle Jeff many, many times about homosexuality and what the Bible says. All the people that I loved the most in my life believed they were born gay, and I believed that was how I was born too, so it was a really hard subject for me. But Uncle Jeff just constantly told me the truth and brought me through so many Scriptures. He talked with me for years over that subject. It took me a long time to accept the truth, but what I want you to know is if you are in this lifestyle, the first and foremost thing you need is to fall in love with Jesus. Your journey out of sin will really be the result of being so loved by God and loving Him back.

When I was baptized in the Spirit, I fell in love with Jesus. Something was different when I got filled with the Holy Spirit, and I couldn't get enough. I would listen to all these teachings, I would read the Word all the time, and at the same time, I was doing a ton of psychedelics. I was sleeping with different girls, and sometimes guys. And I was just a mess. And yet there was this genuine love relationship with Jesus growing and growing.

No matter how far you are from Jesus, turn to Him; start to fall in love with Him. He knows the path to your redemption. Learn about His love for you. Just start getting wrecked knowing that you're so loved by God. Foster that intimacy between you and Jesus. Let Him teach you about Himself; let Him get your heart. Get somebody who will tell you the truth but still let you grow at your pace. I still had a journey to walk out, and that journey was years of more and more knowing the Lord and realizing I couldn't live that way anymore

I found a house church. It was so perfect for me; it was a hippy little place that was just right for me at the time. I would always arrive late; I came off mushrooms and went there. I don't know if they knew I was gay or not, but they just welcomed me with open arms. I didn't open up with any of them, but I just went there, and they loved me. They taught me more about Jesus, and I just couldn't get enough of it. I would party all night on Saturday, and speed to church on Sunday morning just to be there. And I was telling my friends, "I have found Jesus! He's amazing!" All my gay friends were like, "Wow! Cool...okay!" A few of them went to church with me.

But the one person I was asking real questions always told me the truth. Uncle Jeff didn't water anything down; he told me the truth. Toward the end of my fifth year of college was the last time I was with my girlfriend; she was driving away. I was graduating right after that and moving back home. As she drove away, I just knew I was never going to see her again. I don't think I fully knew what was going on with me, but I just knew I had to get out of Iowa City, with its huge gay crowd, and all my friends were there. I really wanted to get baptized. I'd never been baptized, even as a little kid. So, I graduated with my nursing degree, and I moved back in with my parents.

I started going to Northwoods Church in Peoria at that time. I started having supernatural experiences with the Lord that I had no grid for. For example, I *would be in a worship session, and, like, the Holy Spirit was right on me. I was like frozen, and my whole body, parts of my body were tingling; I knew He was healing parts of my body, and I was bawling; I was experiencing God, but I had zero idea what was happening to me. But God started doing those things—even more supernatural-like encounters with me, when I didn't even understand it. I started meeting with Leesa Leslie, a counselor at Northwoods. I really opened up to her regarding lesbianism and the drug scene and all of that. It was really the lesbianism that was the big thing for me. She started really counseling me and telling me the truth about what God says in the Bible. I really fought her hard on it because it really didn't make sense to me. She asked me to agree to stay home with my parents for at least a year. I wanted to get out of Peoria and my parents' house. I was applying for work to every gay place I could find—San Francisco, Asheville—all those places, even though I really loved Jesus. I guess I just didn't want to give that up. I really just didn't understand; I didn't want to understand. But she asked me to promise her that I would stay home for a year. And the church that I left in Iowa City prayed that God would close every door that I shouldn't walk through and open the one that I should.*

And that happened. I didn't get any of the jobs I applied for, even though I was very qualified, had gone to a very good school, and had a great GPA. I didn't get any of the jobs I applied for around the country except for one in Peoria. I was like, "What?" And thank God He did that because I wasn't strong enough in my faith then to leave home. I needed some more help; I needed discipled, and I wanted that too. I was just so back and forth on that fence.

My mom and my dad were also finding Jesus in their lives, and it was amazing. At that time my mom told me (I remember as clear as day), "Katie, you're either all in or you're all out," and when she said that to me, I guess the Lord really gave me grace to hear that. That statement has been one of the most important things for me in my walk with Jesus because I had been still straddling the fence that whole time. I needed to decide if I was going to be all in or all out because I couldn't be in the middle any longer.

God gave me grace for a lot of years, letting me straddle the fence; I guess I wasn't ready to hear that until then. I had been in the middle but now He took me to that point. It's like He said, "It's time. You either got to be all in or you completely leave Me." I think about in Revelation where He spits the lukewarm out of His mouth; that feeling is what I had—that there's not a middle option of being a "kind of Christian." I either had to jump off the cliff and if there was nothing there to catch me, I'd be done, or I could back off; but I couldn't just stand there anymore.

That for me was one of the most helpful things, an idea I still think about all the time: You are either all in with Jesus or you're all out. Don't be that middle person because that is actually one of the most destructive things I think you can be. So when my mom told me that (you're either all in or you're all out), I decided then to be all in.

Shortly after that I called my best friend whom I had been involved with sexually for years. One of the hardest things I've ever done was to say goodbye to her, but I knew I needed to. It was so hard, even after I said goodbye to her; those friends were my family, she was my family. I cried so much after that. My mom was so sweet and understanding, but she would always bring me back to being all in or all out.

I was on fire to get baptized. A baptism service was coming up at Northwoods, and I wanted it so bad. But I knew I couldn't continue a relationship with my best friend. I knew I had to let that go before I was baptized. So that was one of the hardest things I've ever done. I called her just a few days before I got baptized, and I told her (I'm sure I did it all wrong), but she knew I had found Jesus, and I was really loving Jesus. Up until then I was still with her. But I told her on the phone, "I just can't be with you anymore. And I can't even have a relationship at all—not even be friends with you." That's what I felt like I had to do. I know that everybody's journey out of lesbianism might be different, but for me, God was really leading me to make a full break. I knew I wasn't strong enough if I was around her. There was too much history. I called her and told her; she bawled and was so confused and was so sad. I felt like the worst person in the world. She was the closest person I'd ever had in my entire life. I felt so horrible for what I did to her. But I did it, and I knew it was right. I knew that was what I needed to do.

A few days later, I was baptized at Northwoods. I was so, so skinny, but I was so ready and hungry to get baptized. When I came up out of that water (like I said, I had no grid for supernatural experiences), but when I came up out of the water, I felt really light and dizzy. I felt like I was walking on marshmallows. I felt like I went into a whole other realm of the spirit for hours. I didn't want to talk to anybody. People wanted to be together to celebrate, but I said no, I had to get and be by myself with the Lord, outside somewhere. I was like, "What just happened to me?"

Fast forward, years later during a ministry time at Harvest School, the Lord showed me what happened in my baptism. In a ministry time at the school, they instructed us to ask the Holy Spirit to take us back to a memory of anything and let Him show us what He wanted us to know. I saw in this vision (or picture) the scene of my baptism, which I wasn't expecting. But instead of seeing all the people, I saw a ton of angels. They were watching on the shore. Next to me, instead of my pastor who baptized me, were two angels with huge spears. When I went down in the water, they speared through me, and I saw all of these demons get speared out of me; they were left down there on the spears in the water, and I came up out of the water without those demons. That's what He showed me. I then understood why I felt so light and free, and like I was in another realm or something. He had so delivered me in that baptism! It was so holy. That's why I love baptisms so much.

That was my second big moment of freedom. The first time was when I got baptized in the Holy Spirit, when I came back to Jesus. That really empowered me to go after Him and truly find that love relationship with Him. With having left my girlfriend behind, I had taken that next step of baptism when I went all in with Jesus.

So Leesa kept on discipling me at Northwoods. I started working the night shift at the hospital, and on my days off I would ride my bike through the country for hours and hours and just worship and bawl before the Lord. I had a couple of years of just falling in love with Jesus. I stopped all drugs, stopped cigarettes, stopped the alcohol, no more sex. All this stuff was getting out of me, all the witchcraft and the New Age stuff. I was praying and renouncing, and I burned so many things, so many bonfires that freaked my neighbors out. I was so "I'm done!" and I went 1000 degrees the other direction and burned everything I owned—probably some stuff I could have kept, but I tossed anything where I was like "This is not the life I want anymore!"

[After another year Katie joined a mission team to minister with a church in India, which led to a three-month stay with the pastor's family. This was an incredible time of seeing God move in miracles, signs, and wonders. Following that experience, Katie spent three months at Harvest School in Mozambique, Africa, being trained for ministry. She later returned to Mozambique, serving more than two years as a missionary nurse in Pemba with Iris International.]

I want people to know that Jesus is real. He's not just a theory. He's not any of that. He's so real; the Spirit realm is real. He's worth it all. He's worth it to give up everything, even if you don't understand why. Homosexuality—He said not to do that. You might not understand why it's a sin, but He'll get you there. What you really need is that love relationship with Him, that intimacy with Him, and that deep encounter with Him. Just to know that He is there and He's a person, and He's with you. That's why you do everything. You're going to go all in when you fall in love with Him. Just pray that He gives you the grace to love Him and know Him and be known by Him. Give your heart to Him. Jesus is so beautiful, the most beautiful One I have ever seen. He is so kind and pure and lovely and loving. He is the King, and He is so worthy and so righteous and so holy. And all I want to do is just be with Him. I love Him.

If you are wondering about God, when you start to know Him and be loved by Him, nothing else can ever compare to Him. He is so radiant and so lovely that there is no loss compared to getting Him.

Love is the core theme in Katie's story: God's love for her and her love for God. That makes sense when we understand that Jesus taught that loving God is the most important command: *"Jesus replied [to the Pharisees]: 'Love the Lord your God with all your heart and with all your soul and with all your mind. This is the first and greatest commandment'"* (Matthew 22:37-38).

GOD'S LOVE FOR US

The Bible says, *"God is love"* (1 John 4:16), and as a result we can expect His love to be revealed in many ways. Below is a sampling of ways in which God expresses His love for us.

Love Caused God to Act

Romans 5:8 states, *"God demonstrates His own love for us in this: While we were still sinners, Christ died for us."* God acted in your behalf out of love. He didn't wait until you loved Him. He didn't wait until you became more spiritual. He loved you even while you rejected Him. Right now, no matter how far you are from Him, His heart toward you is love, longing for you to return to Him. As Jesus hung on the cross, being mocked by a cruel crowd, He prayed, *"Father, forgive them, for they don't know what they are doing"* (Luke 23:24). That reflects His heart toward you. In Luke 15 as the father runs out to greet his prodigal child who's returning home, he saw past all the child's failures and rebellion and felt only love and joy that his child had come home. That's God's heart for you.

Compassion for the Weak

When Jesus healed broken and diseased bodies, the Bible often notes it was compassion or mercy that moved Him to act. He was gentle with those society rejected, such as lepers, prostitutes, and beggars. This tenderness reflects God's heart because Jesus said, *"If you've seen Me, you've seen the Father"* (John 14:9). If you want to know what God is like, what He feels and how He acts, just look at Jesus. You will learn He has deep compassion for the wounded and weak. The Bible

58

puts it poetically: *"A bruised reed He will not break, and a smoldering wick He will not snuff out..."* (Matthew 12:20).

Parties and Celebrations

God seems to enjoy parties. Luke 15 records three stories about the lost being found, and each story ends with a celebration. In the case of the prodigal son (Luke 15:11-32), his homecoming included a barbecue (*"Kill the fattened calf!"*), music, and dancing. On one occasion I drove to the home of a friend who had just returned to God after a time of wild living. I stopped at Kroger on the way and purchased steaks for him, symbolic of Luke 15.

What do we learn about the heart of God when Jesus's first miracle was to create wine so a wedding feast could continue into the night? (See John 2:1-11.) His first miracle was not an act of judgment but an act of joy. When Matthew began following Jesus, He celebrated his new life with a party at his home (see Luke 5:27-29). There was a party to honor Jesus for raising Lazarus from the dead (John 12:2). The annual Jewish calendar revolved around feast days of friends and food, all ordained by God. And it's the Wedding Feast of the Lamb (Revelation 19:6-9) that will kick off the restoration of God's Kingdom at the end of time. God seems to be biased toward celebrations and joy.

Creation as a Gift

This morning I watched a staggering variety of birds from our home on the Illinois River. There were geese, pelicans, blue herons, Baltimore orioles, red-headed finches, a woodpecker, hummingbirds, and best of all, a bald eagle swooped into the tree in front of our deck. So many styles of flight! Compare the soaring of eagles to the frantic wings of mallards to the V-formations of geese to the pterodactyl-like cruising of herons to the bumblebee-ish hummingbirds hovering at our feeders and then buzzing off to nearby cottonwood trees.

Consider the huge variety of trees: willows, pines, sequoias, apple. Consider the variety of bark on them: smooth birch, deeply etched oaks, circular patterns on palms. Every category of life is jammed with variety. Not sure why all this display feels restorative to the soul, but it does.

Earlier a deer and two fawns moved down the shoreline. One fawn stayed compliantly by mom while the other dashed far ahead, pivoted and sprinted back, passing mom, and then repeated the move over and over. Was mom thinking, "Why can't you be like your brother?!" Why are baby mammals playful? Where'd that blueprint come from? We treasure animals, are drawn to them. That's why there are traffic jams in Yellowstone when one bison is in camera range. That's why a big percentage of TV programming features pets or wildlife. We are fascinated and delighted with the animal kingdom. This attraction to animals is an echo of God's original intention for mankind, that we steward and care for creation, especially the animal kingdom as implied in Genesis chapters one and two.

God created the earth teeming with life. He also filled it with beauty. The night sky. The northern lights. Thunderstorms. Sunsets. The national parks in Utah, turquoise waters in the Caribbean, the fjords of Norway, anywhere in Alaska, Jenny Lake in Grand Teton, Olympic peninsula in Washington state, Mt. Cotopaxi in Ecuador, Karuizawa, Japan, in the winter. Then there's the simple beauty in our backyards. Snowflakes. Dew on spider webs. Every flower. A leaf.

Beauty, wonder, adventure, freedom, playfulness, wildness, mystery—all these traits permeate creation. These qualities feed our souls and delight our hearts. All of this feels gift-like, as if Someone was thinking of us when He fashioned the earth. He cared enough to mix creation with joy and whimsy and splendor and wonder, all calculated to touch us, thrill us, satisfy us. *"What no eye has seen, what no ear has heard, and what no human mind has conceived—the things God has prepared for those who love Him"* (1 Corinthians 2:9).

His Presence

Perhaps in your view, God is Someone distant, unconcerned, hard to please, and frightening. Approaching Him is similar to Dorothy approaching the Wizard of Oz. But King David's great desire was to *"...dwell in the house of the Lord all the days of my life, to gaze on the beauty of the Lord and to seek Him in His temple"* (Psalms 27:4).

When we truly know Who God is, we are drawn to Him. The Bible records how God created Adam and Eve to be in close relationship with Him. And that trait was passed on to you, too. You are hardwired for relationship with Him; your heart yearns for Him. All that search for satisfaction is an attempt to fill the empty place only God can fill. Adam's and Eve's disobedience broke our relationship with our Heavenly Father. But when we repent of our sins and turn back to God through faith in Jesus, the relationship is restored.

David declared, *"Better is one day in Your courts than a thousand elsewhere"* (Psalm 84:10).Think of that: David says one day in God's presence beats 1,000 days on a beach at an all-inclusive resort, or 1,000 days in a fully furnished mountain lake cabin, or 1,000 days at _____ (you fill in your ideal spot). David says being with God just one day is so overwhelming, so take-your-breath-away amazing that 1,000 days at your best imagined place can't top it. This inviting presence of an almighty God speaks of His love. Psalm 16 expresses the lighthearted joy and generosity that we experience in His presence: *"You make known to me the path of life; You will fill me with joy in Your presence, with eternal pleasures at Your right hand"* (Psalms 16:11).

Let David's psalms transform how you see God. He is a loving Father Who will be generous in His kindness to you.

THE NUMBER ONE COMMAND

"Jesus replied: 'Love the Lord your God with all your heart and with all your soul and with all your mind. This is the first and greatest commandment.'" (Matthew 22:37-38)

The greatest command is to love God. Not to SERVE God, but to LOVE Him. The fact that Jesus commands us to love God means that love must be more than a feeling. There must be something about love that is actionable, that requires a willful choice. Actions such as turning toward Him, dropping your resistance, softening your attitude, becoming vulnerable, listening, being teachable. These are actions of the will, and love can't develop without these kind of actions. Think of loving a spouse. Aren't these responses foundational to that love, responses that create the tender heart that love needs in order to grow?

Yet, while love is more than feelings, it seems empty if there are no feelings. Unfortunately, many churches seem to value a strictly rational approach to God that is Spock-like in the way they shun emotion. No wonder so many people feel empty in their church experience and look elsewhere to fill their hearts. There are current worship songs that I sing at our church, with tears streaming down my face and my heart about to burst for the love I feel for God. But then I'll read articles written by other Christians in which those same songs are criticized as "shallow" and "emotion-driven," as more conducive to a rock concert than "true congregational worship," whatever that is. It really saddens me, the way some feel the need to impose their idea of worship on others, when their comments only reflect their personal likes and dislikes. It seems we believers are prone to confuse our personal taste and preferences with the opinion of the Holy Spirit. Why wouldn't our worship experience evoke emotional responses toward God? Why wouldn't our worship include love songs to God?

If Christianity is a relationship with God, and the primary command is to love God, then wouldn't you expect to have relational experiences of love with God? We are to love God with all our heart, but looking at many churches, you'd think the core of Christianity is going to meetings, pursuing academic study, and being against things, with little emphasis on intimacy with the Father, as if that intimacy is an optional category to be pursued only by the few who are feelings-oriented (read "weak-minded").

Love isn't always logical. If it were, you'd never kiss your spouse again, with all the bacteria packed in the human mouth! One time, a woman, out of her deep gratitude for what Jesus had done for her, poured super-expensive perfume onto His feet. Many of His followers, watching this, thought her action wasn't very logical. It was an emotional, silly waste of money. But Jesus? He treasured her for it (see Mathew 26:6-13).

So, let's affirm the soft side of love for God. But having said that, true love for God at its core should have some tough-as-nails qualities too, such as:

Obedience
"Whoever has My commands and keeps them is the one who loves Me. The one who loves Me will be loved by My Father, and I too will love them and show Myself to them."
(John 14:21)

The truest evidence of your love for Jesus is your obedience. When Katie made the hard choice to break off her relationship with her girlfriend, she was expressing love for Jesus over everything. I've sat with husbands while they made painful phone calls to end adulterous relationships with lovers because they knew they were breaking God's commands. Obedience is costly. But love demands it. Taking a stand when Scripture requires it may cost you relationships, popularity, favor with important people, promotions, and positions. But that's just part of the Christian experience as we walk in a world that is not our home. Our allegiance is to the One Who sits on the throne; it's His approval we are seeking.

Devotion

Daniel Chapter 3 tells the story of King Nebuchadnezzar and his demand that everyone worship the idol he created. When three young Jewish men refused, they were arrested and brought before the king. When the king threatened them with death by fire, their response was powerful:

"If we are thrown into the blazing furnace, the God we serve is able to deliver us from it, and He will deliver us from Your Majesty's hand. But even if He does not, we want you to know, Your Majesty, that we will not serve your gods or worship the image of gold you have set up." (Daniel 3:17–18)

Our love for God is expressed by a willingness to suffer rather than compromise. It was seeing this kind of devotion in the lives of persecuted Christians that opened the door for me to become a follower of Jesus. I heard firsthand stories about people in communist lands being tortured or thrown into prison simply because of their faith in Jesus. At that time, I had no interest in spiritual things, but hearing these stories caused me to wonder what was so special about Jesus that people were willing to suffer for Him? Their devotion opened my heart to seek God. Jesus calls His followers to die to self and live for God, to live with a sold-out allegiance to Him. This means we choose to obey Him regardless of outcomes.

Surrender

Because Jesus purchased you with His blood when He died on the cross (Revelation 5:9), you are no longer your own:

"And He died for all, that those who live should no longer live for themselves but for Him who died for them and was raised again." (2 Corinthians 5:15)

A genuine love relationship with Jesus has the surrender of your life at the core. You are no longer at the center of your life; He is. You step down from the throne from which you've ruled your life, and you invite Jesus to take your place, to be your King. That is a reflection of your love for God. Jesus died so you can live. He gave His life for you; now you give your life to Him. All your goals, plans, ideas, opinions, and views you now surrender to Him. You give Him the right to redirect or change anything He desires. That's how it works.

ACTIVATION

A. Jesus's Love for You

In a quiet place consider these verses:

"I have been crucified with Christ and I no longer live, but Christ lives in me. The life I now live in the body, I live by faith in the Son of God, <u>who loved me and gave Himself for me.</u>" (Galatians 2:20, emphasis mine)

"…and walk in the way of love, just as <u>Christ loved us and gave Himself up for us</u> as a fragrant offering and sacrifice to God." (Ephesians 5:2, emphasis mine)

Let these two verses sink into your heart. Pray about them: "Jesus, speak to me about this…Do You love me? Did You give Yourself for me?" Let Him speak to your heart.

B. Correcting Your Ideas About God

Read and think about this passage from Psalm 103:

"The Lord is compassionate and gracious, slow to anger, abounding in love. He will not always accuse, nor will He harbor His anger forever; He does not treat us as our sins deserve or repay us according to our iniquities. For as high as the heavens are above the earth, so great is His love for those who fear Him; as far as the east is from the west, so far has He removed our transgressions from us. As a father has compassion on his children, so the Lord has compassion on those who fear Him…" (Psalms 103:8-13)

Write out a list of the many ways God's love for you is expressed here. Ask Him to correct false ideas you may have about Him.

C. "The Blessing"_Song

Find "The Blessing" song on YouTube. There are various versions online. My favorites are the Hawaiian version and the World edition in which believers from 154 countries sing. Play it and let God speak to you and reveal His heart for you.

CHAPTER 5

LOVING OTHERS

"We love because He first loved us. Whoever claims to love God yet hates a brother or sister is a liar. For whoever does not love their brother and sister, whom they have seen, cannot love God, whom they have not seen. And He has given us this command: Anyone who loves God must also love their brother and sister." (1 John 4:19-21)

"A new command I give you: Love one another. As I have loved you, so you must love one another. By this everyone will know that you are My disciples, if you love one another." (John 13:34-35)

"Dear friends, let us love one another, for love comes from God. Everyone who loves has been born of God and knows God. Whoever does not love does not know God, because God is love. This is how God showed His love among us: He sent His one and only Son into the world that we might live through Him. This is love: not that we loved God, but that He loved us and sent His Son as an atoning sacrifice for our sins. Dear friends, since God so loved us, we also ought to love one another." (1 John 4:7-11)

"But to you who are listening I say: Love your enemies, do good to those who hate you, bless those who curse you, pray for those who mistreat you...But love your enemies, do good to them, and lend to them without expecting to get anything back. Then your reward will be great, and you will be children of

the Most High, because He is kind to the ungrateful and wicked. Be merciful, just as your Father is merciful." (Luke 6:27-28, 35-36)

LOVING ONE ANOTHER

Jesus taught that loving God and loving people are to be the top priorities for His followers. He defined the type of love He had in mind when He said we are to love others in the way He has loved us. How has He loved us? By giving of Himself in sacrificial service, with compassion, generosity, forgiveness, and putting others first.

He said: *"A new command I give you: Love one another. As I have loved you, so you must love one another. By this everyone will know that you are My disciples, if you love one another"* (John 13:34-35). This is a big statement. How will people know you are Jesus's disciple? When they see the love you have for others. In this verse Jesus is giving the world permission to judge if we are Christians by the amount of love they see as we relate to others. But perhaps it is on this point that you left your church. Instead of love, you saw harsh condemnation toward those who were different. You saw division and conflict. You saw unloving church people driving other people away. Maybe that was part of your story.

A HIGH SCHOOL OUTREACH

In high school I attended a Christian youth outreach at which they handed out all the hamburgers you could eat. At the time I wasn't interested in spiritual matters, but I liked hamburgers. After eating, fellow students from my school stood before the crowd and told about their Christian faith and how they needed God in their lives, and they encouraged us to trust God like they did. One student was a popular athlete but as he spoke, I thought, "If that's a Christian, I don't want to be one!" I had watched him regularly bully others at school, often picking on weaker students in the hallways and in P.E. classes. Today, I'd be more sympathetic toward him because now I realize transformation into a new person can be a bumpy process. But in that moment, he seemed like a phony. I suspect many of you have similar stories.

Maybe you became disillusioned as you saw church members whose actions were hypocritical. Perhaps it seemed your church despised anyone with different politics or lifestyles. Maybe you found the church turned inward with little love for the needy or the broken. Instead of inviting everyone to come and meet the God Who loves them, maybe church members were selective in whom they welcomed.

LOVING THOSE WHO ARE DIFFERENT

It seems in every generation the church needs to be reminded to die to itself and sacrificially love others, especially those who are different. The *Jesus Revolution* movie, released in spring of 2023, illustrates this. It tells the surprising story of how, in 1969 on the West coast, at the height of the youth rebellion against middle-class American values, hippies came to faith in Jesus. They were overwhelmed by God's love and forgiveness, and it wrecked them. So they went to churches in California and said, "Help us! We just met Jesus! He saved us and freed us. What do we do next?" Unfortunately, too many churches told the newly saved hippies, "First get a haircut and come back in a suit and tie...and put on shoes!" Thankfully, in some churches, love won out, such as with Chuck Smith and Calvary Chapel, who were featured in the movie.

Lyle Steenis had a similar story. He was a Kansas farmer in the 1960s who felt called to serve Jesus. So Lyle and his wife moved to Southern California and started a church. They worked hard, and by 1969, he was leading 300 white middle-class family folks in a traditional church.

But then it got messy. A born-again hippie visited one Sunday morning and then asked Steenis if he could return with his friends. The next week 21 hippies showed up, and all 21 prayed to receive Jesus. Then they brought their friends who brought their friends. From that point on, beach kids and hippies came and knew they finally found real love in Jesus.

The tidy church with its predictable routines was turned upside down as overnight it filled with barefoot, long-haired types, wearing love beads, surrendering drugs and sin at the altar. Many church members were angry that their traditional church was being thrown into chaos. Some members went out to the parking lot to drive the hippies away, but Pastor Steenis declared, "I'll whip the next guy who tries to run them out!" He told the complaining members, "The church doors swing both directions. If you don't like what's happening, you can leave." And two thirds of his church did leave.

But even for Pastor Steenis, it was all so strange; this didn't look like church as he knew it. However, he kept preaching and praying, and more young people came, and they wanted to pray and sing all night and hold church services daily. All Lyle could do was hang onto God and stay out of His way as hundreds of lives were changed. Today many of these former hippies are in full-time Christian ministry, and hundreds continue to follow Christ faithfully, because they found in Pastor Steenis someone who loved them enough to lay aside his personal comfort and let God have His way.

Fortunately, church leaders like Lyle Steenis and Chuck Smith saw that God was at work, and they dropped manmade religious rules and sought to be led only by the Bible. This is important since many of you abandoned church because you felt beat up by religious rules enforced by leaders. Every new movement of God faces opposition from churches because the new movement typically exposes manmade rules and doctrines. Church leaders must stay humble and teachable, discerning what rules are manmade (e.g., wearing suits to church) versus what is clear Bible teaching.

HATING OUR NEIGHBOR

The most destructive failure to love by churches in our country was during the time of slavery in the American South. Throughout history, slavery has been practiced in many forms in nations and cultures worldwide. However, slavery in the Southern states was some of the most evil ever devised, based on race, with complete denial of all human rights. People were bought and sold like livestock. Rape and torture were common. Children were torn from their mothers, never to be seen again. Unbelievably, this form of slavery was justified and endorsed by Southern churches. In the years leading up to the Civil War, many denominations (Presbyterian, Baptist, and Methodist) broke apart as churches in the North denounced Southern churches for their support of slavery. That so many Southern churches were willing to oppress their brother simply due to skin color was demonic.

Unfortunately, the willingness to oppress fellow human beings knows no boundaries. I live close to Illinois' most popular state park, Starved Rock. The name "Starved Rock" comes from an act of genocide in which two Native American tribes were at war. One tribe chased another to the top of a bluff overlooking the Illinois River, where they laid siege to them until every man, woman, and child died from hunger: Native Americans hating each other. In Mexico, Aztecs enslaved neighboring tribes and used them as human sacrifices. Records tell of a 96-hour period when over 80,000 captives were sacrificed to their gods: Aztecs hating their neighbors. In 1994, there was genocide in Rwanda, Africa, where the Hutu tribe brutally rampaged against the Tutsis, killing 75% of the tribe, with the weapon of choice being the machete: Africans hating each other. In 1975, a Marxist coup in Cambodia led to the mass murder of between one and three million people: Cambodians hating each other. Conflicts between Muslims and Hindus in India and Pakistan have resulted in hundreds of thousands of deaths: Asians hating one another. Add to these the death of millions in the holocaust by Hitler's National Socialist government, and even more millions murdered by Marxist communists in the Soviet Union and during the Cultural Revolution in Mao's communist China. The point is, worldwide, through all history, every culture and race has shown the capacity to hate and oppress their neighbor, That's why we all need a Savior. Instead of vilifying the United States alone, it's more appropriate to vilify the entire human race. The Bible says *"there are none righteous, no not one"* (Romans 3:10)—regardless of race or nationality. Jesus said evil does not begin with a political system or a particular nation, culture, or race; it begins with every human heart:

"For it is from within, out of a person's heart, that evil thoughts come— sexual immorality, theft, murder, adultery, greed, malice, deceit, lewdness, envy, slander, arrogance and folly. All these evils come from inside and defile a person." (Mark 7:20-23)

We all need a new heart.

OUR HERITAGE OF LOVE

When churches and believers are unloving, prejudiced, and/or selfish, they are disobeying their Lord, Who died not only for His friends but also for those who rejected Him. He came to serve everyone through His death, including those who had different ideas of morality and politics. When churches lack concern for others, they are neither following Jesus nor being true to their Christian heritage. Historians point out that the early church had many revolutionary traits that separated it from the rest of the Roman Empire. Roman society was structured with strict separation between the different classes, but the early Christian church was radical in how it mixed the poor, rich, and middle class on equal terms. The church was multi-racial and multi-ethnic. They were committed to caring for widows and orphans, the poor and marginalized. When people fled cities because of outbreaks of plague, it was Christians who stayed and cared for the sick. They fought the common practice of infanticide by rescuing abandoned babies. They practiced radical forgiveness, loving their enemies. That is our heritage. That is who we as Christians are to be.

CONFRONTING INJUSTICE

In America's history, Christians have led the way in confronting injustice. Charles Finney was famous for his revivals in which hundreds of thousands became Christians in the early 1800s. But he also spoke out against injustice. He championed Native Americans, denouncing their treatment by the government as "shameless wickedness" and condemned the Congress for regularly breaking treaties as "outrageous injustice." He also attacked slavery as a "heinous sin." In the decades leading to the Civil War, abolitionists fighting against slavery did so almost exclusively from their Christian beliefs. Historians credit the book *Uncle Tom's Cabin* with stirring the conscience of millions through its depiction of the cruelty of Southern slavery. Its author, Harriet Beecher Stowe, was a pastor's wife who said the book came to her in a vision she had during a communion service. Later, when she met Abraham Lincoln during the Civil War, he reportedly said, "So you're the little woman who wrote the book that made this Great War." Throughout history, slavery was practiced worldwide in many forms, but it was in Western nations that the abolition of slavery started, driven by Christian values.

CHARITABLE GIVING

Since the beginning, the Church has been led by the love of Jesus to be generous in helping the poor (e.g., Acts 4:33-37). This trait is found in the Church worldwide. I've watched poor believers in third-world nations cheerfully give out of the little they have in order to help others. In the United States, in 2022, Christian philanthropy accounted for 70% of all American charitable giving at $300 billion; actual giving is more because much is not reported. Last night at supper, friends told about a needy situation with a struggling family, and it was apparent they were quietly giving money to help. My wife and I give money each month directly to a family in an Asian country to help with the financial pressure they face. In another situation in which we're trying to help, there are poor Asian families trapped in economic slavery; they and their children are forced to work making bricks because they can't pay their debts. We and a handful of friends have been able to help pay off debts and set families free. Because we send monies directly to local churches and not to official charitable organizations, it doesn't get reported and therefore isn't included in the statistics. I know many believers who give and help people in similar fashion.

Whatever people say or think about the Church, it is the primary source of charity and kindness in a world of suffering. It should anger us every time a politician loudly demands more funding for the poor, but their personal tax forms reveal only 1–2% of their personal income given toward charity. Many Christians I know quietly give 10% of their income and go well beyond that.

RECONCILING ENEMIES

It's the gospel of Jesus that has the power to change the human heart and address injustice because at its core is forgiveness and reconciliation. I witnessed a powerful example of this while in Japan. In the 1900s until the end of WWII, Japan ruthlessly colonized Korea, treating Koreans as subhuman. To this day there continues to be bitterness and pain between the two countries. Once while we were in Japan, at a gathering of Japanese church leaders, a Korean friend spoke from the platform, sharing her story of how her family had been brutalized by Japanese soldiers and how she carried resentment toward Japan for most of her life, but now she was a Christian and sought to walk in forgiveness. At that moment, a Japanese church leader interrupted her speech by walking to the stage and then kneeling before her. On his knees he confessed the sins of his nation and asked for her forgiveness. This led to her kneeling before him, forgiving him while confessing her resentment and asking forgiveness. Then it was as if Jesus entered the auditorium because soon, throughout the room, people were kneeling, confessing sins, and being reconciled with each other. It was an amazing moment. Government social justice policies did not create that moment. It was the love and forgiveness of Jesus that was changing human hearts.

BECOMING A LOVING DISCIPLE

Don't let a bad church experience lead you to throw it all out; there's a baby in that bath water! If you were disillusioned by unloving believers, then those people have lost sight of Who it is we follow. When Jesus died on the cross, He gave Himself for everyone, including His enemies and those who didn't agree with Him. If we are His followers, then we too position ourselves to love and serve those whose politics, lifestyles, ethics, and worldviews oppose ours. That's what it means to follow Jesus. We don't compromise truth. We lovingly, humbly, but boldly speak God's truth to a rebellious world. But we love everyone. We extend honor and respect to each person because each is created in God's image. Jesus valued each to the extent He died for them. Jesus died for each person because He loves them and wants them to be restored to God.

We all have the capacity to hate our brother. We all have the capacity to judge others and take offense at others while overlooking our own selfishness, hypocrisy, and pride. However, when we ourselves have dealt with our own hearts through confession of our sins, then our concern for social justice can be rooted in the power of God's love and truth: *"If we claim to be without sin, we deceive ourselves and the truth is not in us. If we confess our sins, He is faithful and just and will forgive us our sins and purify us from all unrighteousness"* (1 John 1:8-9).

Let Jesus, and not the churches you experienced, define what it is to be a disciple.

"Then Jesus said to his disciples, 'Whoever wants to be my disciple must deny themselves and take up their cross and follow me.'" (Matthew 16:24)

Jesus calls people to lay down their lives and follow Him. Don't make your life about yourself; make it about Him.

"And He died for all, that those who live should no longer live for themselves but for Him who died for them and was raised again." (2 Corinthians 5:15)

There is a radical shift in our society around issues of gender, race, justice, and equality. The world emphasizes "my rights," "my body," "it's my choice," "gender is only a construct," and on and on. Much of this clamor is contradictory and self-centered. But Jesus comes to you directly and says, "I called you to be My disciple. It is not about you anymore. Don't be the god of your own life any longer. Deny yourself. Take up your cross. Follow Me."

He hasn't forgotten the prayer you prayed as a child when you gave your heart to Him. The trust you had in Him when you were little, the decisions you made for Him when you were younger are not forgotten. And He is saying, "It's time to return."

ACTIVATION

A. Dealing with Self-Deception

Get in a quiet place and consider 1 John 1:8-9: *"If we claim to be without sin, we deceive ourselves and the truth is not in us. If we confess our sins, He is faithful and just and will forgive us our sins and purify us from all unrighteousness."* This speaks about self-deception. Ask Jesus to reveal to you any areas of self-deception. As He shows you things, take ownership and confess them to Him as sin, asking for His forgiveness and cleansing from them. If you have become involved in other forms of spirituality, ask the Jesus of the Bible to reveal truth about your involvement. You might experience some resistance, especially if you are a spiritually sensitive person. But Jesus warned of spiritual deception, and He will lead you to truth if you set yourself to trust Him.

B. How Do I Follow?

Ask Jesus to speak to you about Matthew 16:24: *"Whoever wants to be my disciple must deny themselves and take up their cross and follow Me."* How does He want you to deny yourself, take up the cross, and follow Him? Ask Him what are the first steps He wants you to take.

HOW DO I PROCEED?

Maybe you are thinking, "I'm so far away from the Lord. My relationships and pursuits and ideas have not made room for the God of the Bible. But I want to return to Him. Where do I start?"

First, surrender your life to God and set yourself to follow Jesus. Pray the prayer at the end of Chapter 3. Ask Him for help and courage. You might experience moments of pain because of the impact your new life will have on your current relationships. This has been true in the lives of all who choose to follow Him. It helps to know you walk with many, many others who have had to lay down their lives and do really hard things out of love and obedience to Christ. Ask the Holy Spirit to guide and help you know what to do next in your life.

Second, start asking Him for help in all the situations and concerns and troubles in your life. Start developing a dependence on prayer. Learn to shoot up short prayers to God during the day, but also begin to regularly set aside more extended time to bring your concerns to Him. For me, spending quiet time with God works best in the morning right after I get up. But maybe evening is better for you. Depend on His promise to answer your prayers: *"Do not be anxious about anything, but in every situation, by prayer and petition, with thanksgiving, present your requests to God"* (Philippians 4:6). Believe

Him for breakthroughs, help, and miracles. *"Ask and it will be given to you; seek and you will find; knock and the door will be opened to you. For everyone who asks receives; the one who seeks finds; and to the one who knocks, the door will be opened"* (Matthew 7:7-8). And don't give up! Keep persevering in your prayers even when you don't see immediate results. *"Then Jesus told his disciples a parable to show them that they should always pray and not give up"* (Luke 18:1).

Start reading the Bible regularly. As you read, ask: "What do I do next, Lord? What is my next step?" You might assume He wants you to immediately walk out of all your current relationships and lifestyle and dive into huge changes. And maybe He will insist on that. But then again, He might say, "For now, I just want to work on your unforgiveness," or "For now, let's deal with your pride," or "Let's address your selfishness." He's a master surgeon Who knows precisely how to heal and free you. Maybe He wants to address your tendency to judge others, or to lie, or to gossip, or to cheat. Or maybe He will say, "For now, I only want you to understand how much I love you and treasure you, and for a season I want to keep you focused on that and growing in intimacy with Me. I want you to experience the healing power of My love in your heart. We'll get to the other stuff later." The point is to follow where Jesus is leading you.

The primary way to do this is through the Bible, letting God mentor you as you read. Position yourself to be responsive, asking Him, "How do I apply this Scripture to my life? What should I do?" Keep your heart soft and open to be corrected, instructed, and guided. Affirm Him as your Lord to be obeyed and your Shepherd to be followed. I think you'll be amazed at how He begins to work within you.

I suggest two approaches to your Bible reading. First, read large chunks of the Bible. When I gave my life to Christ, I soon began reading 10-30 chapters a day (I could read that much because I was a teenager with lots of free time. You may have much less opportunity to read). This is the process of renewing your mind, bringing truth to bear on your thinking. You're not stopping to study details. Instead, you are letting the truth of God wash over your heart and mind. As you read the stories, prophecies, and teaching, you are beginning to correct wrong ideas and opinions you've held about life and God. You are embracing truths and promises that replace fears and worries that have plagued you. Faith and confidence for the future will increase. You are learning the ways of God as you see the life of faith modeled in story after story. I suggest downloading the free Bible app where you will find scores of Bible reading plans that can help you read through the Bible in a systematic way.

The second approach is to read Scripture slowly and ask the Holy Spirit to speak to you in each verse. I suggest you start reading in the New Testament daily. Reading a few verses from a gospel (the gospel of John is a good starting place) and from an epistle (such as Colossians) is a common practice. In this approach, reading less is fine because you aren't focused on the amount you read. Your goal is to hear God. When Paul first encountered Jesus, as recorded in Acts 22:8,10, he asked two questions: "Who are You, Lord?" and "What should I do?" These are great questions to ask as you focus on a few verses. You are asking God to teach you more about Himself (*Who are You, Lord?*), and you are asking Him to show you what to do—how to follow Him and serve Him (*What should I do?*). Thus, as you ponder a few verses, you are speaking to Him, asking Him these questions, trying to listen and understand. In this you are developing a dependence on Him. As you read, expect Him to highlight a promise, an idea, a warning, etc. that is specific for you and your life. As He draws your attention to a verse, stop there and ask the Holy Spirit what He is wanting you to see. What does it mean for you and how does He want you to apply it in your life? (Chapter 12 will discuss the idea of hearing God.) This is allowing the God of the universe to come beside you, to mentor you and shepherd you. And that's pretty cool.

And remember, your goal is not to know the Bible. Your goal is to know the God of the Bible. I say this to help you avoid the error of Jesus's religious enemies, the Pharisees. They were the Bible scholars of the day but Jesus told them, "You neither know Me nor My Father (John 8:19)." Knowing the Bible does not equal knowing God. Keep a clear eyed focus on the chief goal of loving God.

SECTION II
MOVING FORWARD

CHAPTER 6

UNDERSTANDING REALITY

"So we fix our eyes not on what is seen, but on what is unseen, since what is seen is temporary, but what is unseen is eternal." (2 Corinthians 4:18)

"For we live by faith, not by sight." (2 Corinthians 5:7)

"For our struggle is not against flesh and blood, but against the rulers, against the authorities, against the powers of this dark world and against the spiritual forces of evil in the heavenly realms." (Ephesians 6:12)

"Be alert and of sober mind. Your enemy the devil prowls around like a roaring lion looking for someone to devour." (1 Peter 5:8)

"Trust in the Lord with all your heart and lean not on your own understanding; in all your ways submit to Him, and He will make your paths straight." (Proverbs 3:5-6)

As we begin Section 2, I assume that through reading the previous chapters you've made some movement toward God. Perhaps it is a tiny step toward Him with a willingness to listen further, or maybe you've experienced a complete return and surrender of your life to your Heavenly Father. Wherever you are in this journey, I think this section will be helpful to you as it will show how to gain more ground in your life. The following chapters will lead you into healing, restoration, and freedom, especially from your past. We can be stuck in life because we are defined by our past, but Jesus wants to free you and redefine your life.

KNOWING REALITY

In the corridors of major airports, you can find big maps of the facilities with an arrow labeled "You are here," pinpointing your current location. Knowing your location in the facility enables you to choose the right direction in which to move forward. That's the purpose of this chapter: to pinpoint where you currently are—in reality.

Knowing where you are is a big deal because the assumptions and values by which you live are all based on what you perceive reality to be. Is there a "god" who pays attention to our choices and behavior? Or are we all products of impersonal evolutionary forces following no design, only the dictates of natural selection? Who determines what is right and wrong, true and false? What is the purpose of life? What is needed for people to experience their best life? This is the ultimate issue behind all the political, moral, social, and ethical issues that divide people. It is a battle over reality. What is ultimate reality? And who defines reality? Whichever political party is in power? A small, privileged elite? Whomever the media decides to support and protect?

Some time ago I compiled a list of mountain-climbing truths, one of which is: *You can't win an argument with a compass.* A compass is always right; it always points true north. It doesn't matter if I agree with it or not. If I'm mountain climbing and I feel strongly that north is one direction but the compass says north is a different direction, I need to ignore my feelings and follow the compass. If I follow my feelings, I will get lost.

Likewise, the realm of reality is true whether we like it or not. Our feelings for what we want to be true aren't capable of changing reality. If the compass says north is this direction, no amount of feeling, desire, arguing, or wishful thinking can make the compass read what you want it to read. The smart move is to lay down your wishes and submit to the truth of the compass. The sooner you do, the sooner you will be on the right path. Reality is like this. Reality is true whether we like it or not. What we think should be true can't change reality. No matter how strongly you insist on your truth, if it conflicts with reality, you will lose.

The atheistic view of reality says there is nothing outside of the material realm. There is no spiritual dimension, no Heaven, no hell, no throne of God before which we will all stand after we die. Everything began with "the Big Bang": the formation of galaxies, stars, and planets, and the impersonal evolutionary forces that eventually produced you and me. You live and then you die and disappear forever and ever. Whether you model your life after Mother Teresa or Adolf Hitler ultimately makes no difference because no One is watching, no One is assessing your life to judge or reward it. After death there will be no accountability for Hitler's crimes or reward for Mother Teresa's compassion. You make your own truth. Your ethics are a matter of your personal opinion. You determine your behavior, lifestyle, and morality according to what pleases you because there is no standard of right and wrong that all people are called to obey. There is no pesky God telling us how to live our lives. Everybody can live according to their own truth.

Or perhaps you believe a spiritual realm does exist but not as the Bible describes. It is something impersonal, like a Star Warsy Force, or some benevolent power that makes few demands. You've settled on a kind of spirituality that chooses to disregard the commands or teachings in the Bible that you personally find objectionable. The god you believe in brings no judgment but loves and forgives all. Your behavior and lifestyle are all a matter of personal preference, with tolerance as the chief value. (It's curious though, how many who insist on tolerance toward all behavior are quick to cancel, condemn, and deny freedom of speech to anyone whose "truth" doesn't agree with theirs.)

The aforementioned views of reality size up how people in the West often see life. Maybe you find yourself somewhere in these understandings of reality, even though you might hold some unique assumptions and beliefs that don't line up precisely with the way I've presented things. My goal is to get us thinking about reality as I present a Biblical understanding, which will be helpful in moving forward into the destiny God has for you. (The brief discussion above raises many questions about God's existence, truth, morality, etc., which go beyond the scope of this book. For anyone with questions on these matters, I strongly recommend Timothy Keller's book *The Reason for God: Belief in an Age of Skepticism*. Keller does a great job answering common objections against Christianity, with grace and skill.)

REALITY ACCORDING TO THE BIBLE

In 2 Corinthians 12:2, Paul makes an odd statement, saying he was transported to the "third heaven" where he was in God's presence. Apparently the third heaven is the spiritual dimension where God resides as King. It's where His kingdom reigns and His throne is established. Here His love, power, and purposes prevail. Here, in the third heaven, His will, purposes, and plans are never resisted nor thwarted.

While the Bible does not use the terms "second heaven" or "first heaven," it does speak of two more realms: Ephesians 2:2 speaks about the kingdom of the power of the air, in which evil spiritual powers reside, and in Genesis 1:1 we're told that God created the heavens and the earth, which refers to the physical universe, the material realm which we perceive with our five senses. Some Bible scholars deduce that these are the first heaven and the second heaven, though some might debate the matter.

But the point is this: Reality consists of the visible and the invisible, the material and spiritual, the natural and the supernatural realms. You can live denying that an actual spiritual realm exists, but that doesn't make it go away. You must take reality as it is, not as you wish it to be. This perspective is important because the spiritual realm impacts you daily, whether you believe it to exist or not.

When the Apostle Paul used the term "third heaven," he was referring to that place from which God rules the universe. The Bible reveals God's authority as that of an all-wise, all-powerful, loving, and completely good King. Scripture describes several scenes of His throne (see Isaiah 6:1ff, Ezekiel 1:26ff, Revelation 4:1ff). His kingdom rule extends through all the universe, all, that is, except one place, planet Earth, the scene of a rebellion, where the dragon, the fallen angel satan, rebelled against God's kingdom: *"Then war broke out in heaven. Michael and his angels fought against the dragon, and the dragon and his angels fought back. But he was not strong enough, and they lost their place in heaven. The great dragon was hurled down—that ancient serpent called the devil, or Satan, who leads the whole world astray. He was hurled to the earth, and his angels with him."* (Revelation 12:7-9)

Scholars say that in Isaiah 14:12-15, God reveals the fall of satan was due to his pride:

"You said in your heart, ‹I will ascend to the heavens; I will raise my throne above the stars of God...I will ascend above the tops of the clouds; I will make myself like the Most High'" (Isaiah 14:12-15). In the same manner, satan enticed mankind to turn from God when he tempted Adam and Eve with the lie: *"If you eat the fruit you will become like God"* (see Genesis 3:1-6). In following satan's temptation to sin, man opened the door to be dominated and oppressed by him: *"...the whole world is under the control of the evil one"* (1 John 5:19). He comes to steal, kill, and destroy (see John 10:10). This is why repentance and turning to Jesus changes our life. The Bible says Jesus rescues us *"from the dominion of darkness and brings us into the kingdom of the Son..."* (Colossians 1:13).

We live in an imperfect, fallen world, dominated by evil spiritual forces, but once we turn to Jesus in repentance and faith, we transfer allegiances and are freed from satan's rulership. Our reality now becomes that of living in territory occupied by an oppressive, hate-filled enemy, but the good news is Jesus Christ has overcome that foe. We are told in Ephesians 6: *"Finally, be strong in the Lord and in his mighty power. Put on the full armor of God, so that you can take your stand against the devil's schemes. For our struggle is not against flesh and blood, but against the rulers, against the authorities, against the powers of this dark world and against the spiritual forces of evil in the heavenly realms."* (Ephesians 6:10-12)

IMPLICATIONS

The first fact of reality is this: If you are not taking into consideration both realms, the material world and the spiritual world, then you are not dealing with reality, because reality includes both. Both realms impact you every day, whether you believe in them or not. The Bible states, *"We live by faith, not by sight"* (2 Corinthians 5:7). Faith in God means we go through life aware that we don't see all of reality, but that there is an invisible dimension to which we must relate. A starting place for this life of faith is Proverbs 3:5-6: *"Trust in the Lord with all your heart and lean not on your own understanding; in all your ways submit to Him, and He will make your paths straight."* Through faith and submission to the Lord, you will receive His help and direction even when you don't see and understand.

A second fact of reality is: You were born into a war. The Bible assumes you are under some kind of unseen attack: *"Your enemy the devil prowls around like a roaring lion looking for someone to devour"* (1 Peter 5:8). As stated above, we struggle against evil spiritual forces. If we don't understand that we have an enemy who wants to oppress and destroy us, we will misinterpret much of what happens to us. We will blame God, ourselves, and other people for the troubles in our lives when the Bible wants us to understand that there are evil spiritual forces in the equation, too.

Finally, the assault by sin and satan against your life has wounded you, reduced you, and prevented you from experiencing God's original plan. When Jesus said, *"You must be born again"* (John 3:3), He was saying that God wants you to have a fresh start. He doesn't want the past to define your life. Instead, He wants you free from satan's oppression and from the past; He wants you to enter into the identity and destiny He desires you to have. That's why the remaining chapters in this section are all about freeing you from your past and restoring what sin and satan stole from you. In this section, we will deal with past wounds, fears, disappointments, sins, and habits. Our goal is to find freedom and restoration so the past doesn't define and control us. Rather we will move into all the life Jesus intends us to have.

THE GOAL OF SALVATION

The goal of "salvation" is your adoption by God. In salvation God becomes your Father.

"But when the set time had fully come, God sent His Son...to redeem those under the law, that we might receive adoption to sonship. Because you are His sons, God sent the Spirit of His Son into our hearts, the Spirit who calls out, 'Abba, Father.' So you are no longer a slave, but God's child; and since you are His child, God has made you also an heir." (Galatians 4:4-7)

When we repent and turn toward Jesus, placing our trust in Him and giving Him our allegiance, then we are adopted by God and restored to the identity and destiny He originally desired for us. Previously in my ministry, before I fully understood this truth, I focused on raising up leaders for the church. Now my focus is raising sons and daughters, people who enter fully into their new identity and destiny, who learn to walk in all Jesus has won for them.

Repentance, healing, and deliverance all play a role in our lives being restored and our entering into everything God intends for us. Proper diagnosis of your needs is important because different issues require different solutions. A wounded heart requires healing, not repentance. You can't repent of wounds; wounds require binding and healing. We don't heal a willful sin because sin requires repentance. There could be a need for healing from the effects of the sin or the source of the sin, but the starting point is repentance. And we don't heal a demonic stronghold in our lives; we break its hold on us through deliverance, which can be ministered personally or with the help of friends. The chapters that follow in this section will be helpful in beginning to reclaim and restore what you've lost.

ACTIVATION

A. The Lord's Prayer
"Our Father in heaven, hallowed be your name, your kingdom come, your will be done, on earth as it is in heaven. Give us today our daily bread. And forgive us our debts, as we also have forgiven our debtors. And lead us not into temptation, but deliver us from the evil one." (Matthew 6:9-13)

As a first step into the restoration God has for your life, I recommend you begin to pray The Lord's Prayer over your life (see Matthew 6:9-13). Many of us come from church backgrounds in which The Lord's Prayer is recited in worship services every week. However, when The Lord's Prayer is recited routinely in weekly services, it is easy for people to go on autopilot and repeat the prayer mechanically, without faith or focus. This prayer isn't a magic mantra that has power by simply repeating its words. Its power comes when we remember we are speaking to the King, asking and trusting Him to act in behalf of our requests—requests He has ordained.

I think you will find that the effectiveness of The Lord's Prayer comes from understanding that the prayer is a compilation of priorities to which Jesus wants us to give regular attention, matters such as forgiveness and temptation. In The Lord's Prayer, Jesus has given specific topics He wants us to deal with daily.

In your personal prayer life, use The Lord's Prayer as a model of key categories that Jesus is calling you to pursue. There are three specific petitions in the prayer that are tied to your restoration and transformation.

A. Begin to pray the request "let Your Kingdom come and Your will be done" into the various situations you are facing. When you request "let Your Kingdom come," you are asking God to bring His rule and order and kingdom authority into a situation. Whatever trouble, problem, or relational issue you are facing, you can ask God to step in and bring His Kingdom rule into the matter and replace all the chaos and destruction that sin and satan are bringing. And praying "let Your will be done" is a request that the will of God dominates in the problem, that His good and perfect will replaces all the intentions of the devil and forces of darkness. God is for you, not against you. This prayer is for when you don't know what else to pray. You can apply it to every concern and problem in your life ("Lord, in my child's life, let Your kingdom come and Your will be done...Lord, in this problem I'm facing, let Your kingdom come and Your will be done.") Apply it to all the issues that trouble you.

B. A second application of The Lord's Prayer is to regularly pray, "Forgive me my sins as I have forgiven those who have sinned against me." By praying this regularly, you are addressing any bitterness, resentment, and judgment you find in your heart. By regularly declaring your forgiveness over the wounds and offenses you've experienced, you are positioning yourself to love others. Furthermore, you are keeping your heart teachable and humble as you regularly seek forgiveness for your own sins.

C. *"Lead me not into temptation but deliver me from the evil one"* is a third request in the prayer that often applies to us. Every day you are under assault by spiritual forces seeking to lead you into sin, seeking to bring destruction to your life. By praying this regularly, you are inviting God's help and protection into your life. Note how the passage commonly reads: "Deliver us from evil." However, the original Greek wording can also be translated "the evil one," which I, and many translators, think is a better rendering of the passage. This keeps before us the truth that we are under assault by an evil entity, one who desires your destruction. This request seeks God's help against the enemy who is targeting you.

So, in making new movement toward God, make The Lord's Prayer a means of increasing your trust in Him, receiving His help in your daily life, and aligning with the key concerns of His heart for you.

SUGGESTED READING

Keller, Timothy. *The Reason for God*. New York, New York: Penguin Group, 2008.

Keller's book provides solid reasoning for the truth of Christianity while answering common objections people have against it.

Lewis, C.S. *Mere Christianity*. New York, New York: MacMillan, 1965.

Mere Christianity is a classic defense for the existence of God and the Christian faith. This book has helped many people move from atheism to faith in Christ.

Sire, James W. *The Universe Next Door*. Downers Grove, Illinois: Intervarsity, 1976.

This is an amazing book that I first read in 1978—it is now in its 6ᵗʰ edition. Sire catelogs the various worldviews that dominate the world—e.g., theism, postmodernism, pantheism, etc.—and compares them with one another. It is highly readable; you will walk away with a far greater understanding of people around you.

CHAPTER 7

HEALING WOUNDS FROM THE PAST

"The Lord is close to the brokenhearted and saves those who are crushed in spirit." (Psalms 34:18)

"So he got up and went to his father. But while he was still a long way off, his father saw him and was filled with compassion for him; he ran to his son, threw his arms around him and kissed him." (Luke 15:20)

"The thief comes only to steal and kill and destroy; I have come that they may have life, and have it to the full." (John 10:10)

"He heals the brokenhearted and binds up their wounds. He determines the number of the stars and calls them each by name." (Psalms 147:3-4)

FATHERED BY THE FATHER

Read Psalm 147:3-4 again (printed above). It is amazing that the God Who controls 200 billion galaxies is concerned about your wounds. He sees where your heart was assaulted and broken, and He wants to restore it. This chapter might be the chief reason why He has brought this book to you. God wants to make you whole. God wants to step into your life and rewrite your story. Your Heavenly Father wants to father you.

96

The heart of Christianity is this: There is a good and loving Father Who cares deeply and passionately for you. His love for you compelled Him to purchase your life through the death of His Son, Jesus, Who *"loved you and gave Himself for you"* (Galatians 2:20). Through Jesus we have the right to become children of God. He yearns to be your Father now. He will draw near, if you'll let him. He wants to heal the wounds of the past.

"He heals the brokenhearted and binds up their wounds." (Psalms 147:3)

No matter how old we are, our true Father wants us to experience being His beloved child. But it requires opening our hearts, which will take us back into some of our deepest wounds. God does this so He might bring His love and healing to the fatherless child within us.

THE WOUNDS OF THE PAST

What we experience as children has a huge impact on us as adults. Our self-image is a reflection of how we perceive the most important people in our life feel about us. For children, that would be our mother and father.

Growing up, were you treasured by your parents, loved, and delighted in? Did you grow up feeling secure and protected? Did you sense their interest in you and their pride in you? Or were you ignored and neglected? Did you sense they were disappointed in you, or did you feel unimportant? Did one or both abandon you? Was there verbal abuse? Physical or sexual abuse? Or even darker things?

While parents are often a key source of our wounds, other people with authority in our lives, such as teachers, coaches, clergy, bosses, etc., can be the source of much pain. School is a common source of pain. Many people carry wounds received in junior and senior high school. Experiences of rejection, of being left out, of not measuring up, of not fitting in, and of being bullied during our school years can continue to affect us as adults.

The painful treatment we received in the past leaves wounds and gaps in our development that don't disappear over time. We just learn ways to cope and compensate until we receive healing.

God wants to "Father" you. He becomes your Father when you receive Jesus into your life and are born again. The Bible says, *"to those who receive Him…He gave the right to become children of God"* (John 1:12). You become His child and He becomes your Father—a Father Who cares all about you and your life, a Father Who will speak to you and guide you and protect you. Your entire identity and destiny change. Your Father wants to heal your wounds from the past. *"The Lord is close to the brokenhearted and saves those who are crushed in spirit"* (Psalms 34:18).

MY EXPERIENCE AT MOM'S HOUSE

As I now write about my experiences while growing up, I do so only because I've seen how my story has helped many other people. I've spoken at several gatherings and have been amazed at the people who step forward afterwards requesting prayer because my story is their story—details change but they carry the same kinds of wounds I experienced, and they too want healing and freedom.

I want to show respect to my father because we are to honor our parents. Later in life Dad became a Christian, and I saw positive changes in him. People who knew my dad only in his later years saw him as a kind and caring person, who regularly spoke of his gratitude to God for saving him. He truly was a transformed man. Dad recently passed away, but in the last years of his life we had a good relationship in which we were together a few times each year, including several fishing trips to Canada. Those were good years.

But when I was a child, it was a different story. As children, my sisters and I grew up in a dysfunctional home due to our father's narcissistic and abusive behavior. While Dad held a steady job and provided for us materially, we received no encouragement from him, no interest in who we were or what we accomplished. Growing up, we walked on eggshells at home because of his anger or his pouting when he couldn't have his way. There were many times when he would crush us with his words. His abuse took many forms. I cannot remember one warm, happy moment with him while growing up. When I was a freshman in high school, he left Mom and our family and started a new life for himself. He left a wake of destruction in our lives, especially for our mother who never overcame his rejection.

Mom continued to live in the same house that we children grew up in, until her death in 2018. After she passed away, we prepared to sell her house. On the day before the closing, I was at the house alone. I was pondering all the decades the house had been in our family and all the memories while living there; many were not pleasant. As I thought and prayed, I felt God say, "I want to do a work in you. I want you to walk through the house and let Me heal your heart."

What unfolded was this:

- I'd go into a room.
- God would bring up memories of specific moments in that room when Dad said or did something painful to me.
- God would then instruct me to forgive Dad for what he said or did.
- Then God would speak love and encouragement to me: "If I were your father in that moment, here's what I would have said to you…," and the wound would begin to heal with His love and truth.

I started in the kitchen. The first memory was at the supper table in 1971. I was a high school freshman, overweight, and not very athletic, but I wanted to play football. At supper I said I needed $25 for football shoes. Dad got angry about the money and yelled at me, saying, "You're no good at sports so why should I waste my money?" He piled on other similar words in a relentless fashion. That happened nearly fifty years before, but those words still hurt.

Reliving that memory in 2018, I heard God say, "Forgive your dad for saying those things," so I prayed out loud: "Father God, I forgive my dad for what he said and for how it hurt me."

And then God said, "Now, if I had been your father, I would have told you how proud of you I was, proud that you were trying out for football even though you'd never played before, and I would have come to every game, etc., etc." He just spoke how supportive He would have been of me. In that moment I felt much of the pain depart, pain I wasn't aware had persisted. You'd think after fifty years the pain of that moment would be dead. It wasn't dead though, just buried, and the Lord wanted it removed and thus brought it forth for attention.

And this is what I experienced for the next three hours:

- I'd go into a room.
- Specific memories from that room of being mocked by Dad, yelled at, belittled, ignored, mistreated, etc. came one by one. For each incident, God walked me through the same pattern:
- Feel the pain of the memory.
- Forgive Dad for what he said or did.
- And then God saying, "Here's what I would have said to you," or "Here's what I would have done if I had been your father." And in that, His encouragement and healing words replaced the pain.

I started in the kitchen; several memories came. Most events I remembered, but some memories came that I had completely forgotten. God was pulling them out of the past because even though

I was no longer conscious of them, He knew the wound was still there and needed to be dealt with.

I went slowly from room to room, staying in each room until the memories God wanted to address were dealt with, and then I'd move to another room. Sometimes the memory wasn't what Dad had done to me, but it was some incident when he mistreated Mom or one of my sisters. Sometimes it was the pain of what he didn't do. For example, in my bedroom there was a place on the wall where I had hung my ribbons awarded for singing competitions in junior high. Never once did Dad congratulate me or encourage me or ask about the singing competitions, not a word of interest. I forgave him for this, and then my Heavenly Father assured me how proud He was and how He would have praised the accomplishments, etc.

Note this wasn't an afternoon of introspection. I wasn't looking deep within to see what I could find, to uncover whatever issues and wounds from the past I could dredge up. Looking deep and long inside doesn't lead to encouragement but rather to despair. The process I'm describing has its focus on the Lord. I was asking Him what He wanted to highlight and then I'd listen and pay attention to what came to my mind. I've found that whatever He brings before us will have grace on it to be healed. That's His reason for bringing it to our attention.

The memories God brought out that day for me varied greatly. Some were seemingly minor, some were deeply wounding, and a few were very dark things Dad had done. But in each instance, God enabled me to recall it, forgive Dad, and then receive the encouragement He'd give to me.

The result of this interaction was twofold:

First, forgiveness is key toward healing wounded hearts. I'd forgiven Dad over the years but in a more general sense. This process focused on specific moments, singling out individual wounds and dealing with each, one by one. When treating an accident victim with multiple injuries, doctors address each injury according to its need. Likewise with emotional wounds, I saw how each wound required individual attention.

Second, God was rewriting my past. In each memory God was removing the wounds and brokenness caused by my dad's behavior and replacing it with His loving care and support. He was FATHERING me. He was giving me what I needed in a father in each of those memories. What I needed in a dad at age 6 was different from what I needed at age 4 or 11 or 15. In each memory, He replaced Dad's responses and gave precisely what I needed at that age, in that memory. In that experience, even though the events were decades ago, wounds and empty places in my life that should have been filled with the loving attention of a father were healed and filled.

This was one of the most important spiritual experiences I've ever had. It felt strange initially because I'm not someone who dwells on the past, I just keep moving forward, focused more on the future. But as God led me in that experience, I was being freed from past pain. More importantly, I was growing closer to God as being my Heavenly Father. My love and trust in Him increased and went to a new level that I continue to enjoy.

Most of my wounds were inflicted at home. Maybe yours are from school, work, marriage, or church. Whatever the source of your wounds, know you can receive the Father's healing for each wound you've received.

JESUS COMES TO HEAL OUR HEARTS

Jesus came to heal the brokenhearted ("*The Spirit of the Sovereign Lord is on Me, because the Lord has anointed Me, to proclaim good news to the poor. He has sent Me to bind up the brokenhearted, to proclaim freedom for the captives and release from darkness for the prisoners."* [Isaiah 61:1]). It is amazing that His purpose in coming to Earth was to rescue our hearts. Healing broken hearts means we can ask Jesus to touch our past experiences by which our hearts were wounded. Someone said time doesn't heal wounds, but Jesus does. I have found that to be true. Over time, wounds get buried but not healed. A cutting remark or an embarrassing moment from junior high can still influence us forty years later. That time in your past when you were shamed, attacked, rejected, or forgotten...those moments when you were unjustly blamed, ridiculed, or harshly criticized...when you were betrayed... when you didn't measure up...were defeated and mocked...when those who should have protected you and encouraged you failed to do so, or, worse, used and abused you: Jesus came to heal and restore your heart. Maybe you missed this healing in your past church experience. But God's loving purpose for you, right now, is for you to receive the healing work of Jesus. So invite Him into your past.

THE PROCESS

Ask Jesus to take you to the past, to the place of the wounds. Maybe it was a season in your life, such as your junior high years, or the months around a divorce. Maybe your wounds center on your relational experience with a parent, a sibling, an employer, or your ex-spouse. Most of us have a collection of wounds from many people, places, and times in our past. Ask God to highlight what He wants to touch first. He might surprise you and bring incidents to mind that seem minor to you. But follow Him in this and focus on what He brings to you.

When a specific memory is before you, invite God into it. Ask Him to guide you in bringing healing to this wound. You can begin by praying something like: *Father, I ask You to step into that moment when* (name the_person) *did* (describe the incident). *I ask You to heal my broken heart here and make me whole. Please show me what You want me to do.*

Usually your healing will include the need for forgiveness (*"And when you stand praying, if you hold anything against anyone, forgive them, so that your Father in heaven may forgive you your sins."* [Mark 11:25]). So say something like:

Father, I forgive (name the person) *for saying* _____.

I forgive him/her for doing _____.

Be specific, naming what was said or done. Ask Jesus to reveal any other people tied to this wound whom you need to forgive.

God, I forgive my mother for not protecting me in that time of abuse.

Forgiveness can be really tough; I recommend Rodney Hogue's book *Forgiveness* (available on Amazon) to help you through the process. Perhaps you've heard forgiveness described as "setting a captive free and realizing the prisoner was me." It's true that your healing will be hindered by unforgiveness.

Ask God, "What else do You want to do in this memory?" Maybe He will point out feelings of shame. If so, bring those to Him: "Father, please remove this shame. I renounce my self-loathing and I forgive myself." Continue to ask Him: "Is there something more You want to do in this memory?" Pray about whatever else unfolds. Linger in this place and listen, then follow the promptings that you sense.

When it seems He is done, ask Him to fill those wounded places with His love. In the case of the wounds from my dad, many times after dealing with destructive words spoken by my father I'd ask, "God, what would You have said to me?" and I would hear a word of encouragement and love. This is important because God brought His love and healing to the wound in that memory, thus, rewriting my story. Therefore, give Him permission to enter those wounded places with His healing love, and trust Him to walk you into healing.

Maybe as you go forward, you won't feel much or seem to hear much, not in the way I've described. Don't think this exercise is not working for you. Your trust is in God's Word. Reread the Scripture verses at the beginning of this chapter and stand on their truth, whether or not you feel or hear something. Ask the Lord to enter into each wound; ask Him to heal it and restore you. Then ask: "What else do You want to do here?" Pay attention; maybe a thought or an image will come to mind, or you may experience a feeling. Ask God about the impression and listen the best you can. Maybe you'll sense nothing. If so, don't be discouraged. Declare Psalm 147:3 aloud: *"He heals the brokenhearted and binds up their wounds,"* trusting that is precisely what your heavenly Father is doing for you in that moment. Thank Him for what He did in that wound and move on to the next one.

There is great value in this exercise even if you don't feel you've heard the Lord speaking to you during your prayer time. It's valuable because you are developing trust in Him for addressing the intimate places of your life. You are expressing faith in His Word, and faith grows like a muscle every time we use it. You are developing habits of looking to Him. His healing power isn't dependent on our feelings but on His Word, and you are acting on His Scriptural promises to heal broken hearts.

GOD WANTS TO FATHER YOU

Behind this process is a loving Father who wants to "Father" you. The word "father" is both a noun and a verb. Regardless of how your earthly father "fathered" you, your Heavenly Father passionately desires to "Father" you. He wants to heal the wounds of your past so you can move into your future destiny. The Bible has many names for God, but the name Jesus taught us to embrace is "Father"; He wants us to relate to God as a Father. In this truth, Jesus is correcting our false notions of a god who is distant and harsh. Instead, in Luke 15 we find a father so overjoyed at the return of his wayward child that he throws a BBQ party (*kill the fattened calf and let's celebrate!* [see Luke 15:23]). Our Father's huge display of affection for His children is almost embarrassing. In fact, our heavenly Father has planned a great celebration to kick off the restoration of all things at the end of time as described in the book of Revelation. It's called the Wedding Feast of the Lamb (see Revelation 19:7-9). It will be Cinderella's ball, Bilbo's party, the celebrations at the end of Star Wars, and the dancing in the streets on VE Day all rolled into one heart-bursting moment of joy…and He wants you to be there.

THE FATHER SINGS OVER US

"The Lord your God is with you, the Mighty Warrior who saves. He will take great delight in you; in His love He will no longer rebuke you, but <u>will rejoice over you with singing</u>."
(Zephaniah 3:17, emphasis mine)

This verse seemed strange to me. I mean, in what way does God sing over us? But recently, I recalled a moment when I was about 6 years old, playing at my friend Timmy's house. As we were playing, Timmy's dad walked in on his way to another room. As he walked past, he started singing, "I love Timmy, he's my boy" in some silly, made-up tune. And Timmy responded with the same tune, "I love my dad." It's surprising that I still remember something as small as that moment from so long ago, but it left a deep impression on me as a six-year-old because I could not imagine a warm, lighthearted moment like that between me and my dad.

And as I recalled Tim's dad singing about his son, I felt God say, *"That's the way I sing over you. I feel joy when I think of you. That's why I sing over you."* And this is the message of Jesus: There is a good and loving Father who cares deeply and passionately for you; He will heal and restore your life. He wants to rewrite your story.

ACTIVATION

A. Take a journey of healing

I believe the Father has things to say to you as He heals wounds inflicted on you by others. I encourage you to walk through the healing process I described above. Perhaps your wounds occurred in your home or school. Or maybe at your workplace or church. Or perhaps your wounds are better captured in a period of time, such as during a six-month period surrounding a divorce. It can be helpful to do an exercise similar to what I did. You could:

1. Draw a layout or floor plan of your house, school, church, etc. If you prefer, you can instead choose a time frame to focus on (a stretch of months or years) and draw out a calendar.
2. Imagine yourself in one of the rooms—or a month or year, if you are focused on a timeframe instead of a place.
3. Ask: "Jesus, was something said or done to me in this room that You want to heal?" Or: "Was something said or done to me in this month that You want to heal?" Then wait and listen.
4. As memories come into your mind, ask the Lord if there is someone you need to forgive. Then express out loud: "I forgive _____ for saying/doing _____." You might not feel forgiving, but you are making the choice to forgive regardless of your feelings at this moment.
5. Then ask the Lord what He would have said or done in that moment. Listen and see if He has something to say. If an impression or image comes to mind, ask the Holy Spirit what it means for you. If there seems to be only silence, don't despair. Instead, quote Psalm 147:3 over the memory: "*He heals the brokenhearted and binds up their wounds.*" Thank Jesus, and receive healing as you trust the Scripture. Then ask if there is another memory He wants to call attention to.

6. Stay in that "room" or "month" until it seems there are no other memories. Then move to another room or month and repeat the process.

An exercise like this can provide healing for your heart. More importantly, you will draw closer to God, your perfect, loving, heavenly Father Who wants to Father you.

SUGGESTED READING

Below are three books I've found really helpful for experiencing healing and freedom.

Hogue, Rodney. *Forgiveness.* Pennsauken, New Jersey: Rodney Hogue, 2008.

Hutchings, Mike. *Supernatural Freedom from the Captivity of Trauma: Overcoming the Hindrance to Your Wholeness.* Shippensburg, Pennsylvania: Destiny Image, 2021.

Weber, Kimberly Ann. *Jesus and Me: A Journey of Love, Healing, and Freedom.* Self published, available at Amazon, 2018.

CHAPTER 8

THE FEAR OF MAN

"Fear of man will prove to be a snare, but whoever trusts in the Lord is kept safe." (Proverbs 29:25)

"Am I now trying to win the approval of human beings, or of God? Or am I trying to please people? If I were still trying to please people, I would not be a servant of Christ." (Galatians 1:10)

"Yet at the same time many even among the leaders believed in Him. But because of the Pharisees they would not openly acknowledge their faith for fear they would be put out of the synagogue; for they loved human praise more than praise from God." (John 12:42-43)

ST. JOHN LUTHERAN CHURCH

In the spring of 2022, I did an extended spiritual fast from food, wanting to draw closer to God and to receive guidance and empowerment for upcoming ministry. One day during the fast I felt prompted to drive south to the area in Illinois from which my family originally came. I ended up near the small towns of Easton and Topeka, where my parents grew up and where I lived during my first years of life. Then I felt drawn to search for the old country church my mother's family had attended. Eventually I found the

St. John Lutheran Church building, in the middle of cornfields. It had closed years earlier as family farms disappeared and the rural population dwindled in the area. I parked off the blacktop, beside the building. It is the typical white steepled rural church building, now looking abandoned. Its stained-glass windows had been removed and boarded over.

I was far from any major roads, so the only sound was the breeze moving across the fields. As I sat in the car, I asked, "Lord, why did You lead me here?" I had vague memories of the building because when I was a small boy, my mom would occasionally take my sisters and me there for Sunday school when we were visiting our grandparents. As I sat there, a story came to my mind, one my mom had told me long ago.

When I was 4 years old, Mom took us kids to St. John's Sunday school during our visit with my grandparents. I was sitting in a classroom with several other little boys. These boys were all farm kids, growing up on nearby family farms. I was the only "city" kid there as my family had moved to Chillicothe, Illinois, about sixty miles north, because my dad worked at Caterpillar Tractor Company in nearby Mossville. The boys began talking about their family farms, and one boy told how many tractors his daddy had. Then the next boy bragged about how many tractors his daddy had and the farm implements they owned. And then the next boy tried to top that story. When it was my turn, I declared my dad had three tractors and a red combine and how many acres our farm was and so on. Of course, living in town, my family had none of those things, but I wasn't going to be outdone by the other boys. The Sunday school teacher overheard our conversation and she, knowing I didn't live on a farm, got a kick out of my bragging. Later she told my mom what I had said; Mom also laughed at hearing about all of our tractors. Many years later Mom told me this story; it had become for her one of those little memories parents enjoy.

Now decades later, I was parked next to the church building, and that story came to mind, so I asked, "Lord, is there something in this story You want me to see?" I heard in my mind a strong response, almost an audible voice: "That was the first time in your life you gave in to the fear of man." Had I been standing, the force with which His response came might have knocked me down. I had an immediate awareness of what His response meant. The Lord was saying that this moment at age 4 was the first time I felt the need to impress others. As I related with other preschool boys, a desire to measure up and be impressive and be liked had awakened. It was the first time I was concerned with what other people thought of me. Their opinion mattered so much that I was willing to lie. Those are all expressions of the fear of man.

While on one level this experience is just a cute story about four-year-old boys, it reveals the birth of motivations that stretch into a lifetime of effort to please and impress people. The Lord told me that was the first time I gave in to the fear of man. Often when the Lord speaks a sentence to us, it will be accompanied with a download of unspoken information or awareness. With the words He spoke into my mind, I also sensed He was calling me to be rid of this particular fear. "I want to remove the fear of man from your life, so I've brought you back to the root where it all began. It will be important to be free from the fear of man in order to carry out the work to which I'm calling you."

THE FEAR OF MAN

When we speak about the fear of man, we're referring to the concern we have for what other people think about us. For many people this is the dominating motivation in their life. The desire to be impressive, to be well thought of, to be liked, to fit in, and to measure up drives their decisions and goals. Attempts to maintain some persona or image in order to be perceived in a certain fashion are expressions of the fear of man. The need to prove oneself and to look good in front of people and be impressive can all be rooted in the fear of man. This includes comparing yourself with other people, using them as a measuring rod. Am I as successful? As strong? As attractive? As skilled? As well-liked? As popular? As creative? This drive to gain the approval of others can be so strong that people will lie, break the law, or even deny Jesus because of their concern over the opinions of others. The tragedy is the desire to be liked by everyone ultimately reduces your life to one of having little impact on the world; you have squandered your strength and opportunities because of fear.

Maybe when you are honest with yourself, you might find one of the reasons you stopped following the Lord closely was because you knew your friends wouldn't approve of your faith. That's a battle every believer faces. The Bible speaks about people who *"would not openly acknowledge their faith for fear"* because *"they loved human praise more than praise from God."* (John 12:42-43) You need to ask whose approval is more important to you—the approval of God or the approval of people?

Even now, in writing this book, I want to be engaging and helpful, even life-changing for many. I want this book to be well-written. But is my motivation to write well so the book will help people, or is it because I want to be seen as profound, witty, smart, etc.? Motivation is the crux of the matter. Every good thing we do can be motivated by genuine concern for others or by a desire to be seen as having concern for others, an act of virtue signaling.

The fear of man is like other fears: once it no longer controls you, you are free! You are free when you find your value in what God says and not in what the world thinks. That is a state of freedom. That freedom allows you to live according to core values you have chosen, not by the values imposed on you by others.

YOUR CURRENT SPIRITUAL STATE

For some of you, the distance between you and God is the direct result of your desire to be liked by everyone. When you are with Christian friends, you act as if you are a believer too, but when you are with others, you take on a different persona. The fear of rejection and the insecurities controlling your behavior result in a chameleon-type lifestyle, changing your colors according to the people around you. You were not made to live this way! The Bible states, *"For the Spirit God gave us does not make us timid, but gives us power, love and self-discipline"* (2 Timothy 1:7). Freedom is awaiting you!

You start gaining freedom from the fear of man by examining the motivations behind your decisions, behavior, words, and actions. As you get honest and begin to identify what drives your behavior, you can declare to God your desire to be free from any motivation rooted in the fear of man.

Some thoughts on how to proceed:

Love all people without giving them veto power over your life.
We love people and honor them, but we don't give them veto power over our obedience to Jesus. Like Peter said, when addressing hostile rulers, *"We must obey God rather than men"* (Acts 5:9). This doesn't mean we treat people with disdain. That's not love. Instead, we treat every person with respect and honor, including enemies. In doing so, though, we set our hearts to please the Father and not to please people.

Freedom is what you desire; the fear of man is a trap!
"Fear of man will prove to be a snare, but whoever trusts in the Lord is kept safe" (Proverbs 29:25). Wanting everybody to like you is a direct path to disobeying God and disregarding His wishes. Being faithful to Him will put you in conflict with other people. Often

the testing in our lives is the choice of whom we are trying to please—God or people. We feel pressure to be liked by others, to not be misunderstood, and to not look foolish. Yet, in spite of what people think about us, we choose God. It helps when we recognize that much of that pressure is a spiritual attack. You have an enemy who wants to silence you and keep you in a compromised life. Sometimes we have to do things out of obedience even when we feel fear. Sometimes we just have to say to fear, "Get out of my way; I have a work to do!" Though we feel fear, we still have a duty and obligation to act according to God's directives. We cannot allow feelings to control our lives.

Following Jesus means taking a stand, no matter the cost.

Let Jesus describe what it means to "follow Him": *"Then He said to them all: "Whoever wants to be My disciple must deny themselves and take up their cross daily and follow Me. For whoever wants to save their life will lose it, but whoever loses their life for Me will save it. What good is it for someone to gain the whole world, and yet lose or forfeit their very self? Whoever is ashamed of Me and My words, the Son of Man will be ashamed of them when He comes in His glory and in the glory of the Father and of the holy angels"* (Luke 9:23-26). A lot at stake, big deal. Saying yes to Jesus means saying no to the opinions of the world.

Expect pushback!

Jesus's followers have been mocked and attacked since the beginning: It's just part of the deal. The leaders in Jesus's day berated people who were listening to Him: *"You mean He has deceived you also?...Have any of the rulers or the Pharisees believed in Him? No! But this mob that knows nothing of the law—there is a curse on them"* (John 7:45-49). In other words, none of the important people believed in Him! None of your favorite comedians or celebrities follow Him. At school your favorite professors don't believe, so why should you? Only the naive, weak, and uneducated believe. You don't want to look foolish! You don't want to lose your friends!

PERSECUTION AND COURAGE

Thankfully, at this time in America, ridicule and persecution against Christians are fairly mild. If you truly choose to follow Jesus, chances are you'll lose some friends and maybe endure some ridicule personally. Your stance might even impact your job, but for now we generally have the protection of laws. It's not so safe in other places though. As I write this, Harriet and I have been gathering financial aid for Christian friends in an Asian country where mobs in the last two weeks have marched against the Christian community, burning churches and destroying the homes of believers. Another dear friend from Africa had a pistol held against his head by rebel forces in his nation and was ordered to deny Jesus or die. He refused and expected to be shot, but by some miracle the trigger wasn't pulled. God had other plans.

It was hearing about the courage of Christians in the former Soviet Union that compelled me to start following Jesus during my senior year of high school. I heard a young man tell about his ministry serving Christians in communist Russia. He told how the government persecuted Christians and how his friends were imprisoned, tortured, and suffered much injustice simply because they were believers. That caused me to wonder, "What was so special about Jesus that they were willing to suffer like that?" It was their persecution that opened my heart to Jesus and changed everything for me. I'm so thankful they didn't give in to the fear of man but chose to stand for Christ. Their courage and faithfulness moved me to eventually become a follower of Jesus.

When we stand for Jesus and experience ridicule and pushback, remember what Jesus said to His followers: *"If the world hates you, keep in mind that it hated me first. If you belonged to the world, it would love you as its own. As it is, you do not belong to the world, but I have chosen you out of the world. That is why the world hates you. Remember what I told you: 'A servant is not greater than his master.' If they persecuted me, they will persecute you also. If they obeyed my teaching, they will obey yours also. They will treat you this way because of my name, for they do not know the One who sent me"* (John 15:18-21).

Let's embrace the encouragement from the Apostle John: *"And now, dear children, continue in Him, so that when He appears we may be confident and unashamed before Him at His coming"* (1 John 2:28).

ACTIVATION

A. Get alone and ask the Holy Spirit to show you if and where fear of man is a force in your life. Confess and repent of each instance where fear of man has led you to compromise your faith. Ask Him for boldness to stand true for the Lord.

B. Meditate on the following Scriptures. Ask the Holy Spirit to show you how to apply these to your life:

"For the Spirit God gave us does not make us timid, but gives us power, love and self-discipline. So do not be ashamed of the testimony about our Lord or of me his prisoner. Rather, join with me in suffering for the gospel, by the power of God." (2 Timothy 1:7-8)

"Am I now trying to win the approval of human beings, or of God? Or am I trying to please people? If I were still trying to please people, I would not be a servant of Christ." (Galatians 1:10)

"Then He said to them all: 'Whoever wants to be my disciple must deny themselves and take up their cross daily and follow Me. For whoever wants to save their life will lose it, but whoever loses their life for me will save it. What good is it for someone to gain the whole world, and yet lose or forfeit their very self? Whoever is ashamed of me and my words, the Son of Man will be ashamed of them when he comes in his glory and in the glory of the Father and of the holy angels.'" (Luke 9:23-27)

CHAPTER 9

CONFESSION, BREAKING AGREEMENTS, AND FREEDOM

"It is for freedom that Christ has set us free. Stand firm, then, and do not let yourselves be burdened again by a yoke of slavery." (Galatians 5:1)

"...through Christ Jesus the law of the Spirit Who gives life has set you free from the law of sin and death." (Romans 8:2)

"Repent, then, and turn to God, so that your sins may be wiped out, that times of refreshing may come from the Lord." (Acts 3:19)

"The thief comes only to steal and kill and destroy; I have come that they may have life, and have it to the full." (John 10:10)

Let me warn you at the outset. Some of you reading this chapter are going to experience resistance, maybe a lot of resistance. Some of you will begin to feel an increasing desire to stop reading. You might have thoughts or inner voices telling you that this information doesn't pertain to you, that you don't need this, that there's no reason to believe this stuff. You might even experience physical discomfort like a headache that comes from nowhere or dizziness or mental fogginess. Remember, reality consists of both the physical realm and the spiritual realm, and there are spiritual forces that want to keep you captive and trapped (see 2 Timothy 2:25-26). If you begin experiencing anything like this, pray, "Heavenly Father, I want everything that You have for me, so in Jesus's name I command all attack by spiritual darkness against me to end now. I renounce any agreements I've made with lies and deceptions, and I choose to align my life with the truth of God. Amen."

FALSE IDEAS ABOUT CHRISTIANITY

Many people believe that Christianity reduces you into a narrow, negative life. This is a lie. It can be true of religion, but religion is different than life in Jesus. Jesus came to free you from all that enslaves you because He desires you to enter into the life your Father always longed for you to experience. *"You make known to me the path of life; You will fill me with joy in your presence, with eternal pleasures at Your right hand"* (Psalms 16:11). Read that verse again. Does that sound like a stingy, oppressive God, intent on robbing you of happiness?

Religion will restrain and reduce you with manmade rules intended to impose someone's opinion of right and wrong on you. But that's not God, and that's not the life He's calling you into. The God Who created the sweetness of blueberries, the beauty of Maui and Alaska, Who created our hearts to be stirred by music and romance and adventure and good coffee is not a god of petty rules. The God Who calls all the stars by name (the most recent estimate of the number of stars is 2e22, i.e., write the number 2 then write 22 zeros after it) is not small-minded. The lions hunting on the Serengeti, a grizzly fiercely protecting her cubs, the violence of thunderstorms all suggest God prefers what is wild and free. He is not seeking to tame you with religious rules. But He does call you to holiness. He calls you to a life that is free and holy.

"Be holy because I am holy" (1 Peter 1:16). You might need to redefine the word "holy." The word can conjure up images that are not

118

Biblical. Being "holy" might make you think of a joyless, austere, bleak existence of rule-keeping with lots of old-fashioned religious language. Actually, the pursuit of holiness is simply the pursuit of the primary command of Jesus: *"Love the Lord your God with all your heart, soul, mind, and strength"* (see Matthew 22:37, Mark 12:30, Luke 10:27). So pursuing holiness is loving God in our thoughts, words, and deeds. It's finding out what pleases Him and doing it.

THE FUNNEL OF LIFE

The life of Jesus is a good place to start because He always pleased the Father. (*"The One who sent Me is with Me...for I always do what pleases Him"* [John 8:29].) Read the gospels and see how Jesus lived, and set that as a pattern for yourself. Don't read through the filter of religious ideas imposed upon you from the past. In fact, see how often Jesus was in conflict with religious people who tried to enforce their religious rules on Him. Ask the Holy Spirit to give you fresh eyes to see what you missed in the past.

You have an enemy who comes to steal, kill, and destroy. But Jesus came to give you LIFE! Think of your life as a big funnel, like those used for changing your car oil or for pouring ingredients in the kitchen. A funnel has two openings. Whichever opening you enter will determine the course of your life. If you enter the funnel of life at the wide end, that is similar to saying my life has no restraints; it's wide open with no bothersome God telling me how to live! But as you progress into the funnel you find your choices increasingly constrained, increasingly narrowed. Like going on a spending spree with your first credit card, the payments and interest will tighten and begin to restrict your choices. The freedom you thought you had diminishes as your choices become increasingly limited, until at the end you have little freedom and a small life. However, you can enter the funnel at the narrow end. This feels confined and restricted initially, but as you advance, you find increasing space and freedom and movement. Instead of limitation, you find life opening wider and wider. This is equivalent to the life Jesus offers. At the beginning we enter by the narrow path, the one gate. *"I am the gate; whoever enters through me will be saved"* (John 10:9). This choice requires repentance and surrender of our lives to Him. Jesus said, *"I am the way and the truth and the life. No one comes to the Father except through me"* (John 14:6). But as we go forward, we find increasing freedom from the habits and thoughts and forces that were controlling our lives. We enter further and further into the identity and destiny our loving Father wants to restore to us. To live free and holy is to live free from the fear of man, the constraints of religion, and the power of sin, and to be passionately in love with God. In other words, to live like Jesus lived.

FREEDOM

A classic book for mountaineering is entitled *Freedom of the Hills.* It's a good title because mountaineering does free you. Adventure in wild places carries a sense of freedom. When you are climbing a mountain, you are free from the pressures of your job and home. You are unplugged from social media and free from the constant chatter of texts and email. All the common distractions and daily concerns of first-world living are gone, and your life is reduced to the basics of eating, sleeping, and climbing.

However, the freedom of mountaineering does not mean you are without constraints. You are not free to wander aimlessly, because your environment contains deadly crevasses and 300-foot-high cliffs. Years ago, while climbing Mt. Rainier at night, one of our teammates began to walk off to the side of the trail in the darkness to relieve himself. Suddenly our guide shouted, "Stop! Step back!" He obeyed her command, and she then showed him which direction to walk to take care of his business. Later that morning, during our descent from the summit in the light of day, she pointed out the location where she'd ordered the climber to stop. He had been walking toward a cliff, plunging hundreds of feet down.

There is no such thing as total freedom. Appropriate, healthy restrictions on our freedom provides safety. Furthermore, in order to achieve goals, restraints on our freedom are required in the form of discipline. My daughter-in-law Jamie is an amazing violin player. She can play all styles of music freely. But she practices daily; she chooses to limit her personal freedom by submitting to the discipline of practice. But the constraints of practice result in freedom when she plays her violin. My wife had to deal with this while working as a piano teacher. Her students wanted the happy freedom of playing jazz, but before they could experience that freedom, they needed to constrain themselves to the discipline of learning the basics. They had to limit freedom in order to eventually experience freedom. Every accomplished musician and athlete knows that discipline (i.e., constraint) is required if they are to achieve their goals. True freedom is found in choosing the right restraints.

THE TRUTH LEADS TO FREEDOM

Truth is the starting point to walking in freedom. Acknowledging the truth, submitting to the truth, valuing the truth, and championing the truth are all fundamental for a relationship with the true God. Jesus said, *"You will know the truth and it will set you free."* Your enemy the devil wars against the truth. Speaking about the devil, Jesus said, *"...there is no truth in him. When he lies, he speaks his native language, for he is a liar and the father of lies"* (John 8:44).

The apostle Paul, guided by the Holy Spirit, gave a clear explanation of the importance of truth to your freedom in a passage found in 2 Timothy. We looked at these verses in an earlier chapter, but it is helpful to ponder his words again:

"Opponents must be gently instructed, in the hope that God will grant them repentance leading them to a knowledge of the truth, and that they will come to their senses and escape from the trap of the devil, who has taken them captive to do his will."
(2 Timothy 2:25-26)

Please consider all being said here. People who oppose and resist believers are to be gently instructed. They are not to be shouted down or despised or dismissed. That's because they are not the enemy. Paul wrote, *"We don't struggle against flesh and blood but against spiritual forces of evil"* (Ephesians 6:12). People are not our enemies. What we pray and hope for is that God will grant them repentance: in other words, that they can change direction and turn to the Lord. And in turning to Him, they will come into an understanding of the truth, that all the lies and distortions they have believed are exposed, and they will have awareness of true from false, right from wrong. This is the key to freedom because as long as they believe lies about life, about God, about morality, about who they are and why they are on the earth, etc., then they go through life in bondage, in satan's trap. They think they are free, doing their own will, but actually they are fulfilling the will of the evil one. But through repenting and turning to Jesus, His truth sets them free.

The most pitiful sight in the universe is a man or woman shaking their tiny fist at their Creator, screaming, "You won't tell me what to do! You won't tell me what to believe! I'll make my own decisions"; and all the while that little fist is tied with a cord being pulled by forces of darkness. Jesus comes to that person and says, "The truth will set you free...I am the truth."

A PROCESS FOR FREEDOM

What follows is a process by which you can apply the truth and promises of God to specific areas of your life and, in so doing, begin to experience freedom. At the beginning of Jesus's ministry, He announced His mission by quoting Isaiah 61:

"The Spirit of the Sovereign Lord is on Me because the Lord has anointed Me to proclaim good news to the poor. He has sent Me to bind up the brokenhearted, to proclaim freedom for the captives and release from darkness for the prisoners."
(Isaiah 61:1)

Freedom, healing, and restoration are God's desire for you. He is for you and sent Jesus to save you.

GETTING STARTED

I encourage you to get alone with paper and pen and a Bible, and walk through the steps below. This will be a starting point for moving into freedom. If you move through this process, you will experience relief and freedom in many areas that trouble you. However, there can be places in your life where habits and addictions have created strongholds that may require further prayer and attention. What's more, it's not uncommon to find greater spiritual resistance in your life if you've been involved in other religions or other forms of spirituality. But by walking through this process, you are declaring your intention to follow Jesus into the life and freedom He offers; in that, you will begin to experience increasing freedom.

There are two important considerations as we begin: First, our culture currently encourages us to walk in a heightened awareness of grievance. Many people, encouraged by their environment, such as college campuses, walk about finding injustice and offense in whatever direction they look, often singling out people as offenders based only on their identity. We are a people practiced in being outraged and finding offensive behavior everywhere, that is, everywhere except in ourselves. We need to recognize our personal sins. What's more, you will not progress far in Jesus unless and until you begin to respond to people with forgiveness and unconditional love, as Jesus directed. The process of obtaining freedom in your own life cannot proceed without a humbled heart, recognizing your own need for forgiveness. *"If we claim to be without sin, we deceive ourselves and the truth is not in us"* (1 John 1:8).

The second consideration follows from the first: Position yourself to be teachable. It is wisdom to regularly pray, "Lord, correct me. I want Your will and Your truth to prevail in my life, so wherever my thoughts, opinions, or attitudes do not align with Yours, I ask that You correct me." *"But who can discern their own errors? Forgive my hidden faults. Keep your servant also from willful sins; may they not rule over me"* (Psalm 19:12-13).

Hebrews Chapter 12 is a great starting point to position ourselves to receive God's help in freeing us:

"...let us throw off everything that hinders and the sin that so easily entangles. And let us run with perseverance the race marked out for us, fixing our eyes on Jesus, the pioneer and perfecter of faith..." (Hebrews 12:1-2)

Through this passage we can express to God our desire to get free of all the things that hold us back. You can pray something like: "Father, I want to throw off everything that hinders me and the sins that entangle my life. I bring to You all areas of my life. I ask that You deal with any place of unbelief, disobedience, self-indulgence, or rebellion in my life. I bring everything I value, every goal, hope, dream, every relationship and circumstance in my life to the feet of Jesus and say in each one: Let the rule of Your Kingdom come and Your will be done! Correct me in any matter where my opinions, ideas, or attitudes do not align with Yours! Please lead me in this time of prayer and bring me into the freedom that Jesus offers."

REMINDERS

This is also a good moment to remind yourself of all Jesus has done in order to free you and give you a new life. Ponder these truths and thank Him!

"But if we walk in the light, as he is in the light, we have fellowship with one another, and the blood of Jesus, his Son, purifies us from all sin." (1 John 1:7)

"...To him who loves us and has freed us from our sins by his blood, and has made us to be a kingdom and priests to serve his God and Father—to him be glory and power for ever and ever! Amen." (Revelation 1:5-6)

"It is for freedom that Christ has set us free. Stand firm, then, and do not let yourselves be burdened again by a yoke of slavery...You, my brothers and sisters, were called to be free. But do not use your freedom to indulge the flesh; rather, serve one another humbly in love." (Galatians 5:1,13)

"'Then you will know the truth, and the truth will set you free'...Jesus replied, 'Very truly I tell you, everyone who sins is a slave to sin. So if the Son sets you free, you will be free indeed.'" (John 8:32,36)

"For He has rescued us from the dominion of darkness and brought us into the kingdom of the Son He loves, in Whom we have redemption, the forgiveness of sins." (Colossians 1:13-14)

Thank God for the truths above and ask Him to apply them to your life.

TAKING INVENTORY

"Search me, God, and know my heart; test me and know my anxious thoughts. See if there is any offensive way in me, and lead me in the way everlasting." (Psalms 139:23-24)

Now you are going to take an inventory of areas of your life that God wants to address. Ask God to search you and reveal any sins, habits, decisions, attitudes, beliefs, or behaviors that He wants to deal with in your life. Pray for the Holy Spirit to search you and reveal sins, weaknesses, and habits that hinder your life. What fears, addictions, or tendencies are holding you back? Are there patterns of disobedience? Look at Galatians 5:19-21 below; does this list expose any traits in your life that need to be dealt with?

"The acts of the flesh are obvious: sexual immorality, impurity and debauchery; idolatry and witchcraft; hatred, discord, jealousy, fits of rage, selfish ambition, dissensions, factions and envy; drunkenness, orgies, and the like..." (Galatians 5:19-21)

As the Spirit reveals things to you, write them down. Ask the Holy Spirit to reveal any extra details that need your attention.

CONFESS

"Whoever conceals their sins does not prosper, but the one who confesses and renounces them finds mercy." (Proverbs 28:13)

Go through your list and confess each sin to the Lord, asking for His forgiveness. In matters that are complicated, ask the Holy Spirit to guide you, showing you what you are responsible for and asking for God's forgiveness and cleansing.

"But if we walk in the light, as he is in the light, we have fellowship with one another, and the blood of Jesus, his Son, purifies us from all sin. If we claim to be without sin, we deceive ourselves and the truth is not in us. If we confess our sins, he is faithful and just and will forgive us our sins and purify us from all unrighteousness. If we claim we have not sinned, we make him out to be a liar and his word is not in us." (1 John 1:7-10, emphasis mine)

REPENT

"Repent, then, and turn to God, so that your sins may be wiped out, that times of refreshing may come from the Lord." (Acts 3:19)

As you confess each sin, declare to God your intention to repent. This means you are turning away from sin and turning toward God. Declare your intention to turn from all disobedience, unbelief, and self-indulgence. Instead, you have chosen to walk in obedience to Jesus and His Word. Ask Him to cleanse away your sins and free you from their influence.

"Wash away all my iniquity and cleanse me from my sin. For I know my transgressions, and my sin is always before me. Against you, you only, have I sinned and done what is evil in your sight; so you are right in your verdict and justified when you judge...

Create in me a pure heart, O God, and renew a steadfast spirit within me...

My sacrifice, O God, is a broken spirit; a broken and contrite heart you, God, will not despise." (Psalms 51:2-4,10,17)

BREAK AGREEMENTS

An element of repentance is that of breaking agreements. In turning toward God, we often feel resistance. Often this is because we have believed and agreed with lies from the enemy. When you make agreements with the lies of darkness. you give satan a foothold for his purposes. Any power he has over you, is through your agreement with his lies. That's why breaking those agreements is the road to freedom. Repentance includes turning away from those agreements.

There are lies that you and I have believed, such as: "I'll never get free; God doesn't hear my prayers; this problem will never go away;

I'm such a fool; I'm stuck here the rest of my life." The list can go on and on. For example, perhaps you struggle with a particular sin. The thought enters your mind: "You'll never change," and you think, "That's right; I'll never change." You've just made an agreement. The thought enters your mind: "God has given up on you," and you think, "That's right; God has given up on me." You've just made an agreement.

Ask the Holy Spirit what agreements you have made that need to be broken. Ask Him what lie you believed and agreed with. Break the agreement! Declare aloud: "I now reject my agreement with that lie, and I align myself with God's truth and purposes in this matter." Then thank God for His forgiveness and for His help to walk in freedom from lies and instead walk in truth.

You are making a declaration of changed allegiance. *"For He has rescued us from the dominion of darkness and brought us into the kingdom of the Son he loves"* (Colossians 1:13). "I used to walk in darkness, but now I align with the kingdom. I choose Jesus to be Lord over my life. I allow Him to correct my behavior and thoughts and opinions." This is why reading the Bible is so important; it will renew your mind, correct your sense of right and wrong, and prevent you from aligning with deceptions and falsehoods rather than with God's truth.

FALSE RELIGION AND SPIRITUALITY

The need to break agreements and renounce lies is especially important if you've been involved in other religions, witchcraft, or other forms of spirituality. This is because you've been aligning with supernatural powers that do not originate with God, and it might require extra effort to get free. But be confident even if you are feeling resistance; Jesus has all authority in Heaven and Earth. No power of darkness can stand up to Him.

Every book of the New Testament warns against false religious teaching. Much of the Old Testament deals with the destructive forces Israel faced when they turned from God to false religions. Likewise, God warns against witchcraft and sorcery: *"Do not turn to mediums or seek out spiritists, for you will be defiled by them. I am the Lord your God"* (Leviticus 19:3). So, it's important to confess and repent of believing false religious teaching and opening yourself to demonic powers. Note in Acts 19:18-20 how new believers renounced their former religious beliefs and burned all their spiritual texts and religious items as a tangible sign of their surrender to Jesus Christ, repenting of all substitutes for God by removing them from their personal lives.

Throughout church history, new believers worldwide have been prompted to renounce their former beliefs and practices. My wife and I were friends with a strong Christian family in Japan whose Christian heritage began when their grandfather became a Christian. As a young man, to make a bold public declaration of his new faith in their traditional Buddhist/Shinto village, he removed and burned his family gods and shrine in their front yard, announcing to the crowd that gathered that his family now trusted and followed Jesus.

After confessing, repenting, and breaking agreements, thank Jesus for His forgiveness and cleansing. Thank Him for the freedom He has for you. Reread the Bible passages above that speak of His forgiveness and cleansing. Claim those over your life. *"To Him who loves us and has freed us from our sins by His blood, and has made us to be a kingdom and priests to serve His God and Father—to Him be glory and power for ever and ever! Amen"* (Revelation 1:5-6).

PURSUE FREEDOM

We are like onions, and there are more layers below what you're dealing with in this moment. But that's okay. God is patient. Allow Him to lead this process in your life. He may surprise you with what

He wants to deal with first. You might be focused on an addiction or habit or lifestyle choice that seems obviously in need of change and you feel dominates your life. But God could very well say, "Yes, I want you to stand against that big sin in your life, but right now what I really want to go after is your jealousy (or your tendency toward self-pity or the way you exaggerate when you speak or the way you despise your coworker or your impatience toward your spouse). I want to free you from that."

You are entering into the restoration of God. Every time you break agreements, the grip of darkness in your life diminishes. Issues in your heart may be tangled. Maybe cruel and unfair things have been done to you and, unfortunately, these can lead us into resolutions and agreements that need to be broken. Confess the sins He points out and renounce them. Ask Him to reveal any agreements you've made and break them. Ask the Holy Spirit to lead you step by step into those complicated, convoluted issues to sort out what you need to do. Freedom is on the other side! Jesus's blood is powerful to free!

ACTIVATION

After reading through the process above, get alone with God. Consider Hebrews 12:1: *"...let us throw off everything that hinders and the sin that so easily entangles."* Ask the Lord what hindrances and sins He'd like to deal with. What habits, behaviors, attitudes, temptations, etc. does the Lord want to work on in your life?

Here is a tangible way of experiencing freedom. I've walked through this exercise personally several times and have always felt freedom and forgiveness, accompanied by a deeper gratitude for Jesus's death. You will need a pad of tear-off sticky notes and a cross. You can draw a picture of a cross on a sheet of paper, or perhaps you have a cross decoration hanging on your wall. You will use it in this exercise.

Ask God to reveal specific areas of disobedience, unbelief, or rebellion in your life—things you shouldn't have done and things you should have done but didn't. Ask Him to reveal behaviors, attitudes, and opinions He wants you to address. As He reveals these, write each one on a separate sticky note. You are seeking Jesus's forgiveness and cleansing, so as each matter comes to mind, write it down on a sticky note.

Now stick these notes on yourself, on your arm, body, etc. Create a new sticky note for each matter and place it on your body. When you have finished, you will probably have many notes stuck to you. (When I first did this, I laughed at myself with notes stuck all over me and was glad I was alone.) Now, take each note, one by one, and confess whatever sin, unbelief, failure, habit, attitude, or selfish act is recorded on that note. Ask Jesus to forgive and cleanse you *("If we confess our sins, He is faithful and just and will forgive us our sins and purify us from all unrighteousness."* [1 John 1:9]*)* Then remove that note from your body and transfer it to the cross. Whether you drew a picture of a cross or are using one you have hanging on the wall, stick the note on it. This is a tangible way to experience what the Bible says: *"He Himself bore our sins in His body on the cross, so that we might die to sins and live for righteousness; by His wounds you have been healed"* (1 Peter 2:24). He is the Lamb of God Who takes away the sin of the world, and He does this by bearing your sins (and mine) on the cross. So, this act of removing the sticky note from your body and placing it on the cross is a way of demonstrating your trust in Jesus to forgive you, free you, and take your sins away. The act of removing each note becomes a means of experiencing 1 Peter 2:24: *"He himself bore our sins in his body on the cross, so that we might die to sins and live for righteousness; by His wounds you have been healed."* Jesus takes your sins from you and carries them Himself, paying for them on the cross. He truly is the One Who *"loved you and gave Himself for you"*! (See Galatians 2:20-21 and Ephesians 5:2.)

SUGGESTED READING

Eldredge, John. *Free to Live: The Utter Relief of Holiness.* New York, New York: Faith Words, 2014.

Eldredge, John. *Waking the Dead.* Nashville, Tennessee: Thomas Nelson, 2016.

CHAPTER 10

DISAPPOINTED WITH GOD

"How long, Lord? Will you forget me forever? How long will you hide your face from me?" (Psalms 13:1)

«How long, Lord, must I call for help, but you do not listen?" (Habakkuk 1:2)

C.S. Lewis wrote two books that deal with the issue of trusting God while experiencing crushing pain, injustice, and loss. The first book, *The Problem with Pain*, was a scholarly work written to answer the question: "If God is good and all powerful, then why would He allow evil and suffering in the world?" It was a detached, reasoned philosophical argument (which I highly recommend to those grappling with the issue). The second book addressed the same issue from a very different perspective. *A Grief Observed* was his journal reflections of the anguish he endured at the death of his wife to cancer. The loss was so crushing he almost lost his faith as he wondered, "Where was God?"

Maybe disappointment with God is part of your story. In the Bible the man Job was deeply devoted to God, but he lost everything—his children, his wealth, and his physical health. His wife, in her deep pain, urged him to stop following God. Maybe you have gone through a time of loss and pain, and even though you prayed and tried to lean on God, it didn't change—the death, the divorce, the sickness didn't go away. And you decided, "I can't trust God; how can I believe in a God Who allows this?!"

One of our good friends tells her story below. She currently leads a ministry for international missions and has a heart for women and children caught in human trafficking. While there are many twists and complexities in how her life unfolded, disappointment with God was a significant struggle for her.

From the time I was born, I rarely missed church. I remember praying with my mom in the living room at age 7 and asking Jesus to "come into my heart." I would go on walks with Jesus along a path behind my yard as a young child. I had wonderful encounters and conversations with Him which would have been dismissed as daydreaming among the church I was raised in. One thing was certain: Jesus was my best friend and I loved everything about Him. I was also convinced at that time that He loved me and had huge plans for my life.

Every summer I attended the same church camp. At age 10, on the last night of camp, kids were giving testimonies of that week. To my surprise, I found myself standing and sharing that He told me I would be a missionary. I began reading books about missionaries and dreaming with Jesus about the places we would go together.

At this point, you may be admiring the remarkable childhood I had, and in many ways you would be right. From the outside, my life appeared peaceful, normal, and safe. Most people didn't know I was growing up in a violent household where my identity and self-image were demolished daily. I was also being sexually abused by a family member from a very young age, who then gave me to a friend of his who did the same. The things happening in secret and cruel words of my earthly father soon began to drown out those of my heavenly Father. I believed Jesus's words in the Bible to be true; I just wasn't convinced they were true about me.

My father had taught me how to hate myself from a very young age. I know now that he never intended to do so and was only teaching something he had been taught—a generational cycle inherited with no say of his own. Still, I grew up struggling to believe I could do anything right, be it school, sports, friendships, and especially my Christian walk.

After the age of 11 or 12, the encounters I'd been having with Jesus began to lessen until they stopped altogether. I still wanted to be a missionary and please God, but that was the problem: I didn't know that God was already pleased with me. I felt like a failure and never enough for God, no matter how hard I tried. From a young age I struggled with depression, self-harm, and suicidal tendencies. As a sophomore in high school, my mom, sister, and I left my dad's house one night and never went back.

Meanwhile, there was a leader in my youth group who treated me the way I imagined a father figure would. Frank's love for Jesus was inspiring, and I saw a hunger for God inside him that I once saw in myself. Soon after we left my dad's, Frank was diagnosed with cancer and passed away shortly after. On the night of his passing, a friend and I drove to Frank's home where I sat in his daughter's room and watched her begin to grieve the loss of her father. It was in that room that night that I made a vow. The Bible talks about the power of our words and the impact of even the murmurings of our hearts. I decided that night I would never trust God again. A seed of bitterness and offense began to grow inside of me, and I found myself running as far from Him as I could.

I began partying and numbing everything with alcohol and an eating disorder. One night, I overdosed on pain killers and ended up in the hospital. I didn't want anyone to find out since the crowd I hung out with made fun of people with depression. A few weeks later, I went to church camp as usual and ended up sharing about my overdose for the first time with a male camp counselor. Another night, he asked me to go on a walk with him where he then took advantage of me and my vulnerability.

For the next two years, I began believing many lies from this man. I was in shock that night and had learned from a young age how to disassociate in that situation. He convinced me that because I didn't scream for help, I was condoning his actions. I was still in high school, but he convinced me it was now God's will for us to be married. He was studying to be a pastor at that time, and my mom soon believed him to be the answer to her prayers and my rebellion. What she didn't know is that he controlled every detail of my life: where I was allowed to go, who I could talk to, what I could wear, etc. By my senior year of high school, he had isolated me from all other relationships and was pushing for our engagement. I would break up with him only to return again.

One evening after midnight, I drove out into a blizzard on the county roads outside my small town. I hit the gas and began driving down the road as fast as I could when my phone alerted me of a message. I hadn't been talking to anyone; I slid to a stop where I read a message from a young girl who'd previously confided in me her story of abuse. In that message, she shared how she couldn't sleep and felt led to tell me how thankful she was for me and didn't know what she would do if anything happened to me.

I sat in my car, staring at the snow covering my windshield, when I heard the audible voice of God. His presence consumed my car in a way I had never experienced, even as a young child. He spoke five words that would start my prodigal journey home: "I am jealous for you."

After that night, I ended the relationship for good, joined a Bible study and began reading my Bible again. I did everything I knew to please God. However, I was returning to the Lord with an old wineskin, strong enough to hold rules and religion but not the kind of love Jesus died to have with me. He was jealous for all of me.

On Valentine's Day, a few months after that night on the road, I walked into church to hear news I wasn't prepared for. I could feel the roots of anger and bitterness begin to well up inside of me when they began to play the worship song "How He Loves." They were singing the words, "He is jealous for me..." when that same thick presence of God came over me again. I saw Jesus come and sit next to me. He began speaking over me the plans for my life, but most of all, He spoke of His overwhelming love for me. I had never come close to experiencing the love that began pouring over me that day as He shared with *me the truth about me and who He made me to be. That Valentine's Day marked my life more than any other.*

As promised, God took me to the mission field in Thailand where I began to learn about His jealous love for the lost. He doesn't let me forget that His love will not be shared with the love of ministry, man's approval, or any other lover before Himself.

My prayer is that you would allow God to dismantle any roots and lies you may be believing about how He sees you. One of the biggest lies the enemy would use to bring shame and condemnation against me during my prodigal years was that I knew better. I had once walked and dreamed with God on the mountaintops. What worse sin could there be than intimately knowing God and then rejecting Him? Trust me, friend, you are not the exception for which His blood is enough. You are the deep joy of His heart that kept Him going until it was finished. He is not jealous for your servitude or your gifts that He gave you. He just wants all of you. I hope you learn to give Him just that.

Like my friend's story, maybe disappointment with God is in the details of your life. Maybe it's not the biggest issue, but it plays a role in why you no longer follow Him like you once did. And now, as you are making steps to return to Him, it's time to address your disappointment with God. When we feel like God has let us down, we will have trouble trying to move forward spiritually. This needs to be resolved. The feeling won't go away by denying it or pretending things never happened, pretending you're over it. Denial doesn't heal wounds. Time doesn't heal wounds either, but Jesus can.

It will help you to remember Jesus also experienced feelings of deep disappointment with people who walked away from Him and betrayed Him. And when He was hanging on the cross, after three years of obeying and loving His Father in heaven, He is reduced to crying out, "My God, why have You forsaken Me!?" In other words, "Where are You, God!" Many of you have moments when you yelled out at God in the same way Jesus did. Jesus experienced all the feelings of betrayal and abandonment and disappointment we have ever felt, which makes Him the perfect Savior: He understands your heart.

HOW DO WE GO FORWARD?

Be Honest with God

Come to the Father in prayer and be completely honest with Him about your feelings. If you feel that God has failed you—that He didn't keep His promises and has ignored your prayers—tell Him that's how you feel. We read in the Bible about David's frustration with God. We read also about Job, Elijah, and others. Bring into the open your feelings of being angry, hurt, discouraged, or disappointed. You are saying, "I believe the Bible, that You are good and trustworthy, but in this instance, it feels like You abandoned me; it feels like You left me." Bring out everything that remains inside—the feelings, the questions, and the confusion. It might help to write things down and list the experiences and feelings and all the ways your relationship with God was impacted. By doing this, you are coming toward your Heavenly Father and not walking away from Him. You are thus positioning yourself to receive from Him.

Be Aware of Satanic Voices

You have an enemy who will whisper distortions and lies about God, encouraging you to hold grudges and bitterness toward your Heavenly Father. His goal is to separate you from God by gaining your agreement, that you accept his lies as truth ("God abandoned you." "You can't trust Him."). Satan seeks to take advantage of your pain to lead you into resentment toward God. Resist the temptation to accuse and blame God. Instead, in your pain, come to your Father, praying honestly about how you feel but asking your Father to lead you to healing, truth, and restoration.

Don't Demand Answers from God

You probably have a lot of "why" questions for God: "Why did You allow this to happen?" "Why didn't You fix this?" "Why didn't You answer my prayers?" You can ask those questions, and the Holy Spirit may give you some insight. But I encourage you to drop any insistence on understanding the "why" something happened as the prerequisite to restoring your faith in Jesus. In other words, don't require an explanation, because often you won't receive it in this life. We are still in a fallen world, and we have finite and limited ability to understand. Sons and daughters of God have often had to endure great pain and loss without complete explanation, just like Job.

Do Ask for His Help

Instead of insisting on explanations, come to Him asking for His help. Often that comes by His presence drawing near. Perhaps He will highlight a Scripture that will comfort and encourage you, perhaps wisdom from another believer, maybe a prophetic word from another; generally, His help will come from many sources. Oftentimes as you pour out your feelings, His presence simply draws near and strengthens your heart, and you feel His love washing over you. It's as if He says to you, "My daughter, my son, we will discuss this in eternity, but until then I'm giving you comfort and strength through My presence and My Word. I will heal your heart so you can trust Me again."

Declare God's Truth

This might feel counterintuitive, but find Scriptures about God's faithfulness and goodness, and declare those over your life. Speak them out. In this you are taking a stand and saying, "I choose to put my faith in God and His Word. I will not let my experience and my feelings determine what is true. Instead, I choose to trust His Word, and I accept it as true." This is what it really means to live by faith. As you read promises and truths and stories of His miracles, you are rebuilding your faith, and you are taking a stand against the enemy's efforts to separate you from God.

We choose a resilient, bold devotion to God, the kind the Jewish captives showed when they were threatened with a fiery death unless they renounced their faith. Their response to their captors: *"If we are thrown into the blazing furnace, the God we serve is able to deliver us from it, and he will deliver us from Your Majesty's hand. <u>But even if he does not, we want you to know, Your Majesty, that we will not serve your gods...</u>"* (Daniel 3:17-18, emphasis mine). Even if He doesn't intervene, we will stay true to Him.

We live in a fallen world. Not everything we experience is from God. Our obedience does not protect us from loss and pain. Jesus warned us that the enemy comes to steal, kill, and destroy, and there will be loss (see John 10:10). The day is coming when God does restore all things and remove all evil. But we're not in that part of the story yet. Until then, we walk by faith and stay close to our Father.

ACTIVATION

A. Go through the process suggested above. Write out details of your experience and feelings and how they have impacted your relationship with God. Go through the list and talk to your Father. Ask for His help to heal and resolve the feelings and restore your ability to trust and follow Him.

B. It can be helpful to seek the support of others who can walk through a process of healing prayer with you. While I can't endorse specific ministries, many people report being helped at local churches that host Sozo ministry (see bethelsozo.com) or similar prayer ministries. Christian counseling ministries can also be very helpful.

C. David often poured out his feelings to God in the Psalms. In Psalm 6 and Psalm 13, he expresses his feelings that God is letting him down. Meditate on these and use some of the language there to express your own prayers to God.

140

D. A final key to resolving these disappointments might be to extend forgiveness to other people who might have been involved in a matter. Ask the Holy Spirit to highlight any person you need to forgive.

SUGGESTED READING

Johnson, Bill. *God Is Good*. Shippensburg, Pennsylvania: Destiny Image, 2016.

SECTION III
ENTERING IN

CHAPTER 11

YOUR NEW IDENTITY

"But when the set time had fully come, God sent His son, born of a woman, born under the law, to redeem those under the law, that we might receive adoption to sonship. Because you are His sons, God sent the Spirit of his Son into our hearts, the Spirit who calls out, 'Abba, Father.' So you are no longer a slave, but God's child; and since you are His child, God has made you also an heir." (Galatians 4:4-7)

"To Him who loves us and has freed us from our sins by His blood, and has made us to be a kingdom and priests to serve His God and Father—to Him be glory and power for ever and ever! Amen." (Revelation 1:6)

"But you are a chosen people, a royal priesthood, a holy nation, God's special possession, that you may declare the praises of Him who called you out of darkness into his wonderful light." (1 Peter 2:9)

"Therefore, if anyone is in Christ, the new creation has come: The old has gone, the new is here!" (2 Corinthians 5:17)

THE SECOND-MOST IMPORTANT QUESTION

In an earlier chapter we wrote the most important question in life is to know who God is. But knowing who God says WE are is the second-most important question. Too often preachers and teachers focus on developing a Biblically precise doctrine of who God is but have an incomplete understanding of who we have become after we are born again. We fail to let God's Word teach us about how really born again we are and how much of a new creation we have become. This is a big deal because your purpose in this world is dependent on a correct understanding of who you are. Also, it impacts how Christian leaders lead their people. Many of you were wounded by church leaders who did not have a Biblical understanding of the new birth.

SAVED TO SERVE?

A friend of ours is recovering from the abuse she endured in her former church where she was used up and burned out in a never-ending demand to serve the church's needs. She tells how the pastor's mantra was: "You were saved to serve." Therefore, she was expected to make large commitments of time and energy to church activities. "Saved to serve" was repeated often from the pulpit. In practice, the "saved to serve" idea was used to squeeze more work out of church members to fulfill the pastor's vision. She threw herself into serving the many needs of the church, but her efforts never seemed to be enough for the pastor. When she finally said no to one more request, he criticized her severely for her lack of commitment.

That pastor is wrong! You were not saved to serve! God did not save you to make you His employee. God did not save you to fulfill some leader's vision. He saved you to adopt you as His daughter, to adopt you as His son. *God sent His Son...that we might receive adoption* (see Galatians 4:4). Jesus redeemed you through His death on the cross in order to restore your relationship with God. Our sins— our disobedience, unbelief, and rebellion against God's authority— separated us from God. But Jesus removed our sins, taking them on Himself. He truly is *"the Lamb Who takes away the sin of the world"* (John 1:29). When you believe in Him and receive His gift of salvation, then you become a child of God (see John 1:12). God becomes your Father, and you are His beloved, adopted child. *"The Spirit you received does not make you slaves, so that you live in fear again; rather, the Spirit you received brought about your adoption to sonship. And by him we cry, 'Abba, Father'"* (Romans 8:15). Many of you already know that the word *abba* is not referring to an old Swedish pop group, but *abba* is the Aramaic word for "papa" or "daddy." That speaks of an affectionate, intimate relationship with your Father in Heaven.

Your destiny is not a training seminar; you are heading for a wedding feast (see Revelation 19:7)! Weddings are celebrations of love and joy, music and dancing, family and food. The Bible calls it a wedding FEAST! The Bible says you are far more than just a sinner saved by grace. You are a treasured child, more than a conqueror through Jesus Christ, adopted by a King, and now, therefore, you are royalty. That is who you are. When church leaders embrace a Biblical understanding of the people they lead, they will focus more on building big people instead of a big church. We need to let the Bible form our understanding of the new identity into which we are born. In C.S. Lewis's *The Chronicles of Narnia,* the heroes of the stories are school children who become kings and queens. That describes who we are when we are born again; we become children who are kings and queens.

One leader looks at their congregation and sees sinners who must be pushed and driven to serve and give. Another leader looks at their congregation and sees people born again with a new nature and a new heart, who now are naturally generous, prone to righteousness, wired to love and do exploits for God. One leader thinks, "How can I get this person to fill the empty slot in our ministry?" Another leader asks, "What's this person's God-given destiny, and how do I remove barriers and ceilings so he or she can be who they were created to be and do all the Father has called them to accomplish?"

This is why at our Agape school we blitz our first-year students with the truth of their new identity. The first-year books and classes concentrate on building a Biblical understanding of who they are. Many of the students have been Christians for decades, but they come out of the first semester with a life-changing awareness of who God says they are. This is big, because we are intent on developing world-changers! Knowing who you are will determine what you do.

BEING CALLED BY NAME

"Do not fear, for I have redeemed you; I have summoned you by name; you are Mine"
(Isaiah 43:1). One of the foundational spiritual truths is that the God of the Bible knows you. He calls you by name.

In 1977, I felt the need to grow spiritually and get equipped for some kind of ministry. Many people who had been instrumental in my spiritual growth had attended Lutheran Bible Institute in Seattle, Washington, so I felt drawn there. I knew no one at the school, had never been to Seattle, had never been west of Iowa, but I felt God say, "Go!" My sister Sue also decided to attend. Not having much money, we boarded a Greyhound bus and rode three days from Illinois to Seattle. We arrived in an unfamiliar city, in an unfamiliar region with strange names like Snoqualmie and Snohomish. When we stepped onto the busy campus in north Seattle, we knew nobody. Because of that, I began to feel some uncertainty and had second thoughts about the decision to leave home. We found our way to the registration office, and as we entered, a lady at the counter looked up at us, smiled, and said "Hello, Bob; hello, Sue." That was Arlie Rue, the director of admissions. We'd never met before, but she had made the effort to memorize names with pictures on the incoming student applications in order to greet each one by name. To be recognized and known in that moment had a powerful effect on us, pushing away doubts and fears.

IDENTITY THEFT

That God becomes our Father and knows us by name is the core reason we can talk of Christianity being a relationship and not a religion. This is the basis of the new identity we received when we were born again through faith in Jesus. However, we have an enemy who comes to "steal, kill, and destroy" (see John 10:10). One of the primary ways he attacks you is to rob you of your true identity. This has been his goal toward people since the beginning. Genesis 3:1-6 records the fall of Adam and Eve. A careful reading of the account shows how satan's attack was to deceive them about their true identity. He convinced them to disobey God so they could become like God. Yet God had earlier said Adam and Eve were created in His image, and thus they were already godlike. Satan convinced them to turn away from their Heavenly Father in order to become what God said they already were, and in that disobedience, they actually lost their identity and position in creation.

Your Creator holds the blueprint for your true identity. But the enemy's goal is to rob you of your true identity by using the world system, which is designed to separate you from your true Father and substitute false gods. The devil's assault on your identity is constant. Children with abusive parents hear, "You're worthless. You're a disappointment. You won't amount to anything." Many of us have stories from grade school and junior high days in which we were attacked, mocked, put down, ridiculed, embarrassed, and shamed. As adults, our failures and disappointments can tend to define us and rob us of confidence. Identity is at the heart of the gender confusion that has increased in the world. The Bible tells us the world system and the forces of darkness all conspire to diminish us and keep us enslaved to lies about our value, about the identity and destiny God has intended for us.

Years ago on the mission field, I found myself leading a small team that was attempting to start a new church. We had many difficulties and couldn't seem to go forward. Our biggest struggle was trying to rent facilities. We contacted 75 different realtors. Half of the realtors wouldn't work with us because we were foreigners, and when we found realtors who would assist us, the landlords refused to rent to us. It was a tough time. Finally, our mission leaders called for a meeting and told me they had decided to shut the work down. A hard discussion followed, in which the team's failure was analyzed. During the discussion, a fellow missionary said he didn't think I was a leader; he thought I was a good follower but not a good leader, and that accounted for the team's failure. His intention wasn't to hurt me and he spoke gently, but I was devastated by the remarks. I was hurt because I felt a strong call to leadership, but now, people I admired were expressing their lack of confidence in me. In the days that followed I was assaulted by doubts about who I was and my sense of calling for the future. So often our sense of identity is tied to the opinions of the important people in our lives. I floundered for months until another mission friend ministered to me in an extended time of prayer. He broke off the words that had been spoken over me, and my sense of call and identity began to be restored.

The world, the flesh, and the devil will attack you at key points of your identity in order to rob you of God's purpose for your life. This is because when you move fully into what God says about you and how He sees you, and you begin to walk in the identity and destiny He has ordained for you, you are now a threat to satan's dominion. As Ephesians 4:14 states: You will no longer be *"tossed back and forth by the waves, and blown here and there by every wind of teaching and by the cunning and craftiness of people in their deceitful scheming."* You will no longer be caught in *"...the trap of the devil, who has taken you captive to do his will"* (2 Timothy 2:25-26). You are now a free person, secure because now God is defining who you are and what you can do. The weakness, shame, defeat, the "you don't measure up" voices of the past are removed and replaced with God's truth.

GOD WANTS TO REWRITE YOUR STORY

When theologians speak of our salvation, they use words like "justification," "sanctification," and "glorification." While all these words have rich meaning, the bottom-line message is this: The Father wants to rewrite your story. He wants you to experience your own Luke 15 moment (the return of the prodigal son), when you come to Him in surrender and He embraces you, restores your true identity as His child, and grants you access to His kingdom's resources. So many people reduce salvation to "going to heaven when I die" when your Father has far more in mind. He wants to restore your true identity.

At the moment when you repent and turn to God, placing your faith in Jesus, you experience salvation. According to the Bible, at that moment your identity changes:

- From the Father's perspective, you become His royal child.
- From Jesus's perspective, you become His bride.
- From the Holy Spirit's perspective, you become His temple.

Salvation from the perspectives of each of the three members of the Trinity involves a change of your identity. You have become something new! 2 Corinthians 5:17 famously says you are a new creation! The old is gone, the new has come!

THE POWER OF BAPTISM

This newness is what's celebrated and experienced in baptism: *"We were therefore buried with Him through baptism into death in order that, just as Christ was raised from the dead through the glory of the Father, we too may live a new life."* (Romans 6:4, emphasis mine). Instead of a mere religious tradition (to which it's often reduced), baptism is a powerful declaration of transformation as the individual celebrates being delivered from the dominion of darkness and being brought into the Kingdom of the Son. In baptism the person is declaring to the Father, "I praise You for making me Your child!" The person is declaring to Jesus, "I love You because Your death means life for me!" In baptism the person is declaring to the Church, "I am now one of you! I will love you and stand with you!" And to the demonic forces of darkness, the person is declaring, "You no longer have control over my life. I am free and have power to overcome all your schemes!"

These days, I follow the New Testament pattern of baptizing people quickly after they come to faith in Jesus, instead of waiting until it fits the church calendar or after an extended time of study. New Testament practice conveys an urgency for the new believer to be water baptized as soon as possible—and rightly so, as the focus of baptism is the person's new identity: dying to the old life and raised to a new life!

JESUS BARN BAPTISM

In February 1977, I was baptized at the Jesus Barn in Morton, Illinois. Two years earlier, I was a senior in high school. I had no interest in spiritual things and assumed religion was mostly optional—if it helped you, fine, but I myself felt no need for God. However, that summer my friend Steve invited me to a Bible camp in Minnesota. I didn't know what "going to Bible camp" meant, and it didn't sound very interesting, but he pulled a bait-and-switch by stressing how many pretty Scandinavian girls from Minnesota would be attending. So I went. In an earlier chapter I told how I was initially uninterested in all the daily teaching and preaching at the camp until a guy (Tom Eggum) spoke on his work supporting Christians in communist nations who were persecuted for their faith. That led to me wondering what was so special about Jesus that people were willing to go to prison. That awareness softened my heart, and after returning home, Steve and his father led me in prayer to repent and believe in Jesus. That night after praying, I felt a huge shift in my heart, that something powerful had taken place.

However, in spite of that experience, when I left for my first year of college, I began to drift spiritually; before the first semester was over, I was partying and living as I wanted, neglecting any relationship with Jesus. I was miserable inside, though, because I knew something spiritual had taken place in my life, but now I was ignoring God and feeling guilty about it. Because of my inner turmoil, I ended up hurting people and walking away from relationships in those months. I still feel regret over those situations.

In an attempt to get restored spiritually, I dropped out of school and spent four months backpacking on the Appalachian Trail. That endeavor didn't bring restoration, and I returned home spiritually broken and empty. About that time my friend Mike invited me to a service at the Jesus Barn, an alternative ministry started by Bill and Joan Hartseil in Central Illinois for young people whom the traditional church was unable to reach. This experience was toward the end of the Jesus Revolution that swept so many youth to faith in Christ. That night at the Barn my life was changed. God got ahold of my heart as Sammy Tippit preached a message about returning to Jesus. It was exactly what I needed to hear. After the sermon, I went to the altar for prayer, as a broken, empty person, and lay on the floor for much of the evening as God brought forgiveness, cleansing, and restoration to my heart. This was the turning point in my life—a total surrender to Christ—and I've never looked back. I began to regularly attend services at the Barn.

Four weeks later, on a super-cold Saturday in February, there was a baptism service at the Barn for two new believers. The room was packed with young people as Bill preached on baptism. Two people stood by the baptism tank (a horse watering trough from the hardware store), waiting to be baptized following Bill's message.

After preaching awhile, Bill asked, "Is there anyone else who has begun to follow Jesus but hasn't yet been water baptized? If so, what's to stop you tonight from obeying the Scriptures?" Two other people stood, and Bill invited them to line up behind the first two. Bill preached a little more and I felt my own heart being stirred. It felt as if God had entered the room and was touching many people. I had never been baptized as an adult, and I felt compelled to obey the Scriptures. So when Bill asked if there were any others who needed baptism, I arose and joined the line. Bill continued preaching and inviting more people to receive baptism. Each time he asked if there was someone else, more people stood up. By the time he finished, there were 58 of us in line for baptism!

It was an amazing night of celebrating new life. Some of the people being baptized said this was the first time they understood and believed the gospel. Others were new believers who had never received baptism and felt convicted for having not obeyed the Scriptures. We lined up and were baptized in our street clothes. Joan Hartseil was running to find more towels as one by one Bill dunked us in the tank. Because it was winter, people were wearing thick clothing such as sweaters and corduroy pants. This resulted in each person's clothing soaking up water like a sponge. As Bill reached the last few people in line, the water in the tank was so low, Bill had trouble getting them under the water! It was an incredible, joy-filled night of celebrating the goodness of the God Who loves us and saves us.

YOU ARE NOT A MERE HUMAN ANY LONGER

Recently a passage from 1 Corinthians 3 was pointed out to me. It's a passage I've read many times but never caught its staggering implications. (It is amazing how we can continually uncover new ideas from the Bible, even after reading for decades. It truly is a living book!)

The Apostle Paul was writing to the church members in the city of Corinth in order to correct their behavior. He wrote, *"You are still worldly. For since there is jealousy and quarreling among you, are you not worldly? <u>Are you not acting like mere humans</u>? For when one says, 'I follow Paul,' and another, 'I follow Apollos,' are you not mere human beings?"* (1 Corinthians 3:3-4, emphasis added).

This passage is pretty amazing: Paul is rebuking the church members for acting human! He says their jealousies and disputes are the behaviors of mere humans. Implication? You are not a mere human any longer! You have a new identity! You no longer need to respond to life as an ordinary human being!

You are a new creation. You have a new identity as a child of the King; thus, you are royalty. You are seated with Jesus. You have new authority, new rights, and new resources that are supernatural in origin. Living life as a mere human being is no longer acceptable. And that fact changes everything! How you respond to life, relationships, troubles—everything changes!

Math Changes

Earthly math no longer determines the outcomes in your life. For example, now it's possible to feed 5,000 people with 5 loaves and 2 fish. Our math now includes 1 person putting 1,000 enemies to flight, or 2 people causing 10,000 to flee. Now 1 prophet of Yahweh (Elijah) can defeat 400 prophets of Baal. Now, subtracting an army down from 32,000 to 300 (Gideon) creates the right size for defeating the vast Midianite army. And now only 2 or 3 people praying together can move the Creator of the universe to draw close and give His attention and favor. For God's children, you cannot deduce an outcome by counting the amount you have at the start.

Geography Changes

Now for God's children, geography changes. You are no longer restricted by distances because you are no longer a mere person. Now, you can pray in your bedroom in Peoria or at your kitchen table or in your car and directly influence the White House or Thailand or the Ukraine or your family members struggling in Colorado. Distance does not stop your direct influence on a situation.

For several years, Harriet and I have been connected to a group of churches in central Asia, teaching and ministering via WhatsApp and Zoom from our living room in Illinois. Recently as a church gathered at a city in this Asian country for a teaching time, before I called, I asked the Holy Spirit to show me if He wanted to minister to anyone. I received four or five images or impressions about specific people whom I thought the Lord wanted to touch. In one case, an image came to my mind of a middle-aged woman who had either a broken leg or leg problems, and how the Lord wanted to touch her. The only person I knew at the church was the pastor. When we started the Zoom meeting, I could see on the screen the room in the church building was full. Before we started the teaching time, I shared that I thought the Lord wanted to minister to people first. I asked if there was a woman with an injured or broken leg because I believed the Lord wanted to heal her. Everyone got excited, and the pastor explained to me that the middle-aged woman who cleaned the church had just called that morning in tears saying she would have to quit serving because of too much pain in her injured leg. So we prayed for her, and they reported her pain ended; there was a lot of celebrating. Several others were also healed or touched that night. The distance of half a world away wasn't too far to impact. Distance does not limit our influence.

DNA Changes

You have been born again and have become a child of God. With that, your family has changed. Your new family isn't defined by race or nationality but, as the Bible reveals: *"…before me was a great multitude that no one could count, from every nation, tribe, people and language, standing before the throne and before the Lamb"* (Revelation 7:9).

This multitude, this family, was created by the sacrifice of Jesus: *"... You were slain, and with your blood you purchased for God persons from every tribe and language and people and nation. You have made them to be a kingdom and priests to serve our God, and they will reign on the earth"* (Revelation 5:9-10).

Jesus goes on to define those in His family: *"For whoever does the will of my Father in heaven is my brother and sister and mother"* (Matthew 12:50). The Bible explains further, saying God's family consists of those who receive and believe in Jesus: *"...to all who did receive him, to those who believed in his name, he gave the right to become children of God—children born not of natural descent, nor of human decision or a husband's will, but born of God"* (John 1:12-13).

Because your family has changed, you now have new family traits to draw on! Whatever weaknesses or sinful tendencies may have marked your former family, now that you are born again, you have inherited a whole new set of traits and characteristics. You have been born into a family that defeats giants and subdues nations. We speak to kings. We are bold; we don't let the fear of man control us. We walk in love and stand up for the weak and value truth above all. This is who we are; this is how we act in this family. We set captives free; we trust God and stand boldly when odds are impossible. That's who we are; that's what we do.

Caleb facing down a hostile mob; Peter standing in a Jerusalem street, preaching to those who mocked him; Mary who had the courage to endure the criticisms of pregnancy out of wedlock— This is the heritage we've inherited. It's the grandmother Jael who singlehandedly kills the general of the army invading Israel, declaring "You won't destroy my family; you won't destroy my nation!" (see Judges, Chapters 4 & 5.) This is who we are, and this is how we act in this family. And like the successors in every great family, we might wonder if we can measure up and live the same way. You can. It's in you. You can draw on those family traits.

157

We come to the Bible, and we place ourselves in the storylines, because these old stories are also our stories. The strengths and exploits of Bible heroes in the past are ours too because they show what our family does. I am not saddled with the weaknesses or compromises or sins of my past generations! I've been born again and adopted into a new family with new strengths and qualities. Think of an old English manor with centuries-old portraits of ancestors hanging on the wall, and you are the newest expression of that greatness. We hang portraits of heroes of the past to remind ourselves where we come from. In my office I have several pictures of heroes from history, hanging as constant reminders of my roots. And from my family roots, I draw out those traits and qualities that I need in my life and situation.

Our Shakespeare Moment

At the beginning of this book, I said my writing isn't like Shakespeare's. But here's a Shakespeare moment for you!

Shakespeare's play *King Henry the Fifth* tells the story of a brave, young English king leading his small army against an overwhelmingly larger French army. The French soldiers are mocking the English army, laughing at the pitiful King Henry, but a wiser Frenchman says, "Wait a minute; show respect and remember the family this king comes from."

"This is a stem
Of that victorious stalk; and let us fear
The native mightiness and fate of him."

A modern translation might be:

This king is the descendant of a family line of victorious leaders.
So be wary of the courage and strength he has inherited
and of the real possibility he has a victorious destiny in front of him."

This speaks to who you are. Regardless of your circumstances and your current troubles, you are a branch of a mighty family, strong, with an incredible destiny.

In 1997, I was a pastor on a church staff and feeling pretty burned out, beat up and spiritually dry. I put aside several days and went to a spiritual life conference in Kansas City, hoping to be renewed and receive some fresh direction and encouragement from the Lord. Each day there were several opportunities to receive prayer and prophetic ministry; however, as the conference progressed, I grew increasing discouraged because I wasn't finding the help or direction that I'd hoped for. The final day came, and once again I was disappointed at not receiving any fresh encouragement from the Lord. As the conference closed and I returned to my hotel to pack my bags, I was complaining (or "compraying") to the Lord about my disappointment. At that moment, while standing in the hotel lobby, the Lord spoke to me. It came as sentences spoken, not audibly, but into my heart. It wasn't my brain composing some ideas but rather complete phrases coming from outside me and deposited one by one within. He said, "Pray that you have the bold faith of Caleb, the purity of Joseph, the humble, servant leadership of Moses, and the ministry anointing of Philip." That was it, nothing else. But it came with such force, such impact I still remember where I was standing in the lobby and the way it stopped me in my tracks. It was one of the first times I heard the Lord so clearly.

And I understood that He was saying that these traits are what I would need in the future so I should persevere in praying each of these into my life. The bold faith of Caleb speaks to both his courage speaking God's truth before a huge mob of people who opposed him and also, years later, his eagerness to take a hill and fight the giants that occupied it (see Joshua 14:6-12). The purity of Joseph refers to the moment when Potiphar's wife tried to sexually seduce him, but his immediate reaction was: "How can I do this great evil and sin against God" and he fled from her (see Genesis 39:6-9). The humble, servant leadership of Moses is based on the passage in Numbers 12:3. While Moses was the top leader over the nation of millions, he didn't use his position for his own purposes but rather humbly served his nation, giving of himself sacrificially. And the ministry anointing of Philip speaks of his ministry in Acts 8:4–8 in which the Holy Spirit worked miracles of healing and deliverance through him, resulting in the entire town rejoicing over God's love and power.

Since hearing those words in 1997, I have persevered in praying that these traits become reality in my life. Like many of you, I can get excited about an idea or a practice for a while, but eventually the excitement disappears, and the interest wanes until it's all replaced by a new idea. However (and this helps confirm the Lord's hand in this), the commitment to pray for these qualities has not diminished. I can truthfully say that since 1997, I have prayed at least four to five times a week (but usually daily) for God to impart these traits into my life. It is my hope that these qualities will mark who I am.

I share that experience because I believe each of us can ask the Lord for a similar "list" of Biblical traits and qualities found in the earlier generations of our Bible family. The Lord of your destiny knows the unique traits, strengths, qualities, and abilities you will need in your life. Ask Him to reveal those that He wants to grow within you. Ask Him to show you the people in the Bible whose lives exemplify specific qualities and strengths that you will need. After all, you've been born again into this family, and these people are from the previous generations of your family; their qualities are now part of your heritage.

History Changes
History changes in the sense that we are now freed from our past. We no longer need to be defined by our past. In Judges Chapter 6, we are told of a time when the Jewish people were cruelly oppressed by the nation of Midian (located in modern-day Saudi Arabia). The Midianites terrorized the Jews and spread destruction throughout

Israel. Chapter 6 tells of the young man Gideon who was hiding from the Midianites. Gideon seems to be a fearful, defeated man, feeling abandoned by God. In the midst of his troubles, God sends an angel to him who announces, "The Lord is with you, mighty warrior!" Gideon was disappointed, discouraged, and offended at God. But God declared he was a mighty warrior. God came to him saying, "Put all your disappointment and discouragement aside and step into the call I have for you. I do have a plan for you. Stop letting the past control you and give yourself to Me today. Follow Me step by step."

Gideon is a great example of how God doesn't define us by our past but rather by the destiny and identity He has determined for us. God frees us from our past. Gideon looked at himself and saw a weak and insignificant man. God looked at Gideon and saw a warrior and champion. What does God see when He looks at you?

Defeat can be a habit in our lives. But when we get God's perspective, that comes to an end. Weakness, shame, the "you don't measure up" voice, all the wounds and destructive habits—these are replaced with God's opinion as He speaks into our lives, saying who we really are. He begins declaring our true identity and destiny.

Peter had a history of being unstable in his decisions and actions; yet Jesus gave him a new name: "the rock." God sees what's in us and calls it into being. When David's brothers looked at him, they saw a shepherd, a farmhand. When God looked at David, He saw a king.

Don't let the past define you. Don't let your current circumstances define you. Let God define you. Get God's perspective. Ask Him what He sees in you. Furthermore, it's really helpful in your relationships to ask God what He sees in the people in your family, or the people you work with, or the people at your school. Parents, ask God to show you how He sees your children. The result is you will begin to treat them according to God's perspective, not according to what you see in their current behavior and failures. At our ministry school, we teach students to find the gold in people's lives. When we teach students to prophesy and speak into the lives of others, they are to look past the current behavior of people and instead ask the Holy Spirit to show them the gold within the person and speak into that. What is God's perspective on this person? What does He love about them? Even people who have embraced radically antibiblical lifestyles and politics can have powerful encounters with God when someone shares with them what God says about His original purposes for their lives.

YOU BECOME WHAT YOU WORSHIP

There is a principle within the act of worship which plays a role in our transformation into a new person: We become like the object we worship. Psalm 115 states it clearly:

"Our God is in heaven; He does whatever pleases Him.
But their idols are silver and gold, made by human hands.
They have mouths, but cannot speak, eyes, but cannot see.
They have ears, but cannot hear, noses, but cannot smell.
They have hands, but cannot feel, feet, but cannot walk,
nor can they utter a sound with their throats.
Those who make them will be like them, and so will all who trust in them."
(Psalms 115:3–8, emphasis mine)

We become like the God we worship. This is why the true God hates false gods. That's why He hated the Baals and Ashtoreths and all the other false gods written about in the Old Testament. When people worshipped the Baals and other false gods, their values and behavior changed because they would act more and more like the idols they worshipped. So when Jewish people in the Old Testament turned from the living God and began to worship the false gods, their lives began to reflect all kinds of evil.

For example, it was believed that the Baals gave people wealth and power in an amoral way, which led to trampling over the weak and exploiting others for personal gain. Baal worship promoted greed and a ruthless approach to life and relationships, despising the weak and taking advantage of others. The Ashtoreth idols and images were pornographic and promised fertility through indulging sexual lust, perversions, and all forms of sexual immorality. The idol Moloch was especially cruel. He promised favor and economic increase through child sacrifice. Moloch idols were formed from metal, with arms opened wide, and super-heated with fires underneath. Parents would throw their babies into the idol's white-hot arms, sacrificing them in a hideous, painful death in order to receive financial blessing. Worshiping Moloch cheapened human life and deadened the consciences of mothers and fathers as they came to value economic favor over the lives of their children.

Because we become like the god (God) we worship, whenever Jewish people followed these false gods, society became cruel, uncaring, and perverse. The living God hates the worship of false gods because of the way it twists the values and behavior of people. Marriage, family, and children all suffer. The poor suffer. Compassion, generosity, kindness, and justice all diminish.

However, the true God is compassionate and just, champions the rights of others, and cares for the weak. As you read the following Scripture passages that speak of the God of the Bible, consider how the values of a society that worship Him would be impacted:

"The generous will themselves be blessed, for they share their food with the poor." (Proverbs 22:9)

"The Lord watches over the foreigner and sustains the fatherless and the widow, but He frustrates the ways of the wicked." (Psalms 146:9)

"The righteous care about justice for the poor, but the wicked have no such concern." (Proverbs 29:7)

"He raises the poor from the dust and lifts the needy from the ash heap; he seats them with princes, with the princes of his people. He settles the childless woman in her home as a happy mother of children..." (Psalms 113:7-9)

"The Lord is gracious and righteous; our God is full of compassion." (Psalms 116:5)

"Whoever oppresses the poor shows contempt for their Maker, but whoever is kind to the needy honors God." (Proverbs 14:31)

"When you reap the harvest of your land, do not reap to the very edges of your field or gather the gleanings of your harvest. Leave them for the poor and for the foreigner residing among you. I am the Lord your God." (Leviticus 23:22)

"The Lord is gracious and compassionate, slow to anger and rich in love." (Psalms 145:8)

Thus, as we truly worship Him, in Whose image we are created, we become more like Him. Our values begin to reflect His values. Our feelings and thoughts begin to reflect His. He is our Father, and therefore, we, His children, begin to look more like Him.

THE PATH TO GREATNESS

Jesus often taught that to experience God's kingdom we need to become like little children (e.g., Matthew 18:3, Mark 10:15). Typically, when we think of childlike qualities, we think of their humility, their unconcern about what people think, their trusting hearts, and so on. But there's one childlike quality that often gets missed: Children dream of greatness, of doing exploits and of being superheroes. That's why their pajamas have Superman and Disney princesses on them. When they play, they pretend to be Batman and Wonder Woman, Spider-Man and Jedi knights. They pretend to be firemen and police officers doing heroic things to save people. They want to vanquish evil. They want to be powerful. They dream of greatness (until the world crushes it out of them and trains them to accept low expectations and reduced goals).

In Matthew 18 Jesus hears His disciples arguing about who among them is greatest. Jesus comes to them and, pulling a child near, says the greatest among you is the one who takes a lowly position like this child. Greatness in the kingdom is found in humility.

Notice Jesus didn't rebuke them for aspiring to greatness; after all aspiring to greatness is a childlike trait! He simply redefined the path to greatness, that of lowly service to others.

Jesus modeled that to the world. John 13:3-5 is one of those Bible passages that spells out the stark difference between Jesus and every other leader in history: *"Jesus knew that the Father had put all things under his power, and that he had come from God and was returning to God; so he got up from the meal, took off his outer clothing, and wrapped a towel around his waist. After that, he poured water into a basin and began to wash his disciples' feet, drying them with the towel that was wrapped around him."*

Jesus knew He was sent from the throne of Heaven. He knew He had all authority from the Father. And what does that compel Him to do? Kneel down and wash the dirty feet of His friends. This is such a powerful passage, causing us to love Jesus and marvel all the more over Him. He shows us that "greatness" comes from humbly serving others.

ACTIVATIONS

A. Are there truths in this chapter that were especially meaningful to you? Meditate on those and ask the Holy Spirit to correct any false ideas you have.

B. Consider the four Scriptures at the beginning of this chapter. Underline the key concepts you find in each passage and consider how these expand your view of God's intentions in saving us.

C. Ask the Holy Spirit to show you any Bible characters who possessed traits and qualities that God wants to grow in your life. Begin to pray that those traits and qualities become realities in your own life.

SUGGESTED READING

Eldredge, John. *Waking the Dead*. Nashville, Tennessee: Thomas Nelson, 2003.

Vallotton, Kris and Bill Johnson. *The Supernatural Ways of Royalty*. Shippensburg, Pennsylvania: Destiny Image, 2017.

CHAPTER 12

HEARING GOD

"The heavens declare the glory of God; the skies proclaim the work of His hands. Day after day they pour forth speech; night after night they reveal knowledge." (Psalms 19:1-2)

"The Lord came and stood there, calling as at the other times, 'Samuel! Samuel!' Then Samuel said, ‹Speak, for Your servant is listening." (1 Samuel 3:10)

"Whether you turn to the right or to the left, your ears will hear a voice behind you, saying, 'This is the way; walk in it.'" (Isaiah 30:21)

"Keep this Book of the Law always on your lips; meditate on it day and night, so that you may be careful to do everything written in it. Then you will be prosperous and successful." (Joshua 1:8)

"All Scripture is God-breathed and is useful for teaching, rebuking, correcting and training in righteousness." (2 Timothy 3:16)

"In the last days, God says, 'I will pour out my Spirit on all people. Your sons and daughters will prophesy, your young men will see visions, your old men will dream dreams. Even on my servants, both men and women, I will pour out my Spirit in those days, and they will prophesy.'" (Acts 2:17–18)

TRUTH, LIES, AND REVELATION

Christianity isn't a story of man's search for God; rather it's the record of God revealing Himself to us.

As written earlier, we were born into a battle. This battle is primarily a conflict over truth. This battle over truth started at the beginning of time as we see in Adam and Eve's experience:

Now the serpent was more crafty than any of the wild animals the Lord God had made. He said to the woman, "Did God really say, 'You must not eat from any tree in the garden'?"

The woman said to the serpent, "We may eat fruit from the trees in the garden, 3 but God did say, 'You must not eat fruit from the tree that is in the middle of the garden, and you must not touch it, or you will die.'"

"You will not certainly die," the serpent said to the woman. "For God knows that when you eat from it your eyes will be opened, and you will be like God, knowing good and evil."

When the woman saw that the fruit of the tree was good for food and pleasing to the eye, and also desirable for gaining wisdom, she took some and ate it. She also gave some to her husband, who was with her, and he ate it." Genesis 3:1-6

Adam and Eve were confronted with a choice—was God speaking the truth to them, or, as satan said, was God deceiving them? Satan twisted God's words and convinced Adam and Eve they couldn't trust Him. Today, satan comes to you and me with the same strategy, seeking to deceive us about God. In John 8:44, Jesus called the devil a liar and the father of lies. Satan battles against truth because his only power over people is deception. He deceives people by turning them from trusting God and instead to believing his lies.

When we believe satan's lies, then we are under his influence. We are caught in his trap and are his captives. But the Bible says we escape his trap and experience freedom when we repent and turn to God. As quoted earlier, 2 Timothy 2:25-26 expresses this idea: *"Opponents must be gently instructed, in the hope that God will grant them repentance leading them to a knowledge of the truth, and that they will come to their senses and escape from the trap of the devil, who has taken them captive to do his will."* For many readers of this book, you find yourself even now experiencing what this passage from 2 Timothy is describing. You are turning to God, dropping your opposition, and in that act of repentance, you are finding new freedom in your heart and mind.

Jesus said as the end of the world draws near, satan's efforts to deceive mankind will increase. "Deception" is a word the New Testament regularly attributes to him, especially religious deception with false ideas about who God is (e.g., Matthew Chapter 24 which describes Earth's condition before the Lord's return). Furthermore, satan incites the world to silence people who are proclaiming God's truth. The Bible is filled with accounts of persecution and martyrdom of men and women who faithfully stood and declared God's Word. Caleb, Elijah, Jeremiah, Peter, Paul, and, most importantly, Jesus, are some who declared the truth of God when it was not popular. The current practice of "cancel culture" in our colleges and universities is nothing new. Satan hates free speech and has regularly used intimidation, bullying, name-calling, and mocking to silence those speaking truth.

SILENCING THE TRUTH

We live in a mind-boggling time. In my college days, the world was afraid Christians would force their Biblical values and truth on other people. We were told truth is relative and all religions are equally valid; therefore, who were we to say we were right? We were told it was arrogant to say Jesus is the only way to God, and instead we must treat all viewpoints as equally valid. But today, seemingly overnight, the world is guilty of doing the very thing they warned Christians would do. A handful of activists and elites insist all people believe what they believe. Ideologies based on identity, gender, and race, rooted in Marxist interpretations of history and culture, have burst forth, and it is demanded that these interpretations be accepted and celebrated as truth or we will be canceled, ostracized, shouted down, and shamed. America's First Amendment rights of freedom of speech and freedom of thought are increasingly proclaimed as dangerous. Corporations, politicians, and college students find themselves pressured to be silent about their own convictions. In the end, the world seeks to silence truth and replace it with its own ideas.

Silencing those who speak truth is nothing new. Two thousand years ago, John the Baptist experienced the government's attempt to silence him. In his role as a prophet, John publicly called out the government leader Herod for the adultery he committed with his sister-in-law Herodias. Herod silenced John by locking him up:

"...when John rebuked Herod the tetrarch because of his marriage to Herodias, his brother's wife, and all the other evil things he had done, Herod added this to them all: He locked John up in prison." (Luke 3:19-20)

Herod's adulterous new wife was especially incensed at John for exposing her sin publicly.

"So Herodias nursed a grudge against John and wanted to kill him." (Mark 6:19)

Maybe you've read how the whole sordid story played out. While John languished in the dungeon, Herod threw a party for all the bigwigs. At the party his stepdaughter danced for the guests (don't think ballet, think pole dancing). Everyone loved it, and Herod rewarded her, offering to grant whatever she wished. The daughter conferred with her mom, Herodias, who saw the chance to silence John's embarrassing accusations and so instructed her daughter to ask for John's head on a platter, delivered to the party. And Herod fulfilled her wish. The world hasn't changed, as it still wants to shut up those speaking God's Word. The world doesn't want to hear the truth.

That's why this chapter is important. We live in a world of deception, lies, and suppression of the truth. Many of the elites of this world and most of the media have agendas and narratives they want to prevail, and thus they suppress any contradicting facts and ideas. But God has spoken and revealed Himself. Whatever He has said is true, and wisdom is found in conforming our personal thoughts to His truth. As we do this, we will experience freedom (see John 8:32).

There are three primary ways by which God speaks. Theologians call the first two "natural revelation" and "special revelation" and the third, as will be explained, is what some label "supernatural revelation."

NATURAL REVELATION

All people can learn some truths about God by observing the material world around them. Psalm 93:4 says we can deduce from the mighty waves of the oceans that God is powerful; Psalm 104:24 says we can determine from studying all the variety of animal life that God is wise and creative. Acts 14:15-17 indicates we can know that God is kind because He provides regular growing seasons that allows farming. Psalm 8 speaks of how the stars reveal God's glory and majesty.

While we were working with churches in a Tokyo suburb, through another missionary I became acquainted with a Japanese businessman. He was friendly and spoke some English (I spoke very little Japanese at the time), and we had similar interests in backpacking and road biking. Once, while biking in the mountains outside Tokyo, we stopped to gaze at an incredible vista of green valleys and rice fields and mountains stretching into the distance. My friend, who was neither religious nor a Christian, said, "When I look at mountains, I feel thanks in my heart. But I don't know who to thank." That led to our talking about God and His creation, which led to other spiritual discussions. He and his family developed relationships with the church, where they eventually all came to faith in Jesus and were baptized. He went on to become an elder in the congregation. Their transformation started through natural revelation, that God's creative power was *"clearly seen, being understood by what has been made"* (Romans 1:20).

Natural revelation also includes the idea that every human being has some innate knowledge of God, that everyone knows at some level they have a Creator. But they suppress that knowledge, not allowing it a place in their lives (see Romans 1:18). Some suppress their knowledge of God because of wounds and disappointments they received from church leaders and immature or sinful Christians. Some suppress truth about God because of their personal rebellion. They don't want God to exist because they want to rule their own life and not have their behavior accountable to anyone. If there is a God, then they'd have to change the way they live. Others were raised in atheistic environments in which any stirring of interest in God was squashed by the culture around them.

One of my favorite theologians tells of riding in a car with another passenger who was explaining why she was an atheist and how she had no inner sense of God's existence. Suddenly the car hit ice on the pavement and spun out of control. In the midst of their terror, the atheist loudly cried out, "Jesus, save us!" As the car came safely to a stop, everyone stared at her in amazement. Sometimes a moment of crisis can reveal what's deep inside us. For some people reading this book, the call to repentance is to simply acknowledge what you already know deep down but have been suppressing because you didn't want to make room for God in your life.

When I think about my friends who deny God's existence and the concern I feel for them, I've always taken heart by remembering author C.S. Lewis. As a young man, Lewis was an atheist, writing with seeming confidence on how the Christian God didn't exist and how the idea of a god rising from the dead came from pagan religions and the truly brave position was to accept that this material world was all there is and so on. But then through a series of experiences that challenged his ideas, he eventually was forced to the conclusion (unhappily for him at the time) that God was there. And in his career, he went on to write many classic books defending Christian belief. A good starting point in pursuing his ideas is his book *Mere Christianity*. But even more enjoyable is his series of children's books, *The Chronicles of Narnia*. These seven books are packed with humor, profound wisdom, and clear-headed truth about God and life. Harriet and I have listened to these many times on long drives.

SPECIAL REVELATION

When theologians use the term "special revelation," they are referring to the Bible. General revelation enables all people to know some truths about God. However, we cannot know what God is thinking, what His plans are, His wishes and desires, His commandments, or His promises and warnings, unless He specially reveals these, unless He speaks His mind to us. God has done this through inspiring human authors to record His truth in the pages of the Bible.

"All Scripture is God-breathed and is useful for teaching, rebuking, correcting and training in righteousness, so that the servant of God may be thoroughly equipped for every good work." (2 Timothy 3:16-17)

"Above all, you must understand that no prophecy of Scripture came about by the prophet's own interpretation of things. For prophecy never had its origin in the human will, but prophets, though human, spoke from God as they were carried along by the Holy Spirit." (2 Peter 1:20-21)

FEEDING ON THE WORD

Hebrews 4:12 describes the Word of God as "living and active." That's how I experienced it when I first became a Christian. Up to that point, I had never been much of a reader and had never read the Bible, but once Jesus came into my life, it was like someone flipped a switch, and I couldn't get enough of the Scriptures. Their impact on me really felt "living and active." The Bible's words immediately began transforming how I thought about people and the issues in my life. My self-centeredness, resentments and fears, my values and priorities, my relationships and future goals, everything in my life was being impacted by the Bible. I soon made a plan to read ten chapters a day. But some days I'd be so moved by what I read, I'd continue and read twenty or thirty chapters. I was like a sponge, soaking up all the promises and truths and instructions. It really is unlike any other book.

Jesus said, *"Man shall not live on bread alone, but on every word that comes from the mouth of God"* (Matthew 4:4). I felt like a starving man who didn't realize he was hungry. Spiritually I WAS starving, until I began reading the Bible, which became a daily feast. In mountain climbing at high altitude, you lose all appetite and feel no hunger or desire for food. Yet your body is deceiving you because it is actually in desperate need of nourishment since you are expending thousands of calories when climbing and you are in dire need of energy. That's how people are when they have no regular input of God's truth. They feel no need for God's Word, but spiritually they are starving inside.

When reading the Bible, it's helpful to remember it isn't one book. Rather it is a collection of 66 books written by some 40 authors over hundreds of years. So don't expect it to read like a novel in a continuous line from cover to cover. Rather, think of the Bible as a mini-library in your hand; when you read, you are selecting one of its books off its shelf and opening it. While at times we do study the

Bible in an academic fashion to grow in understanding doctrines, truth, and principles, we need to regularly read it simply to learn how to personally know God and how to walk with Him. The Bible records case study after case study of people walking with Him in hundreds of situations, giving you examples of how to trust, obey, and follow God in your own life. We open the Bible and ask, "Holy Spirit, please mentor me. What do you want me to see? What do you want to say to me?"

TRUSTING THE BIBLE

It goes beyond the scope of this book to discuss all the attacks on the Bible's reliability. But of all the reasons to believe and trust the Bible, I think the most important is the example of Jesus's own attitude toward the Scriptures. He treated the Bible as completely true and trustworthy. For example, He said, *"Do not think that I have come to abolish the Law or the Prophets; I have not come to abolish them but to fulfill them. For truly I tell you, until heaven and earth disappear, not the smallest letter, not the least stroke of a pen, will by any means disappear from the Law until everything is accomplished. Therefore anyone who sets aside one of the least of these commands and teaches others accordingly will be called least in the kingdom of heaven, but whoever practices and teaches these commands will be called great in the kingdom of heaven"* (Matthew 5:17-19). Here's the deal: If Jesus is your Lord, then He has the right to correct your views and beliefs. If you claim Him as your Lord, then He has every right to insist you believe the Bible the way He does. How can someone say, "I believe in Jesus and He's my Lord" and then say, "No, Lord, You are wrong about the Bible! Don't you know it contains a lot of mistakes?"

As you read the Scriptures, you will find ideas you might not understand. Don't get hung up on those; just lay them aside and come back to them another time. There may be ideas that you initially don't agree with. Actually, you should expect this because you hold specific beliefs and values that originate in the culture in which you were raised. However, the Bible's truth and values are universally true regardless of place and time and will often come into conflict with the values and beliefs of a given culture. For example, people in our Western culture like the idea of a God Who is forgiving and loving, but we tend to be offended at the idea of a God Who brings judgment and punishes sin. However, in many traditional cultures, we find the reverse; in those cultures, people naturally assume God will punish wrongdoing, but the idea that God will freely forgive wrongdoers is offensive. Yet both the forgiveness of God and the judgment of God are Biblical ideas. Thus, the Bible challenges the biases of both cultures.

Taking this thought a bit further, the Bible contains moral law such as we find in the Ten Commandments (see Exodus 20) that extends universally to all cultures and nationalities. The Bible teaches this moral law is also found in the heart of every person, expressed through their conscience. For example, every culture agrees you can't take what doesn't belong to you. That law is understood and modified in various ways in different cultures, but the prohibition against theft is never completely dismissed in any culture. It is a universal commandment for which all people young and old, rich and poor, every race, nationality and class, is accountable to obey. However, currently in many cities in our nation, people are being allowed to shoplift without consequences, depending on the race or economic class of the perpetrators. Allowing people to go free without consequences is saying these people are exempt from the commandment "You shall not steal" (Exodus 20:15). It is destructive to society when our government allows two-tiered justice toward theft based on race and class and ignores a universally held moral law that applies to all people.

Romans 12:2 speaks of no longer being conformed to the world but instead being transformed into a new person by having our minds renewed. It is the truth found in Scripture that is the primary source of renewing our minds. Recognize there are many beliefs you've picked up from your culture. Allow the Bible to challenge your beliefs and opinions. If you get upset when you read something you disagree with, then are you assuming God will have views that agree with only your viewpoint? It's hard to hear God if you've already decided what He should say. If you don't trust the Bible to challenge and correct your thinking, then the source of truth in your life will only be your personal opinions and feelings. Many in our culture today believe that personal feelings are more valuable than the truth. But the blessings of growth and transformation come only by being teachable and applying truth to our lives. So allow the Bible to challenge and correct your opinions. A great daily prayer is "Correct me, God. Show me where lies, deception, and misconceptions have formed my opinions and convictions." I personally pray "Correct me, Father" throughout the day. The key to spiritual growth is maintaining a humble, teachable, and responsive heart toward God and His Word.

Remember that the end goal in your pursuit of the Scriptures isn't to know the Bible; it's to know God. Be careful that knowing the Bible doesn't become more important than loving the God of the Bible. Remember Jesus said loving God with all your heart is the first commandment. He did not say knowing the Scriptures is first. The fact that the Pharisees, who were experts in the Scriptures, also hated Jesus is warning enough that we can develop a "relationship" with the Bible and miss God. This is why talking to the Holy Spirit as you read Scripture is a helpful practice in nurturing a dependent, responsive, loving heart toward God.

TAKING HIM AT HIS WORD

As I wrote earlier, when I first read the Bible, I was soaking it up and being transformed in my thinking. I had never read the Bible before, though my family were nominal church members and I had gone through confirmation classes that the denomination held for junior high kids, as many of my friends had. But when I began reading the Bible, it felt like everything was new. There were so many ideas about God that I was reading for the first time. For example, all the Bible's teaching on the Holy Spirit, the baptism of the Spirit, and spiritual gifts was new to me. While these things were maybe mentioned in confirmation classes, I had no memory of them. I was really amazed to read about how the Spirit works in our lives. After reading the book of Acts, I simply assumed the filling of the Holy Spirit was really important for every Christian and that churches should expect miracles when Christians pray in Jesus's name. I believed all the powerful gifts of the Spirit were supposed to be part of normal Christian life. It was the Bible that led me to those beliefs. Later, though, I was surprised to learn that many Christians have a different understanding of the Holy Spirit, one that seemed greatly diminished from what I saw in Scripture. They believed the more dramatic supernatural gifts of the Spirit were only temporary and we shouldn't expect to see them any longer. I found that puzzling as my reading of the Bible didn't lead me to that conclusion.

I read about a spiritual gift called "speaking in tongues" in 1 Corinthians. I had never heard of speaking in tongues before and had no personal experience of hearing someone speaking in tongues. But simply based on Scripture, I assumed it was a gift we should find in the church and one that should be valued because the Bible speaks so highly of it. But later, Christian friends wanted to convince me that God no longer gave this gift to the church and that seeking it was a sign of immaturity. Some of these friends would ridicule those who spoke in tongues as being shallow and unintelligent, which seemed strange to me because Paul, who wrote the deepest theology in the New Testament, also wrote about how valuable tongues were to him. In 1 Corinthians 14, Paul writes about the gifts of prophecy and tongues. Here, you'll find statements from him such as, *"I would like every one of you to speak in tongues…I thank God that I speak in tongues more than all of you…do not forbid the speaking in tongues."* I think the safest position is for us to value what the apostles valued, even if it makes us (or others) uncomfortable or seems strange. I'm only using speaking in tongues as an example; my main point is that we must let the Bible form our beliefs. We must value whatever the Bible values, and not let our feelings, experience, or tradition trump Scripture.

We want to treasure what He treasures, value what He values. We want to saturate ourselves with Scripture for this purpose. We might have a tendency to limit our beliefs and practices only to what we're comfortable with and what aligns with our personal opinion. But as we engage the Bible, let's bring our opinions and ideas and biases to Scripture and say, "Father, correct my thinking wherever it doesn't agree with Your Word."

WHATEVER YOU ASK FOR

One area that challenges us is the incredible number of promises that Jesus made concerning prayer. Why settle for a faith and practice that assumes miracles are rare? The Bible doesn't lead us to that conclusion. Jesus constantly invites us to believe for miracles. Ponder His words:

"Therefore I tell you, whatever you ask for in prayer, believe that you have received it, and it will be yours." (Mark 11:24)

"...if you have faith as small as a mustard seed, you can say to this mountain, 'Move from here to there,' and, it will move. Nothing will be impossible for you." (Matthew 17:20)

"If you believe, you will receive whatever you ask for in prayer." (Matthew 21:22)

"...whoever believes in Me will do the works I have been doing, and they will do even greater things than these..." (John 14:12)

"If you remain in Me and My words remain in you, ask whatever you wish, and it will be done for you." (John 15:7)

"And I will do whatever you ask in My name, so that the Father may be glorified in the Son." (John 14:13)

Jesus calls us to extravagant, outlandish levels of faith. But all too often the modern church comes behind Him, like a press secretary cleaning up the mess of an exaggerating politician, telling the world He didn't really mean what He said. Often, attempts to explain these verses feel more like an effort to reduce expectations so as to justify our current mundane experience and keep us comfortable with the status quo. However, I think Jesus is pleased when we take Him at His word and try to bring our level of experience up to what He says is possible rather than reduce what He said to something reasonable, something that aligns with our current experience of predictable routines and low expectations.

So, if your previous church experience was unsatisfying, let the New Testament redefine "normal Christianity" for you. Read the book of Acts as an example of what God intends normal Christian experience to be. Treat it as a series of case studies from which we learn how the Holy Spirit works in the church and let it increase your faith for His miracles. Let Scripture correct your beliefs, values, and opinions. God the Father has never changed. Jesus Christ has never changed. And His Word hasn't changed (*"…the Word of our Lord endures forever."* [Isaiah 40:8]). Let your beliefs and practice flow out of Scripture and align with Scripture. Don't allow any tradition or teaching be imposed on top of Scripture, reducing it to something less, something more mediocre. Take Jesus at His Word when He says, *"Whoever believes in Me will do the works I am doing"* (John14:12-14). The Greek word for "works" is the same word used elsewhere in the Bible to describe His miracles of healing and deliverance. He's inviting us to minister supernaturally! Ask Him to remove all filters of fear, unbelief, and bad teaching through which you read the Bible and that have limited your experience of God. Let's be believers who believe. Let's fully receive everything the Bible says God has for us.

HOW TO BE MENTORED BY GOD

The Bible is at the center of your return to God and the chief instrument for the transformation you need. You come to the Bible and ask its author, the Holy Spirit, to mentor you. Let Him use the Scriptures to correct and transform your behavior, thoughts, feelings, ideas, convictions, attitudes, practices, beliefs, values, choices, opinions, relationships, goals, priorities, dreams, hopes, lifestyle, decisions, everything that makes up your worldview, everything that forms your political, spiritual, social, economic, theological, and scientific views. You position yourself under the Holy Spirit's direction, encouragement, and support so that your life will align with God's truth and His purposes. This is a surrender of ownership, recognizing you have been purchased by the blood of Jesus. You are not your own and your heart's cry is: "Father, in all that I am, let Your Kingdom come (to rule and reign over me) and let Your will be done (not my will or the world's will) in every area of my life."

The Holy Spirit will mentor you if you will allow Him. As you open the Bible, position yourself to be receptive with a listening ear. Ask the Holy Spirit to speak as you read. You're not soaking up knowledge right now; you are listening and expecting God to talk to you. Ask the two questions that Paul asked when he first met Jesus: "Who are You, Lord?" and "What do You want me to do?" (see Acts 22:8,10). These are great questions to ask every time we come to the Bible, because generally God wants to tell you more about Himself, and He wants to give you direction on what to do and how to live. It's here that He is mentoring you. Perhaps you have some huge behavior issue in your life, and it has all your attention. But the Lord might be saying, "I'm not dealing with that big thing right now. Instead, I want to deal with your bad temper (or your critical spirit or the way you are so impatient with your spouse or the way you exaggerate when talking or the way you despise Republicans [or Democrats])." Or, maybe, "Right now I just want you to know Me better" or "Right now I want to bring healing to the heartbreak in your life." Let Him mentor you and lead you step by step, day by day, into the areas of your life He wants to touch. He knows when to tell you to roll up your sleeves and tackle the big issues in your life and when to tell you to sit back and let Him comfort you. He loves you and knows the path you need to walk and the speed by which to walk it. This isn't a one-size-fits-all process. He will tailor-make a discipling process for you.

SUPERNATURAL REVELATION

The term "supernatural revelation" describes the many ways God speaks to believers personally and directly in order to encourage, guide, and warn them in their daily lives. It also refers to revelation given to help minister to others. Of course, both natural revelation and special revelation are also supernatural in that they originate with God. But there is revelation by which God speaks to people through dreams, prophetic words, impressions, visions, and other forms that are specific and direct to individuals. It differs from the natural communication we experience in our lives; it proves itself to come from outside this natural realm; hence, it is supernatural.

Both by Biblical examples and teaching, God's intention is for His children to walk in personal, supernatural revelation. When the Holy Spirit was poured out on the followers of Jesus on the day of Pentecost, the first trait of the Spirit to be highlighted was the supernatural revelation He would give to believers:

"In the last days, God says, I will pour out my Spirit on all people.
Your sons and daughters will prophesy,
your young men will see visions,

your old men will dream dreams.
Even on my servants, both men and women, I will pour out my Spirit in those days, and they will prophesy." (Acts 2:17-18)

The Bible declares that all believers, regardless of age or gender, can expect to receive supernatural revelation as they walk with Him.

A PIVOTAL PROPHETIC WORD

Years ago, I joined the staff of a church which I soon discovered was in ongoing conflict and dysfunction. After two years I found myself so discouraged by all the turmoil that I was ready to quit. I wanted to join friends in the Seattle area to help begin and lead a new ministry there. The elders of the church, though, asked me to take a week and pray before making a final decision to quit. During that time of prayer, in spite of my wishes to leave, I felt God prompting me to stay where I was. I didn't like that; I wanted to quit, but I surrendered my will to Him and remained in my staff position.

The strife continued for another two years, with lots of tension, division, and drama. In late November of the fifth year, Harriet and I went to a conference for spiritual refreshment. While there, one of the speakers had a prophetic word for us. It contained a lot of detail, but in summary we were told to "Get ready because God says you will soon be leading. It's going to happen suddenly, and it's going to happen very soon but don't be afraid of what's coming." We both felt it was a genuine word from the Holy Spirit. We also both thought it meant that the Lord was releasing us from our current ministry so we could move to Seattle and help lead a new church there. As a result, we began mentally preparing for a big change and thinking through our departure. I planned to submit my resignation from the church at the next elder meeting, which would be in early January.

But that never happened. Four weeks later, in the last part of December, unexpected events suddenly and surprisingly burst forth in the church. This resulted in a leadership change and by December 31, I was co-senior pastor of the church, where I stayed for the next fourteen years.

Some thoughts here: First, this is an example of receiving a correct prophetic word but then misinterpreting its meaning. Everything that was declared to us at the conference came to pass. But we were mistaken in how we interpreted it. We should have prayed for more clarity instead of assuming the big change involved us leaving for Seattle because that was the only possibility that made sense to me at the time. I had so wanted to move to Seattle that I hadn't considered any other possible fulfillment of the prophecy.

Secondly, despite misinterpreting the prophecy, this word was so helpful as we were mentally prepared for the major change when it came. We were anticipating a big transition and had positioned ourselves to accept it when it arrived.

Finally, the prophecy gave me great confidence that God was in all the changes that were being made. This was especially helpful when making painful and difficult decisions during the leadership transitions at the church. I knew God was behind it and that He cared for everyone involved, but above all, He was bringing healing to the church that had suffered for so many years.

VALUING THE HOLY SPIRIT'S HELP

I am so thankful for prophetic ministry. Especially in these last ten years, prophetic dreams and prophetic words for my wife and me have been so helpful and powerful in major issues and decisions. In daily ministry situations, the Holy Spirit will give directions and knowledge on how to pray for a person or guidance for some problem or concern that I would never have known naturally. The Bible assures this supernatural revelation is available to every believer.

As I have opportunities to preach and minister to groups, I'm learning to lean on the Holy Spirit in times of ministry. When at a ministry gathering, I silently ask the Holy Spirit for impressions about the people present, to see if there is anyone He wants to touch. Some call these impressions "words of knowledge" from 1 Corinthians 12:8.

Recently we had a Zoom meeting for training with a church in Central Asia. But before teaching, I prayed silently, asking the Holy Spirit if there were any individuals He wanted to touch. I felt Him give me four or five impressions about people and the church, including a mental picture of an older man in grimy mechanic's overalls, whose hands were dirty with grease, and some other details. The image came with an awareness that he was in spiritual darkness, the Lord loved him, and a battle was going on for his salvation. I was ministering to those gathered before beginning to teach, and I asked if this image made sense to anyone, as I thought the Spirit wanted to encourage them that this specific man was on the Lord's heart. The pastor got excited and shared he had an appointment that evening to meet a man who fit the description, a man insignificant to the world but highly valued by Jesus. The pastor was very encouraged to be bold and confident that the Lord was in this appointment. My understanding is the man came to faith in Christ that evening. It is amazing that God would speak to a guy in Illinois in order to let a mechanic with grimy hands halfway around the world know he was important to God.

We have a wonderful Savior Who knows all about us. He goes out in search of missing sheep, calling them to follow Him. That may be why you find yourself reading this book, that you are on His heart, and He is calling you to Himself.

SCRIPTURAL ASSURANCE OF
PERSONAL REVELATION

The Bible assures us that God speaks to His children. In the Scriptures God spoke to Noah, Abraham, Moses, Samson, Deborah, Samuel, David, Elijah, Mary and Joseph, and scores and scores more. After Jesus rose from the dead, He birthed the church with the outpouring of the Holy Spirit, Whose arrival was announced in Acts 2:17-18, as referenced above.

The Holy Spirit has many traits and ministries in the Church, but at the very beginning, the focus was on supernatural revelation, that He would release dreams and visions and prophetic words to believers. The Spirit's gifts to Christians are further described in 1 Corinthians 12, with many involving God speaking through tongues, interpretation of tongues, prophecy, discernment, words of knowledge and so on. Hearing God personally is the birthright of every believer.

Some Christians insist that God speaks today only through the Bible and we shouldn't expect Him to communicate directly to people as He did in Scripture. But there is no Scripture passage that tells us God stopped speaking. Before I ever experienced receiving a prophetic word or prophetic dream, I already believed in them because the Bible led me to that belief. The Bible convinced me God wants to speak to us personally. Furthermore, reading the Bible awakens a hunger to hear God just as the heroes in the Scriptures did. I saw the Bible as my foundation for life and the primary way that God spoke to me. But my daily life has also been shaped by ongoing revelation of dreams, impressions, and prophetic words, and I try to nurture a heart that is listening and responsive to the Holy Spirit while going through my day. The first verse I ever memorized was Proverbs 3:5-6: *"Trust in the Lord with all your heart and lean not on your own understanding; in all your ways submit to Him, and He will make your paths straight."* This verse has far more heft in my life when I actively seek and listen for God's direction, knowing He does speak and that this is the heritage and inheritance of every believer.

Maybe you became disillusioned with church and the Christian faith because you saw little evidence of God's presence or activity. While you heard all the talk about Christianity being a relationship with God, what you really saw was a church structure that operated like any secular business, with church programs that were routine and predictable. You saw ministries that were copied from what some flagship church was doing. Leadership meetings reached decisions like any secular organization, through debate, with the strongest personalities in the room tending to win. This left you wondering if there was any evidence that God was guiding. In Acts 13, in the midst of a leadership gathering, the Holy Spirit spoke and gave directions. Yet there seemed to be little expectation that He might interrupt your church's meetings. Perhaps you wondered "Where is the supernatural? Where is God? If it's a relationship, shouldn't we expect our Father to speak to us?" You hungered to experience spiritual reality, but the church left you unsatisfied. So, you either lowered your expectations to match the experience of the people around you, or you left the church in search of something more. That might have led you into New Age experiences, to psychics, Wicca, or other forms of religion and spirituality. These supernatural experiences are rooted in forces of darkness, but your hunger to experience the supernatural is a legitimate desire because you were made to walk with your supernatural Creator.

If you have engaged in other religions and spiritual practices but are now returning to Jesus, you might find spiritual resistance as you begin to follow Him. Jesus calls you to renounce any involvement you've had with other religions, and He will help free you from them. Every book in the New Testament warns against false teaching and spiritual deception by which satanic forces deceive and entrap sincere people who are looking for spiritual reality. These forces won't give you up easily. You might need prayers of others to help you get free. But the biggest source of freedom will be filling your heart and mind with the truth of Scripture (see John 8:32). My advice is to press hard into the Bible. Fill yourself up on Scripture. Let it transform your thinking and renew your mind with its truth. Consider the two verses below:

"All Scripture is God-breathed and is useful for teaching, rebuking, correcting and training in righteousness, so that the servant of God may be thoroughly equipped for every good work." (2 Timothy 3:16-17)

"Do not conform to the pattern of this world, but be transformed by the renewing of your mind. Then you will be able to test and approve what God's will is—His good, pleasing and perfect will." (Romans 12:2)

ENCOURAGEMENT FROM SCRIPTURE

The Bible creates a hunger and a hope that I too can hear God. It does so through the stories of the many ways God spoke to people in the Scriptures. Here is a sampling:

In 1 Samuel 16:1-5, God sends the prophet Samuel to anoint David as the new king. Samuel discusses this assignment with God because he's concerned the current king will kill him, so God gives him specific instructions on how to safely proceed.

In 2 Samuel 5:17-25, David asks God if he should attack an invading Philistine army. God says yes and David defeats them. When the Philistines invade a second time David asks the Lord if he should attack again. God says yes but tells him this time to attack in a different manner.

In Acts 8:26-29, Philip has his successful ministry in Samaria interrupted by an angel who gives him specific directions to leave and then where to travel. On the way he sees a foreign dignitary, and the Spirit tells Philip to approach him, which leads to the man's conversion.

In Acts 9:10-16, in a vision, the Lord has a conversation with a disciple named Ananias, instructing him to go and heal the church persecutor Saul who had just encountered Jesus on the Damascus Road.

In Acts 16:6-10, Paul and his missionary companions have their plans changed and their journey redirected by the Holy Spirit. Eventually the Spirit gives them a vision that directs them to the city of Philippi, where they start a new church.

There are dozens of examples we can pull from the Bible, but the point is made. The Bible itself leads us to expect God to speak to us. Note how God had specific instructions for the situations mentioned above. Those heroes couldn't turn to a page in a Bible to find the directions they needed for each of their situations. They needed fresh direction for the unique situations they were facing, and their stories encourage us to believe God will speak to us too.

JESUS'S DEPENDENCE ON HEARING GOD

It's especially instructive to see how much Jesus Himself needed to hear His Father. He regularly spoke of how much He depended on the Father's direction:

"... that the world may learn that I love the Father and do exactly what My Father has commanded Me." (John 14:31)

"...Very truly I tell you, the Son can do nothing by Himself; He can do only what He sees His Father doing, because whatever the Father does the Son also does." (John 5:19)

189

"...The words I say to you I do not speak on My own authority. Rather, it is the Father, living in Me, who is doing His work." (John 14:10)

"By Myself I can do nothing; I judge only as I hear, and My judgment is just, for I seek not to please Myself but Him who sent Me." (John 5:30)

"For the one whom God has sent speaks the words of God..." (John 3:34)

PROMISES OF GUIDANCE

If Jesus, in His perfection, needed the voice of His Father, how much more do we! Jesus modeled a life that reflected the many promises God has made to us. We can trust He will speak to us because He has promised He will. Here are a few of those promises:

"Whether you turn to the right or to the left, your ears will hear a voice behind you, saying, "This is the way; walk in it." (Isaiah 30:21)

"I will instruct you and teach you in the way you should go; I will counsel you with My loving eye on you." (Psalms 32:8)

"If any of you lacks wisdom, you should ask God, who gives generously to all without finding fault, and it will be given to you." (James 1:5)

"Lord, I know that people's lives are not their own; it is not for them to direct their steps." (Jeremiah 10:23)

"Show me Your ways, Lord, teach me Your paths. Guide me in Your truth and teach me, for You are God my Savior, and my hope is in You all day long." (Psalms 25:4–5)

RANDY AND THE CUPCAKE

One person who has inspired me to press into this place of listening to God is my roommate from Bible school, Randy Wiant. In 1977, Randy and I were thrown together in Seattle as we shared a room at Lutheran Bible Institute, and we stayed connected over the years. Whenever we would call and talk, I always came away wanting to trust God more and take more risks for Him. That's the kind of impact Randy had on people. Randy passed away in 2020. Shortly before his death, he self-published a book on hearing God. Below are a couple of stories from his book (shared with permission from Randy's wife, Kristi):

One Sunday morning after the first service at our church, I thought, I'll buy some cupcakes to bring home to share with Kristi and Kim. At the store I located the packages of cupcakes, which came four to a pack. I picked out the chocolate cupcakes with white frosting, paid at the self-check, and proceeded to walk out of the store. At the exact same time I was walking out of the door a young woman was walking in. Two steps past her I heard that inner voice say, "Give her a cupcake."

That's silly I thought and ignored it. Two more steps and I felt these words rising up from deep down inside, "I said give her a cupcake!" Again I ignored the prompting voice. What would it look like for me to approach a young woman in a store aisle and say "I'm supposed to give you a cupcake!" I kept walking to my car. As I unlocked my car, I heard the voice for the third time: "She needs you to give her a cupcake!"

I turned and walked back in through the doors, praying under my breath, "Lord, I am obeying You. Help me find her!" I looked through the first four aisles, and on the fifth there she was. Walking up to her with the nicest smile I could muster, I asked, "Can I give you a cupcake?" She seemed startled and took a step back. Shaking her head she said, "No!" "You don't understand" I said, "The Lord wants me to give you a cupcake." I took a cupcake out of the container and stretched out my hand with the cupcake in it toward her.

I saw she was crying as she took the cupcake. She said, "God answered my prayer today." Through her tears she said, "Before I went to church today, I asked God for a cupcake. You see my dad passed away not too long ago. It was our special thing to go buy cupcakes and drive to the beach in Edmonds and eat them together."

Now I had tears in my eyes. As the tears rolled down her face she looked at me and said, "Chocolate with white icing is my favorite." Then she added, "You have my father's eyes!" She lost it, I lost it, and we were both crying and praying together on aisle five at a Fred Meyer grocery store.

She told me her name was Tami. I gave her my business card and an invitation to church and walked back out of the store, minus one chocolate cupcake with white frosting. Sitting in my car I said to the Lord, "I get it." I promised to obey Him from then on, with all my heart and determination.

A few weeks later I was surprised to get a call from Tami. "I'm wondering if you could meet me and my mom for a cup of coffee?" she asked. When we met, Tami and her mother said, "We need your opinion on something." Tami asked, "Do you think it would be okay if we used my dad's life insurance money to pay part of my tuition to CBN University?" "Yes, use it!" I said. "Your dad would be proud of you! Honor your father by doing so."

I have kept in contact with Tami over the months and she is doing great. By the way, she asked me, "If it works out, would you stand in for my dad and walk me down the aisle when I need it?"

This is what walking by faith looks like. We might get a prompting and act on it, and maybe we got it wrong and so we might look a little foolish. So what? Most of us can benefit by having our pride humbled! But it could be that acting on a simple inner impression might lead to something wonderful that's being orchestrated by the

Holy Spirit, and you will have the joy of being an agent of God's love.

GOD TOUCHES ANNABEL

Another Randy story takes place on the Saturday before Easter 2018 at another grocery store and involves a lady named Annabel. It's another account of being available and sensitive to God's promptings.

Needing a few items, I stopped on my way home from Bible study, planning to be in and out of the store quickly. As I was walking to the entrance, I smelled an odor first, then saw a homeless woman a few feet from the door. "Spare change?" she asked as I neared.

I'm used to giving spare change out but knew I wouldn't have any until after I shopped. I'll let her know, I thought. But as I walked up to her, (feeling prompted) instead I asked, "Can I pray for you?"

"What?" she asked.

"Can I pray for you?" I asked for a second time.

"No, get away from me. God doesn't care for me. Never did, never will." Then she walked into the store.

"I'll follow her," I thought, "just in case." I looked in my wallet, took a twenty out and put it in my front left pocket. It was what I usually do with just two or three dollars at a time when there are homeless people around. As I followed her around the store I didn't make it obvious. I felt like I was kind of being God's secret agent of grace. I picked out my items all the time watching the woman. When she went up to the checkout stand, I slid in behind her quickly.

When the checker added up her food items, the total came to over eighteen dollars. The homeless lady took a handful of change out of her pocket

193

and laid it on the counter. She said, "That's all I've got." It looked to be about two dollars, maybe a little more. I took the twenty dollar bill from my pocket and waved it at the checker, signaling I would pick up the difference.

The woman left the store as I paid for my items. The cashier told me, "I have never seen anything like that." Taking my bag I went to the exit and there she was. She leaped toward me and shouted, "Why did you do that? This wasn't any of your concern!"

"God wanted you to know He does care and used me to show it to you."

"Why would God care about me?"

"Because He does! You got a gift from Him today."

Again I asked her, "Would you let me pray for you?"

"Okay but don't touch me."

I prayed a simple prayer for God to make Himself real to her.

Something was happening as I prayed. Annabel immediately said, "What's that?! I feel warm! Like nothing I ever felt before!"

God was touching her, loving her. Again I was His instrument to kindle hope in a lost soul.

With tears in her eyes she asked me, "Can you take me to church tomorrow?"

"Yes, of course," I said. "Be ready at 8:30 and I will pick you up right here."

The next day, Easter Sunday, I picked her up and took her to a church close to the store. I figured it would be easier for her to get back to a church nearby. She sang along with the worship music, listened to the announcements, and listened to the Word being preached. When the pastor asked for anyone who *needed Jesus in their hearts to come forward, she almost ran to the front, and a group of ladies followed her.*

I walked forward too with tears of joy and amazement rolling down my face. Here was someone who the day before was saying "God doesn't care for me," now asking God to forgive her and inviting Jesus into her life forever. It blows me away that God's love can do that. This was God's doing, His timing, and I was available.

Annabel is now doing things to help herself get over the pain of her past. Though it is a struggle she is still living for Jesus. The church helped her in many ways: buying her some clothes, helping her get a place to live, and teaching her more about God's love. Annabel is a life changed by God's Grace!

I still follow up and try to connect with her every few weeks. Recently I saw her at the same store where we first met. She ran up to me and said, "Randy, smell me! I am even wearing perfume!"

"Wow," I said, "You do smell good!" Annabel now has a part-time job at the very store she was standing in front of asking for spare change. What a story of transforming redemption!

HOW DO I BEGIN TO HEAR GOD?

Below are a few ideas on how to start but I strongly encourage you to read the books listed below as they will give more detail and answer questions that I'm unable to address in this short chapter.

A. Believe the Bible affirms God does speak to His children. Let the Scriptures form your expectations. Don't form your theology and practice based on your experience. (*"I don't hear God and my church doesn't believe this; therefore, I'll create a theology that justifies my current level of experience."*) Don't form theology out of your fears (*"I don't know if it's God or my imagination…I might make a really foolish decision based on a spiritual feeling…I might be deceived by satan…this is how cults*

195

start...I might look really foolish," etc.). To hear God is your heritage and inheritance if you are His child. Don't let the devil steal that!

Let the Bible build your faith in this matter and seek to bring your experience up to the level Scripture says is available. Read the verses and passages and Scriptural promises written in this chapter. Let them strengthen your faith and shape your beliefs.

The Bible is absolutely authoritative and trustworthy in all it says. God is not a liar so any word, prophecy, or impression that claims to be from God will not contradict what the Bible teaches. For example, you are married but you've met a new person that you feel is your true soulmate. However, if you think you hear God giving you permission to divorce your spouse and marry this new person, you are dead wrong. The Bible forbids that. Regardless of how strongly you feel God is leading you, it is a false feeling and needs to be corrected by Scripture («*'The man who hates and divorces his wife,' says the Lord, the God of Israel, 'does violence to the one he should protect,' says the Lord Almighty. So be on your guard, and do not be unfaithful."* [Malachi 2:16]).

B. Ask the Lord to lead you and grow your ability to hear Him. The Bible tells us to value and pursue prophetic ministry: *"Follow the way of love and eagerly desire gifts of the Spirit, especially prophecy"* (1 Corinthians 14:1). You can pray with confidence that your request to grow in hearing God is aligned with His will for your life. So ask Him to lead you into more. James says, *"You do not have because you do not ask God"* (James 4:2). He likes it when we ask!

C. Pay attention to dreams, impressions, thoughts, images, etc.
As you receive dreams and impressions, ask the Lord if they are from Him. Ask Him what they mean and if you are to do something. If you are like me, initially I didn't think I was hearing anything or receiving anything. But keep persevering! Let the Scriptures

encourage you! As you begin to identify dreams, impressions, etc. that might be from the Lord, ask Him to confirm them. Ask Him to correct you if you aren't hearing Him. As I wrote earlier, *"Correct me, Lord, if I'm wrong"* is a great prayer to pray regularly!

If you think the Holy Spirit is giving you a word about someone, before sharing it, ask Him for permission. If you share, there's no need to thunder like an Old Testament prophet. Use words like, *"I might be wrong, but I think maybe the Lord is showing such and such about this matter—does that make sense to you?"* We teach our Agape students that any word they share with someone must strengthen, encourage, or comfort the person, in accordance with 1 Corinthians 14:3. They are forbidden from sharing any negative, condemning, or destructive word. If they think they are receiving a word for someone that feels negative, they are taught to keep those to themselves and assume they are to pray in behalf of the individual. If they are troubled by a word they think they've received, they can speak with a leader.

For years I've kept a log in which I write down dreams and prophetic words that have been given to me. It is a source of encouragement and helps guide my prayers. Keeping a log demonstrates you value prophetic revelation. It seems to be a spiritual principle that those things we value, pursue, and are thankful for will increase in our lives.

WALKING WITH GOD

This chapter is about learning to walk with God. You might have received Christ 40 years ago and have attended church for decades; you may be able to outline the book of Revelation from memory and read Hebrew, Aramaic, and Greek, but if you can't remember the last time God spoke to you personally, then you are missing a big part of your relationship with Him. Aren't we "followers of Christ"? Isn't He a Shepherd and His sheep know His voice? Then, by all means, let's listen to Him and let Him lead us. His primary way to speak to us is through the Bible. And it's the Bible that encourages us to grow in hearing His voice in our personal lives. He really does want a personal relationship with us. Let's actually seek Him and learn to hear Him. Not ideas about Him. Not just His principles. Him.

The point in this section on supernatural revelation is to assure you that God is with you and He is not silent. His promises to speak to His people aren't just for the spiritually elite or a handful of oddball Christian mystics. Read Acts 2:17-18 again. He intends single moms and college students and retirees and Sunday school kids to hear Him. Don't let the traditions of men that say "God doesn't do this any longer" rob you of what the Bible says is yours. If this is all new and strange, then read the books listed below. They are solid, Bible-based, and good teaching on how to proceed.

ACTIVATION

A. Go outside!

Go for a walk in a park or woods and go with the intentionality of walking with God. Talk to Him as you walk and ask Him to teach you about Himself as you experience your surroundings. What do the wind, the temperature, the sounds, clouds, sun rays, a leaf, a bug reveal about God? Try to position your mind not to think up answers but to receive answers, just as when you converse with a friend. You ask a question and listen to their response. Likewise, as you walk, ask Him to show things to you. When your attention is drawn to something, ask Him what He wants to reveal to you and then listen. You might receive a thought, a mental picture, or some impression. Maybe a Scripture verse or a quote might come to mind, or some feeling might be evoked, or a memory may come into your head. If its meaning isn't clear, ask Him to explain. If you seem to hear only silence, or it feels more likely it's your own imagination speaking, that's okay. Tell that to the Lord and ask Him to lead you into genuine experiences of hearing His voice. Don't give up. Stand on the Bible promises found in this chapter. Read the books below for more help.

As a side note, besides going outside for the exercise written above, go outside simply because nature is life-giving! You receive healing and restoration simply by going outside! Your mental and physical health requires big doses of nature. (I could go on about the need to regularly go off the grid, deep into the wilderness, into the mountains or forests, but that's another book.)

B. Let God mentor you.

Maybe you are not ready to go back to a church, but you can let God begin to mentor you through reading the Bible. Return to the final pages of Section One and reread the suggestions on how to proceed. Here you will find thoughts on how the Holy Spirit can mentor you through the Bible. To practice being mentored, read Romans Chapter 8. As you read the chapter, ask the Holy Spirit to give you answers to the two questions: "Who are you, Lord?" and "What do You want me to do?" I think you'll be amazed at the ways He will answer those questions. Walk through the chapter reading and talking to the Holy Spirit, asking Him to answer those two questions. Ask Him to explain the answers. By doing this, you are nurturing the habit of depending on the Spirit of God.

SUGGESTED READING

The books below will lead you further into experiencing supernatural revelation.

Deere, Jack. *Why I Am Still Surprised by the Voice of God*. Grand Rapids: Zondervan, 2022. (*Jack Deere was a seminary professor who taught God no longer did miracles in this day, until his life was radically transformed through encounters with the Holy Spirit. This book gives great explanations and encouragement about how to grow in hearing God.*)

Eldredge, John. *Walking with God*. Nashville: Thomas Nelson, 2016. *(John Eldredge wrote the great book* Wild at Heart, *but he has also written much about hearing God. This book focuses on listening for God's direction for your daily life decisions.)*

Seng, Jordan. *Miracle Work*. Downers Grove: InterVarsity Press, 2013. *(I think this is the best one-volume summary of how to understand and experience supernatural ministry. It is especially helpful in answering questions for those whose previous church experience had little emphasis on the supernatural. The chapter on the ministry of prophecy is really helpful.)*

Vallotton, Kris. *Basic Training for the Prophetic Ministry*. Shippensburg: Destiny Image, 2014. *(This is our foundational training book for teaching prophecy at our Agape school.)*

CHAPTER 13

POWER IN THE CHURCH

"For the kingdom of God is not a matter of talk but of power." (1 Corinthians 4:20)

"...how God anointed Jesus of Nazareth with the Holy Spirit and power, and how He went around doing good and healing all who were under the power of the devil, because God was with Him." (Acts 10:38)

"By faith in the name of Jesus, this man whom you see and know was made strong. It is Jesus' name and the faith that comes through Him that has completely healed him, as you can all see." (Acts 3:16)

"But you will receive power when the Holy Spirit comes on you; and you will be My witnesses in Jerusalem, and in all Judea and Samaria, and to the ends of the earth."
(Acts 1:8)

"Finally, be strong in the Lord and in His mighty power. Put on the full armor of God, so that you can take your stand against the devil's schemes. For our struggle is not against flesh and blood, but against the rulers, against the authorities, against the powers of this dark world and against the spiritual forces of evil in the heavenly realms."
(Ephesians 6:10–12)

POWER IN THE EARLY CHURCH

The Bible says the kingdom of God is not a matter of talk but of power (1 Corinthians 4:20), and the early church was a living example of this. Time and again believers, walking in the power of the Holy Spirit, supernaturally healed the sick and cast out demons. Uneducated, unknown blue-collar kind of people filled with the Holy Spirit prevailed over those unbelieving educated elites who were holding political and religious power.

The church was birthed in power. After Jesus conquered death and walked out of the grave, He told His followers He would send them out to change the world, but they were to first wait until they were clothed with power from Heaven (see Luke 24:49). His concern wasn't that they learn more and study more. His concern was that they received spiritual power (see Acts 1:8). Then, on the day of Pentecost, the Holy Spirit's power came upon the group of Jesus's followers who were hiding from their enemies in Jerusalem. With that power they abandoned their hiding place and went boldly into the city streets, preaching with Holy Spirit manifestations confirming their words. The day began with 120 followers cautiously hiding and ended in the streets with 3,000 new people joining them, saying, "Teach us this new life!" A lot can change in one day when the Holy Spirit shows up.

I believe it is God's intention that there will always be miracles, signs, and wonders in the life of the church. The need for God's supernatural power has never changed, but many churches have changed their beliefs, concluding that miracles are rare and God doesn't work often in powerful demonstrations like He did in the Bible. Maybe this contributed to your drifting away from faith in Christ. Maybe you encountered a faith that was so committed to a rational experience that it seemed hostile to the supernatural, to emotions, and to spiritual mystery. I've listened to Christian teachers fight tooth and nail to defend the validity of the miracles recorded in the Bible, but then turn around and ridicule claims that God still heals and performs miracles, signs, and wonders today. This strikes me as an odd position. Christian faith is rational but it's far more than that. Perhaps the Christian faith you experienced left you disappointed. Maybe you found little evidence that God was at work in your church so, unsatisfied, you left, hoping to find spiritual reality elsewhere. Hopefully this chapter will point you back to a Biblical faith that embraces all that God intended His church to walk in, all the expressions of His loving, supernatural power that He offers to us.

KEVIN'S STORY

Kevin and Dawn Kuykendall have been Harriet's and my good friends for many years. Kevin is a lawyer, and we serve together on the board of a ministry that creates jobs for the underemployed and for people coming out of prison. What follows is Kevin's story of God's loving power bringing deliverance to him:

Like most individuals born into a home where Jesus is not present, I grew up in a dysfunctional home. This dysfunction was the cause of great mental strife for me that manifested itself in many ways, including anger, fear, anxiety, and depression—usually in that order. My brother, Jason, is seven years younger than me. I can remember going to school in the fourth grade and being so afraid my brother would not be home when I got there that I would get sick at school. This anxiety would lead to depression. I would cry on weekends thinking about having to go back to school on Monday and not being with my brother. I thought if I was around my brother, I could protect him. My parents were not abusive, but they were young parents, and they had their own issues. There was a lot of yelling and arguing, and while I know my parents loved me, for whatever reason it was very hard for them to show it.

My anxiety and depression continued when I went to middle school. I almost never went to church as my parents never took us. I did go to Bible school one summer while I was in middle school; I remember having such peace there. I really didn't understand why I had peace, and I had no concept of who Jesus was or why I was going, but I did feel such peace. I hated school; I felt like most people did not like me, so many times I isolated myself. As I entered high school, my anxiety and depression worsened and became chronic. Home was not comfortable for me as there was so much tension and bad feelings between family members. During the day, both of my parents worked so they were not at home. I would often skip school so I could be at home alone. I did not want the tension, but I also did not want to go to school and be around people. I would sleep for hours on end. I was surprised I graduated from high school due to the number of days I missed my senior year. After graduation, I left for college. That is when things really fell apart for me.

I left college after my first semester. I could no longer be around people. I simply could not function due to anxiety and deep depression. My mother finally took me to a doctor, and I was given medication. This was in the early '90s when anti-depression medications came into vogue. The side effects were horrible, but it was supposedly the clinical answer to all my problems.

It was about this time that I gave my life to Jesus. I really had no idea what I was doing, but I knew I needed help, and I was willing to try anything. My commitment to Jesus was not strong after He saved me. I really knew nothing about God, and I knew nothing about the Bible. I got married and had children. I got divorced, and the depression intensified. However, over the years I slowly began to trust Jesus, and I continued to take my medication. Sometimes the medication worked and sometimes it didn't.

As I grew stronger with God, I many times thought about giving up the anti-depressants. I thought God could take away my depression. He could set me free. Jesus was always setting people free in the Bible. I remarried—a Christian girl who believed in the gifts of the Holy Spirit. We lived our life and I continued to take my medication. I believed Jesus could get me off medication, but I didn't know if He was willing. The anti-depressants were my crutch. What if I tried to get off my medication and I crashed? What if I had to go into the hospital? Those thoughts were always circling my mind. Maybe it was just better to keep taking the pills until I died.

In December of 2019, my wife and I were blessed to take a vacation to Honolulu, Hawaii. I had recently been in a Bible study where the group had studied a book by Pastor Jordan Seng. Pastor Seng leads Bluewater Mission Church in Honolulu. My good friend suggested I visit the church while I was there, so my wife and I made it a point to go on a Sunday morning.

I remember walking into the church. We sat in the third or fourth row in a crowded auditorium. Jordan Seng came up to the stage and started talking. It wasn't five minutes into his talk that he began saying someone was going to be set free from having to take mental health medications, someone who had been on them a long time. I had been taking anti-depressants for almost 30 years. The unbelievable thing was that the entire time Jordan was talking about someone gaining their freedom, he was looking straight at me. In that crowded auditorium he never took his eyes off me. Pastors usually go back and forth and look at all the people while they talk. Not this time. He looked straight at me for about 45 seconds as he proclaimed God was freeing someone. I knew it was for me and I stopped taking anti-depressants that day. It was my miracle! That was in January of 2019. I remember feeling just an unbelievable sense of freedom, not having to feel like my life would fall apart without medication. I've taken no meds since, and I'm never going back!! Freedom for the captives—me!

Kevin's story is a great example of what I believe God intends to happen when His church gathers. Jesus has promised to show up when believers gather in His Name (see Matthew 18:20). He is present, and when given the opportunity to touch people, His loving power can manifest. Jesus Christ is the same today as yesterday (see Hebrews 13:8). His compassion hasn't changed. His miracle-working power hasn't changed. His wonderful promise to be with us until the end of the age hasn't changed. Why wouldn't we expect Him to heal, deliver, help, and save people when we gather in church and small groups? Why wouldn't we make room in our worship services for Him to be our Savior, Healer, and good Shepherd Who cares for His sheep? Why do we create church services each Sunday that talk about Jesus as if He's not in the room? (Kevin didn't mention this in his story but we recommend checking with your doctor before stopping your meds, in order to confirm your healing).

THE COMPASSION OF THE MESSIAH

It helps to remember what Jesus said His mission was all about. Isaiah 61, a prophecy written hundreds of years before Jesus came, describes His mission as the Messiah Who was coming to the world.

"The Spirit of the Sovereign Lord is on Me,
because the Lord has anointed Me
to proclaim good news to the poor.
He has sent Me to bind up the brokenhearted,
to proclaim freedom for the captives
and release from darkness for the prisoners." (Isaiah 61:1)

Notice it doesn't speak of the Messiah coming to teach profound religious truth or bring world peace (which will be true of Him), but rather His priority in coming was to use His compassionate power to restore and deliver people. He still desires to do this today as He looks over the people gathered in our churches.

Hundreds of years later Jesus announced the beginning of His ministry by standing before people and reading from the same passage:

"He stood up to read, and the scroll of the prophet Isaiah was handed to Him.
Unrolling it, He found the place where it is written:
'The Spirit of the Lord is on Me,
because He has anointed Me to proclaim good news to the poor.
He has sent Me to proclaim freedom for the prisoners
and recovery of sight for the blind,
to set the oppressed free,
to proclaim the year of the Lord's favor."

Then He rolled up the scroll, gave it back to the attendant and sat down. The eyes of everyone in the synagogue were fastened on Him. He began by saying to them, 'Today this scripture is fulfilled in your hearing.'" (Luke 4:16–21)

Jesus declared Himself to be the Messiah of Isaiah 61. He then demonstrated what Isaiah 61 meant by healing the sick and casting out demons.

"Jesus went through all the towns and villages, teaching in their synagogues, proclaiming the good news of the kingdom and healing every disease and sickness."
(Matthew 9:35)

"At sunset, the people brought to Jesus all who had various kinds of sickness, and laying His hands on each one, He healed them." (Luke 4:40)

"When Jesus landed and saw a large crowd, He had compassion on them and healed their sick." (Matthew 14:14)

"... A large crowd of His disciples was there and a great number of people from all over Judea, from Jerusalem, and from the coastal region around Tyre and Sidon, who had come to hear Him and to be healed of their diseases. Those troubled by impure spirits were cured, and the people all tried to touch Him, because power was coming from Him and healing them all." (Luke 6:17–19)

"When evening came, many who were demon-possessed were brought to Him, and He drove out the spirits with a word and healed all the sick." (Matthew 8:16)

Above are a few samples of summary statements in the gospels about Jesus's ministry. He healed all who came to Him. He never told anyone who came to Him, "I want you to keep this sickness because it's building your character." He never told anyone, "Your problem is too complicated for Me." He never told anyone, "Come back after you've cleaned up your life, after you've earned My help." Never! When people came to Him, He healed them. The most-often stated reason given in the Bible for His healing is His compassion and mercy. He was moved with compassion as He saw the needs.

THE COMPASSION OF GOD

What is so helpful in our understanding of God is that the compassion of Jesus is the compassion God the Father feels toward us. Some teachers say Jesus is perfect theology. That statement may be puzzling until we consider what theology is. Theology is the study of God, the pursuit to know what God is like. Jesus said, *"Anyone who has seen Me has seen the Father"* (John 14:9). The apostle Paul wrote in Colossians, *"The Son is the image of the invisible God…For God was pleased to have all His fullness dwell in Him"* (Colossians 1:15,19). So, the most perfect picture of God is seen in Jesus. Do you want to know what God is like? Then look at Jesus. Look at how He responds to those with broken hearts and broken minds, broken bodies and broken dreams. Every response of Jesus is a precise reflection of the heart of your Heavenly Father.

Read through the four gospels and see how Jesus lovingly healed people and set them free. When you read the miracle stories of Jesus, do so without the religious filters telling you Jesus doesn't do this any longer. Read without the filters of church experience that create a low expectation of God caring for you and working miracles in your life. Read the gospels with new eyes and let them build faith that maybe, just maybe, His miracle-working power doesn't have to be as rare or conditional as so many churches make it out to be. Maybe He's a lot more generous and compassionate than our experience has been.

A few years back, Harriet and I were on a ministry team of over 100 people, serving with Randy Clark and Global Awakening in São Paulo, Brazil. The team had the joy of seeing many people healed, including blind eyes opening and people getting out of wheelchairs. But we could see the tender love of God in the less dramatic moments too. A young lady came to Harriet and me in the prayer line asking for healing because she regularly suffered from migraine headaches. After asking her permission, we placed our hands on her head and prayed against the headaches in Jesus's name. As we prayed, I silently asked, "Holy Spirit, besides her migraines, is there anything else You want to do?" I "heard" in my heart, "She's trying to make a big life-changing decision." Not sure if it was my imagination or the Holy Spirit speaking, I asked her, "I might be wrong, but are you trying to make a big decision right now?" Her eyes got big, and she immediately burst into tears. I then "heard" in my heart Psalm 37:4: *"Take delight in the Lord, and He will give you the desires of your heart."* I said to her, "I think the Father is saying He wants to give you the desires of your heart." With that, she began crying pretty much uncontrollably. After a while she calmed down and explained, "I'm an architect and I love what I do, and I want to get better at it. I really want to go to Europe or America to study more, but I keep having these thoughts that God is against it, like it's just a selfish desire of mine. And I want to obey Him, so I've been struggling and praying for an answer. But now I feel His approval, that He will bless my studies!" It was a big moment for her. (By the way I'm pretty sure her migraines ended too; I seem to remember getting a text from her weeks later saying that her migraines had disappeared though I couldn't track the note down to confirm this). Maybe this is what you missed in church the first time, the experience of God showing He really is *"...gracious and compassionate, slow to anger and rich in love"* (Psalms 145:8). We really have a God Who is tender and kind and concerned even about the heart and desires of a young Brazilian woman.

POWER IN THE CHURCH — THE HOLY SPIRIT

The book of Acts records the birth of the Church. We believe Acts contains the prototype for churches to follow today. It records the values, priorities, and practices God intends His Church to maintain until Jesus's return. And one constant theme throughout the book is the loving supernatural power of the Holy Spirit in the life of the Church.

In the early Church, power was expressed in the filling with the Holy Spirit. While the book of Acts is usually understood to be the acts of the apostles, many think it is better understood as the acts of the Holy Spirit because the Spirit's work is evident on almost every page. It is clear the early Church valued the Holy Spirit. Unfortunately, when the world today desperately needs the Church to be saturated with the Holy Spirit's power, too many of our churches have developed structures, practices, and beliefs that replace our dependence on the Spirit.

Much of the training in the seminaries and religious institutions of our Western world increase the theological knowledge of students but don't train students to hear God and walk in His power. It is a common story that Western missionaries in Asian and African nations often find their church members going to village shamans or witch doctors when they need healing or have trouble with evil spirits because they don't find the supernatural power they need in their church.

When Harriet and I prepared for missionary service in Japan, we had to appear before a screening committee of church leaders and seminary professors. One of the professors told us his story of missionary service. He was a young missionary sent to an African nation to teach in their seminary. He told how he taught the curriculum that he'd learned in the States. One day after lecturing his class on proofs for the existence of God, students came up to him and asked, "Why are you teaching us these things? Everyone in this country believes in God! What we really need to know is how to cast out demons and how to combat curses placed on our church members by witch doctors and how to heal the sick." The professor said he was stuck because he never learned those things in the American seminary.

Miracle-working power comes from God (Psalm 62:11), and He says come to Him for it. Seminary won't make you powerful; God will. A title or position won't make you powerful; God will. Unfortunately, in this world, diplomas and titles give the illusion of power. But the kind of power that is recognized in Heaven and hell comes from God. Go to Him for it.

"But you will receive power when the Holy Spirit comes on you; and you will be My witnesses in Jerusalem, and in all Judea and Samaria, and to the ends of the earth." (Acts 1:8)

Jesus told the disciples to wait and don't go out into ministry until they received power from on high. (That's good advice for every person wanting to serve in ministry.)

"I am going to send you what My Father has promised; but stay in the city until you have been clothed with power from on high." (Luke 24:49)

We see Jesus fulfill this word on the Jewish festival of Pentecost:

"When the day of Pentecost came, they were all together in one place. Suddenly a sound like the blowing of a violent wind came from heaven and filled the whole house where they were sitting. They saw what seemed to be tongues of fire that separated and came to rest on each of them. All of them were filled with the Holy Spirit and began to speak in other tongues as the Spirit enabled them." (Acts 2:1-4)

We see God intends that every believer knows the power of the Holy Spirit!

"In the last days, God says, I will pour out my Spirit on all people. Your sons and daughters will prophesy, your young men will see visions, your old men will dream dreams. Even on My servants, both men and women, I will pour out my Spirit in those days, and they will prophesy." (Acts 2:17)

"Peter replied, "Repent and be baptized, every one of you, in the name of Jesus Christ for the forgiveness of your sins. And you will receive the gift of the Holy Spirit. The promise is for you and your children and for all who are far off—for all whom the Lord our God will call."" (Acts 2:38)

SEEKING THE HOLY SPIRIT'S EMPOWERMENT

Some theologians have reached the conclusion that every believer is baptized in the Spirit the moment they are born again through faith in Christ, and so they already have all of the Spirit's power from that moment. Therefore, it is concluded that there is no need to seek additional experiences with the Holy Spirit. The trouble with this reasoning is that the early Church received the empowering of the Holy Spirit, whether called "the baptism of the Spirit" or "the filling of the Spirit" or "being clothed with power," as a secondary experience, apart from salvation. The passages below demonstrate this:

"But when they believed Philip as he proclaimed the good news of the kingdom of God and the name of Jesus Christ, they were baptized, both men and women...When the apostles in Jerusalem heard that Samaria had accepted the word of God, they sent Peter and John to Samaria. When they arrived, they prayed for the new believers there that they might receive the Holy Spirit, because the Holy Spirit had not yet come on any of them; they had simply been baptized in the name of the Lord Jesus." (Acts 8:12, 14-16)

"...Paul took the road through the interior and arrived at Ephesus. There he found some disciples and asked them, 'Did you receive the Holy Spirit when you believed?' They answered, 'No, we have not even heard that there is a Holy Spirit.' So Paul asked, 'Then what baptism did you receive?' 'John's baptism,' they replied. Paul said, 'John's baptism was a baptism of repentance. He told the people to believe in the one coming after him, that is, in Jesus.' On hearing this, they were baptized in the name of the Lord Jesus. When Paul

placed his hands on them, the Holy Spirit came on them, and they spoke in tongues and prophesied. There were about twelve men in all."
(Acts 19:1-7)

God has ordained that the Church pursue personal encounters with the Holy Spirit as the means of acquiring spiritual power. This isn't being Pentecostal; this is being Biblical. We must value and pursue the Holy Spirit to the same degree the early Church did.

For this reason, my friend Pastor Stifan Sanganahalli makes the filling of the Holy Spirit the first priority at his ministry school in India. The people attending his school are typically newer converts, often being radically saved out of Hindu backgrounds. They love Jesus and are on fire to serve the Lord, but they have little background in Christianity. Pastor Stifan's curriculum starts with the baptism of the Holy Spirit. They simply look at what Jesus said about it and how the early Church experienced it. He teaches this is normal Christianity, so they receive it. Their theology is not so sophisticated as to define the baptism of the Spirit into something less than how it was experienced by the Church in Acts. They simply read how people experienced the Holy Spirit in the Bible and assume that's how we do it.

The next topic in their curriculum is the 28 chapters of the book of Acts, again, presented as what normal Christianity should look like—strongly valuing the Holy Spirit for guidance and power, miracles, and breakthroughs. No one has told them God doesn't work this way any longer. The book of Acts gives the students the case studies and ministry models of how they can expect God to work in their own ministry. Instead of developing deep theological sophistication, they focus more on how to preach with power, how to heal the sick, how to cast out demons, how to hear God, and how to disciple new believers into the life and destiny God has given them. They can't quote Karl Barth, but they can say with power, "In the Name of Jesus rise up and walk."

POWER IN THE CHURCH —
THE NAME OF JESUS

This leads us to another source of power highlighted in the book of Acts and that is the authority and power found in the name of Jesus. It's striking what a central role the name of Jesus plays in the opening chapters of the book. Let's walk through Acts Chapters 3 and 4.

Chapter 3 opens with Peter and John headed to a prayer service:

"One day Peter and John were going up to the temple at the time of prayer—at three in the afternoon. Now a man who was lame from birth was being carried to the temple gate called Beautiful, where he was put every day to beg from those going into the temple courts. When he saw Peter and John about to enter, he asked them for money. Peter looked straight at him, as did John. Then Peter said, 'Look at us!' So the man gave them his attention, expecting to get something from them. Then Peter said, 'Silver or gold I do not have, but what I do have I give you. In the name of Jesus Christ of Nazareth, walk.' Taking him by the right hand, he helped him up, and instantly the man's feet and ankles became strong. He jumped to his feet and began to walk. Then he went with them into the temple courts, walking and jumping, and praising God." (Acts 3:1-9)

Notice that Peter did not so much pray in Jesus's name but rather commanded in His name. The result was legs that had never walked became strong and healthy at a command given in Jesus's name. This caused a big commotion at the temple, and the worship routines were disrupted over the excitement of a miracle. (When God shows up at church, routines tend to get disrupted!) People hearing the commotion gathered around and were amazed at seeing this man, whom they recognized as the lame guy, running and jumping and hanging onto Peter and John:

"They recognized him as the same man who used to sit begging at the temple gate called Beautiful, and they were filled with wonder and amazement at

what had happened to him. While the man held on to Peter and John, all the people were astonished and came running to them in the place called Solomon's Colonnade. When Peter saw this, he said to them: 'Fellow Israelites, why does this surprise you? Why do you stare at us as if by our own power or godliness we had made this man walk?'" (Acts 3:11-13)

Note how Peter dispelled the notion that he was holy enough or spiritual enough to create the miracle, thus helping us understand that supernatural power is not earned by being religious enough. Peter was quick to point to Jesus.

"The God of Abraham, Isaac and Jacob, the God of our fathers, has glorified His servant Jesus. You handed Him over to be killed, and you disowned Him before Pilate, though he had decided to let Him go. You disowned the Holy and Righteous One and asked that a murderer be released to you. You killed the author of life, but God raised Him from the dead. We are witnesses of this. By faith in the name of Jesus, this man whom you see and know was made strong. It is Jesus's name and the faith that comes through Him that has completely healed him, as you can all see." (Acts 3:14-16)

In a staggering statement, Peter claimed it was Jesus's name that has the power to heal, staggering because a miracle through His name confirms that Jesus was alive and His name has authority in heaven to release supernatural power on earth. This would have definitely shaken things up for the guys responsible for killing Jesus on the cross.

So Peter boldly preached to the crowd, calling them to repent, turn to God, and put their faith in Jesus. Around 5,000 people believed. But the leaders got wind of what was happening and reacted:

"The priests and the captain of the temple guard and the Sadducees came up to Peter and John while they were speaking to the people. They were greatly disturbed because the apostles were teaching the people, proclaiming in Jesus the resurrection of the dead. They seized Peter and John and, because it was evening, they put them in jail until the next day." (Acts 4:1-3)

Think of the threat the religious leaders felt. They showed no power to heal this man who begged at the gate that they had walked through for years. But now they had to explain how blue-collar fishermen with no theological training, walked onto their turf and demonstrated authority and power beyond anything the leaders could muster. And these newcomers claimed this divine power came in the name of the Man Whom the leaders labeled a fraud and had sentenced to death.

"They had Peter and John brought before them and began to question them: 'By what power or what name did you do this?' Then Peter, filled with the Holy Spirit, said to them: ‹Rulers and elders of the people! If we are being called to account today for an act of kindness shown to a man who was lame and are being asked how he was healed, then know this, you and all the people of Israel: It is by the name of Jesus Christ of Nazareth, whom you crucified but whom God raised from the dead, that this man stands before you healed.'" (Acts 4:7-10)

One characteristic of being filled with the Holy Spirit is boldness. Peter and John stood before the people who had all the political power but did not shrink back. Peter says, "You guys who claim to speak for God are guilty of killing this Man, by Whose name God healed this lame beggar. Apparently, you are completely wrong about Jesus!" Pretty gutsy stuff. Going further Peter declared boldly, *"Salvation is found in no one else, for there is no other name under heaven given to mankind by which we must be saved"* (Acts 3:21). The Savior of mankind is Jesus and there is no other.

What angered the religious leaders was that less than two months after they'd killed Jesus, thousands of people who once looked to them for spiritual leadership were now running to these unknown, uneducated people who worshipped and preached the very name of the One they'd crucified. Miracles, healings, signs, and wonders were being performed through His name. Maybe even more worrisome was that thousands were being baptized in His name (see Acts 2:38). This was huge as baptism was a line in the sand that these people stepped across, leaving behind their allegiance to the Jewish religious leaders. This is why baptism is a big deal for you and me as it is crossing the line and departing false gods and religion, false beliefs and allegiances and opinions. Now being baptized in His name, we are declaring our commitment, trust, obedience, surrender, submission, and allegiance to Jesus. You are rejecting the former life and embracing Jesus Christ.

"When they saw the courage of Peter and John and realized that they were unschooled, ordinary men, they were astonished, and they took note that these men had been with Jesus. So they ordered them to withdraw from the Sanhedrin and then conferred together. 'What are we going to do with these men?' they asked. 'Everyone living in Jerusalem knows they have performed a notable sign, and we cannot deny it. But to stop this thing from spreading any further among the people, we must warn them to speak no longer to anyone in this name.'" (Acts 4:13-17)

Here is a prime example that even the undeniable evidence of a divine miracle isn't enough to overcome all unbelief, that a person can have such a hard heart and hold such hostility toward God that no miracle can convince them to repent. That's pretty scary. While it seems Peter and John were on trial, the ones on trial actually were these leaders. Each had a decision before them. Based on the evidence of the miracle, do they humbly admit they were wrong about Jesus and ask God for forgiveness, or do they double-down and continue to deny God and justify themselves? Maybe you've reached a decision point while reading this book, that it's time to humble yourself, confess you've been wrong about Jesus, and turn to God in surrender to Him.

After the leaders talked it through, they called Peter and John back into the room.

"Then they called them in again and commanded them not to speak or teach at all in the name of Jesus. But Peter and John replied, 'Which is right in God's

eyes: to listen to you, or to Him? You be the judges! As for us, we cannot help speaking about what we have seen and heard.' After further threats they let them go. They could not decide how to punish them, because all the people were praising God for what had happened. For the man who was miraculously healed was over forty years old." (Acts 4:18-22)

When miracles occur through the name of Jesus, people give praise to God. That alone is a great reason for believers to pursue healing and miracles—because of the glory they bring to God.

The entire Church gathered after this incident. They did not call a meeting to debate among themselves what to do. Instead, they met to pray and express total dependence on God. When confronted with increasing opposition, the early Church didn't ask God to hide them, nor did they pray that God give them better sermons. They prayed for boldness and for supernatural power to manifest in healings, signs, and wonders. In this day when so many reject Christianity and oppose Christian ideas, why wouldn't we follow the early Church and cry out for the same thing?

"On their release, Peter and John went back to their own people and reported all that the chief priests and the elders had said to them. When they heard this, they raised their voices together in prayer to God.

"'Sovereign Lord,' they said, 'You made the heavens and the earth and the sea, and everything in them. You spoke by the Holy Spirit through the mouth of your servant, our father David: "Why do the nations rage and the peoples plot in vain? The kings of the earth rise up and the rulers band together against the Lord and against his anointed one." Indeed Herod and Pontius Pilate met together with the Gentiles and the people of Israel in this city to conspire against your holy servant Jesus, whom you anointed. They did what your power and will had decided beforehand should happen. Now, Lord, consider their threats and enable your servants to speak your word with great boldness. Stretch out your hand to heal and perform signs and wonders through the name of your holy servant Jesus.'

"After they prayed, the place where they were meeting was shaken. And they were all filled with the Holy Spirit and spoke the word of God boldly." (Acts 4:15-31)

Notice the different reactions of the religious leaders and the believers to the power of the Name of Jesus. The Sanhedrin recognized that the name of Jesus threatened their religious authority and thus ordered the Christians to stop all preaching and teaching in His name. In direct opposition, the Christians, recognizing His name as the source of their power and authority, asked God for greater boldness to proclaim His word and for more miracles through the name of Jesus.

AUTHORITY HAS BEEN GRANTED US

So what's going on here? Why is praying and ministering in the name of Jesus such a big deal? It's all about authority. Jesus Christ conquered death in His resurrection, thus He has authority over life and death. He has been given all authority in heaven and earth (see Matthew 28:18-20), and at His name every knee will bow, and every mouth will declare He is Lord of all (see Philippians 2:10-11). He does not share this authority with any other religious figure. He had the authority to bring history to an end and to initiate His return when all the earth will be brought into submission to His rule. He has the title "King of kings and Lord of lords." He will sit on the throne at the final judgment where all who rejected Him will be cast away from the Kingdom of God. No demon nor disease can overcome His authority. His authority is such that *"nothing is impossible for God"* (Luke 1:37).

So, when we recognize the authority Jesus has, we will begin to understand how amazing the following promises are:

"And I will do whatever you ask in My name, so that the Father may be glorified in the Son. You may ask Me for anything in My name, and I will do it." (John 14:13-14)

"Until now you have not asked for anything in My name. Ask and you will receive, and your joy will be complete." (John 16:24)

"You did not choose Me, but I chose you and appointed you so that you might go and bear fruit—fruit that will last—and so that whatever you ask in My name the Father will give you." (John 15:16)

Understanding the authority which Jesus possesses is what makes these such amazing promises. He is giving us permission to use His name. If a president or king gave you permission to use their name as a reference, you'd probably see doors open for you. In the spiritual realm, the use of Jesus's name has power to produce results. Using His name gives us authority to tap into the unlimited resources and power of heaven.

This is much like me giving my sons the right to use my credit card. By authorizing them to use my name, I am giving them access to my resources (meager as they are!). Jesus gives us the right to use His name and thus grants us access to the resources of Heaven. Not only access to resources, but Jesus allows us to use His name to exert His authority in situations. It is like the authority my son Jeremy has as a police officer. He wears a uniform and drives a squad car, but that in itself does not give him authority to arrest people, uphold the law, and act as a police officer. He can enforce laws because he has been granted authority by the governing powers, i.e., the state.

When my older son, Stephen, was commissioned as an officer in the United States Army, he had authority to command bestowed on him. In his commissioning ceremony, there was a moment that powerfully illustrates this. In the military, enlisted soldiers are to acknowledge the command authority of officers by saluting them. Before he was commissioned as an officer, Stephen and the rest of his ROTC college group were trained by older sergeants who had seen warfare and had accumulated decades of military experience. The sergeants were in charge of training those young inexperienced students to become soldiers and officers. When two years of training ended and the day of their commissioning came, Stephen and the other students stood in their dress uniforms on a stage. They swore a commissioning oath to serve the country after which they were declared to now be officers in the Army. Then came the moment known as "First Salute." All the sergeants, the older guys with all the experience, lined up on stage and faced the young students and saluted them. For the students, it was the first time their new authority as an officer was acknowledged. The sergeants were showing the roles had changed, and they were submitting to the command authority that had just been bestowed on the students. They were the first to acknowledge the new authority as officers by saluting them. (It was fun to watch how awkward the students looked being acknowledged in such a way.)

This is a further example of the authority Jesus has given us in using His name. Our authority is not because we are personally stronger or wiser. We don't achieve it, we receive it.

AUTHORITY DEPENDS ON RELATIONSHIP

So there is power in the name of Jesus. But it is powerful only for those who have surrendered themselves to live under His authority. You only have authority to the degree you submit to authority. Our use of the name of Jesus releases authoritative power only when we are in a relationship with Him, submitted to His authority. His name can't be used like magic, like people in a horror movie who hold up a crucifix to stop the vampire. His name has no power in the mouth of unbelievers as the following Bible account shows:

"God did extraordinary miracles through Paul, so that even handkerchiefs and aprons that had touched him were taken to the sick, and their illnesses were cured and the evil spirits left them. Some Jews who went around driving out evil spirits tried to invoke the name of the Lord Jesus over those who were

demon-possessed. They would say, 'In the name of the Jesus whom Paul preaches, I command you to come out.' Seven sons of Sceva, a Jewish chief priest, were doing this. One day the evil spirit answered them, 'Jesus I know, and Paul I know about, but who are you?' Then the man who had the evil spirit jumped on them and overpowered them all. He gave them such a beating that they ran out of the house naked and bleeding. When this became known to the Jews and Greeks living in Ephesus, they were all seized with fear, and the name of the Lord Jesus was held in high honor." (Acts 19:11-17)

You must have a relationship with Jesus as your Lord in order to use His name. That begins with the first time you call on His name, asking Him to save you: *"All who call on the Name of the Lord shall be saved"* (Romans 10:13).

Demons react strongly to the name of Jesus, but only when the name is invoked by a follower of Jesus. Demons hate the name of Jesus. That's why they've made it a swear word, leading people to use it when cussing. If you are using the name of Jesus as a swear word or when cussing, ask God for forgiveness and for power to break this habit, because you are aligning yourself with darkness when you reduce Jesus's name to a swear word. Remember the command: *"You shall not misuse the name of the Lord your God, for the Lord will not hold anyone guiltless who misuses His name"* (Exodus 20:7). How you use His name is a pretty big deal to God.

POWER IN THE CHURCH—DOING THE WORKS OF JESUS

In John 20:21, Jesus told His followers, *"As the Father has sent Me, I am sending you."* He said, *"Whoever believes in Me will do the works I have been doing"* (John 14:12). Jesus expects His people to go into the world as He did, caring for the world as He did, seeing people through His Father's eyes, changing lives as He did by repeating the works He did. And what were those works? The gospels are clear that

He gave Himself to teaching, preaching, healing, and deliverance. When Christians actually believe what He said and pursue all the works of ministry He did, wonderful things can happen.

TALULA'S STORY

Talula is one of our Agape students. Recently she shared how God worked through her while at her job:

I was working at a gas station in Creve Coeur [a nearby town]. We had various product representatives come into the station, driving their routes and checking on their products being sold at the station. One man who I got to know was a cigarette rep, who would stop in each month. He was a big man, maybe 6'3" or so, very healthy-looking and we became acquainted with one another during his monthly visits.

Over time, during his visits, I noticed he was gradually getting thinner. After three months of this, when he showed up again, I was alarmed at how thin he was and asked, "Are you ok?" He said, "Well, not actually. I can't eat anything, and everything I do eat comes back up. I have problems using the restroom, and I'm in terrible pain. I don't know what's going on and I don't know how to fix it. The doctors want to try a trial medicine, but next week they might start me on a colostomy bag."

I told him, "This is terrible! Can I pray for you? I believe God is a big God and He can do miracles, and if you are willing, I'd like to pray for you." He said he was at a point of desperation and willing to try anything. So I prayed for him. I didn't lay my hands on him and had to pray a very short, fast prayer, because I could hear the door buzzer, indicating customers were coming in, so I felt pressure and rushed. I prayed fast: "Jesus, You parted the Red Sea and You made the deaf hear and the blind see and there's no thing so small that you don't care about and he's in pain and I ask that You would heal him in Jesus's Name." The prayer was short and rushed. He got up and said, "Well, thank you" and left as I had to wait on customers. I

223

thought, "Oh my goodness, that was a terrible prayer! There was no power or faith and I didn't say it right. He really needs a miracle, but I just really messed that up. I should've put my hands on him and should have prayed a better prayer, but I was so rushed! He didn't get the time that this needed, and his life and job are at stake, but I just dropped the ball and messed this up so bad." I was very upset at myself for the next few days, and I continued praying for him at home.

However, a month later he came back, and I saw he'd gained weight and had more color to his face, and I said, "You look so much better." And he said, "Can I give you a hug? Whatever you prayed, it worked! I didn't know what was going on, but God healed me and I just love you for what you did!" He told my bosses, "You guys are all alright but this girl right here, she's amazing!" He gave me another hug, and then left. And I heard the Lord tell me it isn't about how well we pray, but it's about what He when we are obedient that is important.

Jesus said, *"Whoever believes in Me will do the works I do."* That includes not only pastors in churches but also people working in gas stations.

PREACHING ACCOMPANIED WITH POWER

Power was also demonstrated in the church through the preaching of the Word as it was accompanied with the miraculous. Jesus set the stage for the church's ministry in Matthew Chapter 9:

"Jesus went through all the towns and villages, teaching in their synagogues, proclaiming the good news of the kingdom and healing every disease and sickness. When He saw the crowds, He had compassion on them, because they were harassed and helpless, like sheep without a shepherd. Then He said to his disciples, 'The harvest is plentiful but the workers are few. Ask the Lord of the harvest, therefore, to send out workers into His harvest field.'" (Matthew 9:35–38)

Jesus was speaking into the future mission of the church. Out of His compassion for the lost, He wanted His work expanded so more people could experience God's love. And His work, as defined by this passage, was teaching, preaching the good news of the kingdom, and healing the sick. He wanted to raise up more workers to accomplish those works. That is what we find in the early Church. They preached the Word, accompanied with demonstrations of God's power to heal. An example is found in Acts 8:5-8:

"Philip went down to a city in Samaria and proclaimed the Messiah there. When the crowds heard Philip and saw the signs he performed, they all paid close attention to what he said. For with shrieks, impure spirits came out of many, and many who were paralyzed or lame were healed. So there was great joy in that city." (Acts 8:5-8)

Notice how the miracles in Philip's ministry had two effects. First, miracles endorsed his words. If God is favoring this man by working supernaturally through him then his message about Jesus must be true. Secondly, there was great joy in the city as families saw their loved ones set free. Who knows how long a daughter or son was trapped in demonic oppression? How long a family member suffered in physical pain? But then the power of a loving Savior changed everything!

During a ministry trip to India, we visited a pastor at a new church, which was meeting in a small rented building. While taking our seats and making introductions with the pastor, we were served tea by a smiling, gray-haired lady. As we visited with the pastor, we asked him to tell us about his ministry. He had graduated from Pastor Stifan's school (which I mentioned earlier in this chapter) and moved to this town to launch a new church. Initially it was difficult to reach people with the Gospel. But one day a desperate grandmother, accompanied by her teenaged granddaughter, came to his door. She told the pastor that her granddaughter was oppressed with a demon who was destroying her life. It would manifest in various ways including violent behavior and speaking in masculine voices. Being a Hindu, the grandmother took the girl to temples and holy men seeking help, but no one was successful in freeing her. Finally, having no other option, she decided to try the Christian God. The pastor prayed over the girl and cast the demon out. She was set free in a moment of time as God demonstrated His loving power through prayer in Jesus's name. In their joy, the grandmother and granddaughter both received Jesus as their Savior, and many other family members moved toward faith in Christ. The pastor then told us that the lady who had served us tea was the grandmother. He called her into the room, and she told us her story, how Jesus changed everything for her family.

By most accounts, miraculous events are prime reasons for why the Church is growing in Asia, Africa, and South America. A family member goes to a church or a meeting and gets healed or delivered. They become a Christian, and then they bring their family members. They tell of a God Who still heals, delivers, and saves, and how Philip's story in Acts 8 is being repeated worldwide. These churches are expecting God's power to show up in their ministry, as these verses indicate:

"Our gospel came to you not simply with words but also with power, with the Holy Spirit and deep conviction..." (1 Thessalonians 1:5)

"...When I came to you, I did not come with eloquence or human wisdom as I proclaimed to you the testimony about God...My message and my preaching were not with wise and persuasive words, but with a demonstration of the Spirit's power, so that your faith might not rest on human wisdom, but on God's power." (1 Corinthians 2:1, 4-5)

"I will not venture to speak of anything except what Christ has accomplished through me in leading the Gentiles to obey God by what I have said and done—by the power of signs and wonders, through the power of the Spirit of God. So from Jerusalem all the way around to Illyricum, I have fully proclaimed the gospel of Christ." (Romans 15:18-19)

"...This salvation, which was first announced by the Lord, was confirmed to us by those who heard Him. God also testified to it by signs, wonders and various miracles, and by gifts of the Holy Spirit distributed according to His will." (Hebrews 2:3-4)

The testimony of the early Church is that of preaching the gospel, not only with words but also with miraculous deeds. The Scriptures give every indication that supernatural ministry was to continue in the life of the Church until Jesus returns.

HEALING POWER OF THE CROSS

It's important that we embrace all that Jesus accomplished on the cross. Hundreds of years before Jesus's birth, the prophet Isaiah predicted the Messiah would die as a substitute in our place, paying for our sins with His own life:

"Surely He took up our pain and bore our suffering,
yet we considered him punished by God, stricken by Him, and afflicted.
But He was pierced for our transgressions,
He was crushed for our iniquities;
the punishment that brought us peace was on Him,
and by His wounds we are healed.
We all, like sheep, have gone astray, each of us has turned to our own way;
and the Lord has laid on Him the iniquity of us all."
(Isaiah 53:4-6)

This prophecy, written some 800 years before Jesus's birth, reveals the love of God in Christ. On the cross, He was pierced with nails for our transgressions. His body was crushed for our iniquities. God loves you and me to such an extent that He gave His Son, Jesus, to take the punishment that our disobedience and rebellion deserved. While we were still opposing, resisting, and ignoring God, Jesus died for us. He was the perfect Lamb of God without sin and blemish,

Who took our sins on Himself. He did this out of love for you and me. But not only did He pay for our sins on the cross, He also paid for our healing. The gospel of Matthew speaks of this:

"When evening came, many who were demon-possessed were brought to Him, and He drove out the spirits with a word and healed all the sick. This was to fulfill what was spoken through the prophet Isaiah: 'He took up our infirmities and bore our diseases.'"
(Matthew 8:16-17)

Remember God will not withhold healing from you because you don't deserve it. And He doesn't heal you because you are good. He heals because He is good. He will heal you because of what Jesus did on the cross.

For many of you this chapter raises questions about miracles in the church today, especially if supernatural ministry was ignored or denied in your earlier church experience. I encourage you to turn to the books I suggest at the end of this chapter as they will address common objections and questions that people have. More importantly they will raise your expectations and faith in a loving Father Who still saves, delivers, and heals in response to the prayers of His people.

DEALING WITH DISAPPOINTMENTS

Maybe you have personal disappointment about healing. Maybe you've received prayer for healing, but nothing happened. Perhaps that has led you to conclude it is not God's will to heal you, or that God doesn't really care about your troubles, or that God wants you to keep your disease or injury to teach you some lesson, or that you remain sick because you didn't have enough faith. Recognize that a lot of bad theology is created when Christians feel the pressure to explain unanswered prayers. I encourage you to hear the words of Jesus from the gospel of Luke:

"Then Jesus told His disciples a parable to show them that they should always pray and never give up." (Luke 18:1)

Jesus's encouragement to persevere in prayer implies there is resistance, opposition, or other factors that hinder answers to prayer. An unanswered prayer is not due to God's unwillingness to act. Instead of giving up on God or creating some rationale by which you accept your sickness as God's will, Jesus says keep coming to Him. It's not uncommon for someone to be prayed for many times without effect, only to receive prayer one more time and have a powerful healing take place. We might correctly identify some reasons that delay or prevent healing, but so much of it is conjecture and mystery. That's why I always encourage people to look at Jesus Who was always willing to heal and to lean into Luke 18:1. Let that be our response to unanswered prayer.

YOUR KINGDOM COME, YOUR WILL BE DONE

A simple starting point for asking God for healing, one that is accessible to all believers, is The Lord's Prayer. Jesus taught us to pray, *"Your kingdom come, Your will be done on earth as it is in heaven"* (Matthew 6:10). Jesus has given us a great gift in these words because when we don't know what to pray, this is always an appropriate request. In whatever trouble or situation you are dealing with, you can pray: "Father, into this matter may Your kingdom come and may Your will be done!" What are we requesting when we pray these words?

First, when we request "Your kingdom come," we recognize the kingdom of God isn't geographical, but it is spiritual. The word "kingdom" is formed by shortening the phrase "king's domain." Therefore, the kingdom is wherever the king's rule and reign are established. Thus, wherever God is acknowledged as King and His rule is obeyed, that's where God's kingdom is found.

229

When we pray "Your kingdom come" as Jesus instructed us, we are asking that the rule and reign of God come into a situation. If there is some problem, trouble, or issue that you are facing, Jesus invites you to pray: "God, into this situation let Your kingdom come." In other words, "Lord, bring Your rule and reign into this problem, into this relational breakdown, into this medical report. Let Your kingdom come and bring Your rule replace the darkness, confusion, and chaos of this moment. Bring Your kingdom power and authority against all the destructive work of the evil one in this matter."

Next, Jesus tells us to pray: "Your will be done on earth as it is in heaven." This is an amazing prayer. Jesus is giving us permission to request that, to the extent God's will is obeyed in heaven, let His will be obeyed here. This is huge. Where is the greatest expression of God's will? It's in Heaven! In Heaven the will of God is fully realized, fulfilled, and manifested. Everything we see in Heaven is a direct expression of God's will. And what do we find there? Maybe the better question is: What do we not find in Heaven? According to Revelation 21:4, there is no death, sorrow, pain, or tears. There is no sickness, disease, or despair. No poverty, oppression, no addictions or abuse. All mental illness, depression, and hopelessness have vanished. Every broken mind and broken body are restored. It is a huge request when we pray, "Your will be done on earth as it is in Heaven," because we aren't asking God to make things a little better. We're asking, "Father, into this trouble we're facing, let Your will be fully expressed and obeyed to the extent it is obeyed in Heaven!" Jesus is telling us to pray big and bold.

The God Who controls 200 billion galaxies has lovingly tied Himself to our lives through prayer and has told us that miracles are released by our prayers. The people we love who are lost, broken, addicted, and oppressed can find miracles of freedom and new life through our prayers. Diseases and disabilities that seem permanent are healed through our prayers. Broken marriages and broken relationships find new beginnings through our prayers. These things happen as we follow Jesus's instructions and cry out to God that His will be done and that His kingdom rule comes to replace the hopelessness in the situations that break our hearts. This is all in the context of warfare against an enemy who is relentless but is already defeated by the blood of Jesus on the cross. Therefore, we stand firm so that no matter how dark and impossible a situation seems, we will always pray and never give up.

ACTIVATION

A. Read the book of Acts. You can do so in 45-60 minutes in one sitting. Ask the Holy Spirit to help you read it as if for the first time. Underline every passage where the name of Jesus or the Holy Spirit is mentioned. What did you learn? What actions do you feel prompted to take? Are any of your personal convictions and beliefs challenged?

B. Practice praying: "Your kingdom come, and Your will be done" as Jesus instructed. You can pray this over yourself: "Lord, let Your kingdom rule be established in my life! Rule over all my thoughts, emotions, attitudes, actions, all my plans and goals, over my career, my relationships, my future. In all of these let Your kingdom come and Your will be done!" You can pray this over the situations and people in your life that need God's help, whether they are battling sickness, addictions, relational issues, or financial troubles. We see Jesus in the Gospels always willing to heal, deliver, and help. In this prayer, we are calling on Jesus to intervene and work miracles. In the lives of people we love who are afflicted with disease, injuries, and disabilities, we are reminded that the fullest expression of God's will is in Heaven, so we request that sickness is banished and disease is destroyed. Just as Your will for health and wholeness is obeyed in Heaven, so let Your will be accomplished here in this situation!"

C. On YouTube you will find recordings of the song *"I Speak Jesus"* by several musicians. Choose one and listen, letting the words speak to your life.

D. In your desire to walk in God's loving power, begin to pray John 14:12 and Acts 1:8 to become realities in your life. This is your role and calling, to experience God's power and purpose in your life.

SUGGESTED READING

Blue, Ken. *Authority to Heal.* Downers Grove: InterVarsity Press, 1987. *(This is the first book I'd read that gave positive theological and practical understanding of healing ministry. It addresses common unhealthy and unhelpful ideas about healing while explaining how healing is an expression of God's Kingdom.)*

Clark, Randy. *Eyewitness to Miracles.* Nashville: Thomas Nelson, 2018. *(Randy Clark was a Baptist pastor who came into the power of the Holy Spirit and today has helped tens of thousands experience supernatural ministry through his writings and the work of his ministry, Global Awakening. He has written dozens of books; we use several as texts in our school.)*

Deere, Jack. *Why I Am Still Surprised by the Power of God.* Grand Rapids: Zondervan, 2022. *(Jack Deere was a seminary professor who taught that God no longer did miracles in this day, until his life was radically transformed through encounters with the Holy Spirit. This book is especially helpful in addressing theological arguments claiming God has ceased working miraculously as He did in the Bible. Also, the book contains a lot of wisdom on how to move into supernatural ministry.)*

Deere, Jack. *Why I Am Still Surprised by the Voice of God.* Grand Rapids: Zondervan, 2022. *(This book gives great explanations and encouragement about how to grow in hearing God.)*

Hutchings, Mike. *Supernatural Freedom from the Captivity of Trauma.* Shippensburg: Destiny Image, 2021. *(My friend Mike has written a powerful book specifically to release healing over trauma-related issues such as PTSD.)*

Keener, Craig. *Miracles Today: The Supernatural Work of God in the Modern World.*

Grand Rapids: Baker, 2021. *(Keener, professor of New Testament at Asbury Seminary, is recognized as one of the top theologians in America today. This book is a condensed version of his two-volume work on miracles, widely deemed to be the definitive word on miracles both in the Bible and in today's church.)*

Seng, Jordan. *Miracle Work.* Downers Grove: InterVarsity Press, 2013. *(I think this is the best one-volume summary of how to understand and experience supernatural ministry. It is especially helpful in answering questions for those whose previous church experience had little emphasis on the miraculous.)*

CHAPTER 14

CHURCH AND COMMUNITY

"...I will build My church, and the gates of Hades will not overcome it. I will give you the keys of the kingdom of heaven; whatever you bind on earth will be bound in heaven, and whatever you loose on earth will be loosed in heaven." (Matthew 16:18-19)

"Every day they continued to meet together in the temple courts. They broke bread in their homes and ate together with glad and sincere hearts." (Acts 2:46)

"And let us consider how we may spur one another on toward love and good deeds, not giving up meeting together, as some are in the habit of doing, but encouraging one another—and all the more as you see the Day approaching." (Hebrews 10:24-25)

"Keep on loving one another as brothers and sisters." (Hebrews 13:1)

From the very beginning when Christianity was first birthed at Pentecost, God has led believers to join together into groups. This was a new thing for the followers of Jesus. During Jesus's earthly ministry, He had a group of twelve disciples plus other supporters who traveled with Him. But as far as we know, as Jesus went from town to town, He did not leave behind groups of disciples organized to continue meeting together. That all changed on the day of Pentecost. From that day forward the believers began gathering into groups. Acts 2 tells the story of how the Holy Spirit came to Jesus's disciples, empowering them to go into the streets of Jerusalem and preach. This resulted in 3,000 people repenting and placing their faith in Jesus. Those new believers entered an ongoing relationship with each other:

"Those who accepted his message were baptized, and about three thousand were added to their number that day. They devoted themselves to the apostles' teaching and to fellowship, to the breaking of bread and to prayer. Everyone was filled with awe at the many wonders and signs performed by the apostles. All the believers were together and had everything in common. They sold property and possessions to give to anyone who had need. Every day they continued to meet together in the temple courts. They broke bread in their homes and ate together with glad and sincere hearts, praising God and enjoying the favor of all the people. And the Lord added to their number daily those who were being saved." (Acts 2:41-47)

This was a new thing. As people carried this new faith to other towns and regions, those who believed the gospel banded together in each location.

This became the pattern for Christian faith in every nation throughout history. Someone—a factory worker, a housewife, a student—has their life changed by Jesus, and they are compelled to tell others, whose lives are also changed, and then they begin gathering regularly to support each other in living this new life. This morning I was on a WhatsApp call with a church leader in Central Asia who asked for prayer as he was leaving for a distant village to help a group of 50 new believers form a church in an area where the dominant religion is hostile toward Christians. Last week I had lunch with two people I consider my heroes, one from Kenya, the other from India. They were meeting each other for the first time, yet we discovered they were doing similar ministry in their respective countries. They go into villages that have few Christians and hold outreach meetings. They preach, heal the sick in the village, and deliver people from demonic powers. This results in villagers becoming followers of Jesus. Then the new believers are gathered into a group which continues meeting for spiritual growth, and leaders are raised to shepherd the group. My Indian friend has started close to 200 churches, and my Kenyan friend, who is younger, has planted 15 churches. In every nation the Holy Spirit reveals God's desire for His people to band together to love and support one another.

Also, from the beginning, enemies of this new faith have sought to outlaw or destroy these gatherings. But being together is so important to believers that even today, millions of Christians risk imprisonment and physical violence simply to be with one another. Millions know the experience of meeting in secret, whispering prayers together in order to avoid detection by hate-filled opponents.

And yet, while the church is so central to Christian faith, for some people, it has been a source of pain and trouble. Maybe you were wounded deeply in a church and, while you may be returning to God, the idea of stepping into a church building is intimidating. What you experienced in the past makes it difficult for you to trust churches and leaders. I encourage you to keep doing the things that help you grow in your relationship with God. But understand that it is your Father's intention that you eventually enter into relationship with other believers. You share the spiritual DNA of a worldwide family, and God desires you find a place among them.

Below, two of my friends share their journeys back to God and how they each found a place of healing and help in a local church.

A FRIEND'S STORY

This story tells how a good friend found her way back to the Lord. I think readers might see themselves in this story as many people come from families that were broken, and so they learn to look for affirmation elsewhere, often in unhealthy places and ways. Her story also shows how important the help of a local church was in her spiritual growth.

As a child, I grew up in a family in which my parents believed in the Lord, but faith wasn't a priority for us. We didn't attend church, and I really had no understanding of what faith truly meant or how faith can be the core value of your life. As I reflect back, I don't hold any resentment towards my parents for not raising us in a faith-based home. Both faced difficulties in their lives that challenged their beliefs in a higher purpose. My dad had suffered extreme and unthinkable abuse growing up, and I believe that abuse stopped him from engaging in life fully. My mother turned from her faith when her older brother was killed in a family car accident. Both events went on to shape some of who they are today.

Fast forward into my teenage years and I found myself looking for validation and approval in unhealthy ways. Although my dad loved his family with all his heart, he was often emotionally disconnected. His inability to stand firm as a father coupled with my own physical disability drove me to seek out ways to be recognized. I worked incredibly hard in school, always trying to be at the top. I sought approval in my relationships and my work. I spent years climbing the corporate ladder and chasing after that next promotion. It wasn't until later that I would find that corporate power and recognition was actually empty and lonely.

By the time I had married, I knew that something was missing in my life, and I knew that ultimately God was the answer. I had toyed with church off and on during my teenage years but hadn't really taken it seriously. As a newlywed I served at a local church service and longed to connect deeper with the Lord. I got engaged in small groups and began praying more. But I hadn't truly rooted my life in God's Word, and ultimately that path fell away as well.

It wasn't until I hit my mid-30s that faith came to the forefront of my life. One Saturday morning, my husband (a nonbeliever) looked up at me from the breakfast table and told me he wanted our kids to be in church. He mentioned that he had seen some apologetics videos on Facebook, and he was compelled to learn more about the Gospel. He further shared his interest in raising our children with a firm value system. At that moment, I didn't realize how a Facebook video would be such a pivotal turning point in our lives.

We found a nearby church, and God's grace and mercy immediately felt overflowing. We got connected in small groups, joined the volunteer team, and my husband got baptized. The past 2 years have been the absolute most fulfilling and joyful years of my life. During this time, we started to really dig into our faith. It became the center and core value of my life, and it wasn't until I became immersed in God's Word that I truly began to have a real relationship with my father. The funny thing is that while these have been the best 2 years of my life, they have been the hardest 2 years as well. Over the course of this time, my family has faced unexplainable trials, but God was faithful at every turn. We faced financial hardship when there was a property tax error in the closing of our new home, my son contracted a very rare and serious sickness that rocked our family's core, and my integrity was challenged at work based on a false accusation against me. One might look at those 2 years and feel bad about that time. But I look back on these 2 years with unending gratitude. At every turn, and every hardship, God showed up in big ways. The Lord has brought a peace and fulfillment that I have never known. A fulfillment that no academic education or corporate title could ever fill. He brought covenant love into my marriage. He delivered my husband from anxiety and anger. My children know what it means to pray over a meal, lay their head to rest trusting in God, and sing songs of praise to their Maker.

Looking back, I only wish I had gotten serious about my faith sooner in life. Looking forward, I want nothing more than to serve the Lord and seek His will. I hope to one day engage in ministry full time.

MIKE'S STORY

My friend Mike Harms and I served together for many years. Early in his life, though, he had become disillusioned and hostile toward the Christian faith after an initial attempt to follow Christ. He found, as perhaps you are too, that while we try to forget God, He never forgets us and is at work to bring us back to Himself.

As a child I attended church regularly with my mother and grandparents. It was a mainstream Protestant denomination, and I was confirmed and baptized at the age of 12. But it wasn't until I was 19 years old that I found my faith in Jesus. My parents were in the middle of their divorce, and I felt like my world was crashing around me. God had placed a coworker in my life who was a believer, and he shared the gospel message with me. On my knees in his apartment with him and his fiancée, I accepted Christ as my Lord and Savior.

Unfortunately, I seemed to be the seed cast on the rocky soil. I was excited about my new life and dove into the Word and prayer. I didn't get fully connected with a body of believers though, and I soon withered and died spiritually. That spurred anger, and I turned my back on the Lord. I spent many years declaring that I wanted nothing to do with those "born again" Christians.

Nearly ten years later I found myself four years married with a nearly two-year-old and my marriage heading the wrong direction. My wife had been raised Catholic, and we regularly attended Mass. I was just trying to be a good husband but spiritually I closed off from God. After service one Sunday in February 1984, at the age of 28, my wife and I had a fight; she expressed that she was looking for more from church and God than what she was getting. She stated, "There has to be something more." In my frustration, I told her to just pick a church, any church, and I would take her there! In my ignorance I thought that if she would just get happy, our marriage would be okay.

Within a couple of days, she came to me and said she had decided she wanted to try Nancy's church. This was not what I wanted to hear at all. Nancy and her husband, Vince, were neighbors two houses down. My wife had become friends with Nancy, and I had no problem with that, but I didn't really want to hang around with them because it had become obvious that they were some of those "born again" Christians I wanted nothing to do with.

I was trapped. I had given her a choice, and I had to honor my commitment to take her to any church she picked. The very next Sunday we walked into a grade school gymnasium, the temporary location of a budding new congregation, Hill Fellowship Church. My first impression was that everyone was very nice, maybe a little too nice. I smiled, and we found seats near the back. I was hopeful that it might not be too bad; most of the people were our age, and there were drums and guitar amps on the stage. I don't remember exactly, but two or three songs in, I heard a voice in my head as distinct as I've ever heard, say to me, "You're home." I was overwhelmed and began to sob, the sloppy kind. My wife was taken aback, wondering what was going on with me.

The Father had spoken to me, not words of rebuke or scolding, but a welcome home. I stood there and repented through my tears, receiving love and forgiveness. I also determined that I was never leaving home again.

My wife's transformation took a few months; she was not prepared for the change in me. At the end of that service, I told my wife we were coming back next Sunday. When I got home, I dug out the Bible my friend had given me when I first got saved and began to read it again and pray. Within a few weeks, someone asked if we were going to come Thursday night? I asked, "What's Thursday night?" We were told about a Bible study, and I quickly responded, "We'll be there!"

My wife wasn't fond of the husband I had been previously, but she wasn't quite sure of this new husband she had brought home. We continued to attend as a family and take it all in like a sponge. My wife was drawn by the Holy Spirit to come forward and make a commitment but hesitated because she didn't feel worthy. Finally on a Sunday in August, a member of the worship team shared that there was someone holding back because they felt they needed to get it together before coming to Jesus. He encouraged that none of us ever have it together but to come to Christ just as we are. She went forward that morning and gave her life to Jesus. We continued to attend and pursue our newfound relationship. We jumped in and served wherever we were needed and began to find God's leading and realize the talents He had given us. We went on to a successful marriage, raising four children and are blessed with seven grandchildren.

YOU ARE DESIGNED FOR RELATIONSHIPS

The stories of my friends above mention how important churches were in helping them return to the Lord. God will also lead you to join other believers and develop ties of friendship and support. That might occur at a mega-church with three parking lots, or it might simply be with a few people meeting in a living room, or perhaps it's something in between. But the Spirit of God will compel you to connect with other believers because you are now a child of God with lots of siblings. He intends for you to grow in a family of His children.

You are designed for relationships and community. This is because you are created in the image of the triune God. The true God is a Trinity, meaning in the nature of the one God are three Persons—Father, Son, and Holy Spirit. Thus, God in His nature is a community of three Persons relating to each other. Because you are created in God's image, you too are made for community.

If your previous church experiences left you wounded, disappointed, or disillusioned, ask the Holy Spirit to lead you to a group of believers that is functioning in love and truth. It may take time but recognize it is Jesus's intention for you to be in relationship with other believers, so don't settle into an independent spiritual life.

THE AMERICAN CHURCH UNDER ASSAULT

Since the beginning, the Church has been attacked on two fronts—by persecution from the outside and sin from the inside. There are spiritual forces assaulting the Church from the outside, working to silence, isolate, and diminish the Church. While Christianity is expanding rapidly in many parts of the world, polling shows the influence of Christians in the United States is currently declining. But America has seen times in the past when Christian faith seemed to be faltering, only to experience a national spiritual revival. Historians tell of "great awakenings" in our past, when spiritual and moral revivals turned the nation around. Many of us believe we're poised for another such awakening.

But along with attacks from the outside, there has also been sin assaulting the church from inside. In the last five years, some of the most influential ministries in the nation have been devastated by the sinful behavior of their leaders. These are leaders who many of us had admired. But now they've been exposed as being abusive, immoral, and unfit for leadership. What is even more troubling is the manner in which their ministry boards handled the leadership failures, with responses that were inept, callous, and ungodly.

ADOPTING BUSINESS WORLD SYSTEMS, PRACTICES, AND VALUES

For example, today as I write this, a famous church is being taken to court by one of their members who is accusing a church employee of sexually assaulting her. The church board tried to keep the case out of court by offering the member a cash settlement, provided she sign an NDA—a non-disclosure agreement. This would have legally prevented her from disclosing any information about the case. The church was attempting to buy her silence with money. NDAs come from the corporate world; their use might be appropriate in protecting a company's technology secrets, but the use of an NDA to protect a church from being held accountable for its failures is an idea from hell. Jesus calls His people to humble themselves, confess their sins, bring their failures into the light, bless their enemies, seek forgiveness that restores relationships, and speak the truth in love. Here, the use of an NDA is to protect people in power by keeping deeds hidden, with no admission of guilt, and the ministry leadership is never held accountable. Not to be overly dramatic, but keeping matters in the dark is satanic. The reporting of major church scandals in recent years commonly mentions how NDAs were used to silence victims and whistleblowers, with churches demanding their staff members sign NDAs if they wanted to receive their severance pay.

How did the use of NDAs ever become common practice for churches? This is an example of how practices from the corporate world have worked their way into many American churches. This is important because ministry scandals in the past were usually about the personal failings of an individual, but more and more churches are imploding because of the ungodly behavior of leadership teams. This behavior reflects values, practices, and culture borrowed from the world of corporations and business and not the values of Scripture.

We've misidentified the Church, thinking principles and practices that worked in managing corporations and industries would improve churches. But the Church is a supernatural body and not a business. I think this is one reason why many young people have rejected the modern American Church. They intuitively know something is wrong. They can sniff out that which is carnal and manmade. They want the real thing.

A flagship church, which I and thousands of other church leaders looked to for best practices in creating healthy ministries, was exposed as being horribly unhealthy. They were famous for their annual leadership conferences which influenced leaders worldwide but then they were exposed as being terrible at leadership, led by a man who behind the scenes was abusive, narcissistic, and sexually immoral. Furthermore, their leadership team attacked whistleblowers and mistreated victims over a long period before the team finally admitted the charges against the lead pastor were true.

Recently a prayer ministry with worldwide impact was toppled when its leader was shown to have a decades-long history of grooming and seducing young women. And again, the leadership team of that ministry responded terribly to the situation. They placed the needs of the organization over the needs of the victims, and thus re-victimized these individuals.

An internationally known apologetics ministry was destroyed when its deceased founder was exposed as having been immoral and deceptive, with a history of manipulating vulnerable people for his sexual pleasure. What was more destructive to the ministry, though, was how horribly their leadership board responded to the situation. Their actions were lawyer-driven, attacking and slandering victims, and denying any charge of wrongdoing. It was ugly and ungodly.

Many of us feel betrayed by the leadership teams of these ministries who did not hold their point leaders accountable and then mismanaged the crisis when their leader's wrongdoing was exposed. As credible charges of wrongdoing were presented, instead of responding with contrition and repentance, leadership teams used the weight of their mega-church or mega-ministry resources to crush opposition and avoid scrutiny. In case after case, the actions and decisions of boards were rooted in corporate or business world values, void of the fruit of the Spirit and the love of God. Their governing boards allowed narcissists to lead, and then they went into attack mode in order to protect the organization against all threats and to control narratives, regardless of the truth of the accusations.

RETURNING TO THE SCRIPTURES

The prevailing practice of turning to the corporate world for ideas on developing and leading churches isn't serving the American Church very well. I write as a person who valued those ideas for years. Along with many of my fellow pastor friends, my bookshelves were packed with an odd mixture of texts from both business schools and seminaries. Developing mission statements and vision statements and five-year strategic plans and a host of other practices that originated in the business world seemed like a good idea as we tried to lead and grow churches. But in those years, at least in my case, my dependence on the Holy Spirit for church direction and solutions diminished greatly. However, these days I'm committed to keeping the Holy Spirit's presence, power, and direction as the top priority in the ministry I'm leading, and I'm in a season of going back to the Bible in order to determine what Jesus had in mind when He said, "I will build My church."

We need a radical change in how we understand Church. Linguistically, the word "radical" comes from the Latin word meaning "root." Words like "fundamental," "foundational," and "original" are associated with the term. In this sense, a radical change involves a return to the roots. So, let's be radicals and return to the root, to what God originally had in mind when He birthed this thing called "church." Let's erase everything we think we know about "church" and erase all current practices and programs and structure commonly found in churches. Instead, on a clean whiteboard, let's record what we discover in the Bible. If we had no earlier experience of "church", no exposure to "church" as practiced in North America and only had the Bible to guide us, what would emerge? While what follows is by no means an exhaustive study of all that the Scriptures teach about the Church, here are a few concepts from the Scriptures that may be overlooked or downplayed currently in many churches. Maybe for those of you who are returning to faith, the following can help you evaluate and choose a church home that aligns with Scripture in its practices and priorities.

I WILL BUILD MY CHURCH

"When Jesus came to the region of Caesarea Philippi, He asked his disciples, 'Who do people say the Son of Man is?' They replied, 'Some say John the Baptist; others say Elijah; and still others, Jeremiah or one of the prophets.'

'But what about you?' He asked. 'Who do you say I am?' Simon Peter answered, 'You are the Messiah, the Son of the living God.' Jesus replied. 'Blessed are you, Simon son of Jonah, for this was not revealed to you by flesh and blood, but by My Father in heaven. And I tell you that you are Peter, and on this rock <u>I will build My church, and the gates of Hades will not overcome it. I will give you the keys of the kingdom of heaven; whatever you bind on earth will be bound in heaven, and whatever you loose on earth will be loosed in heaven.</u>'" (Matthew 16:13-19, emphasis mine)

There is a concept in Bible study called "first mention." Theologians say we should pay attention to the first time Scripture mentions a topic because often core truths are revealed in the first mention, truths that are intended to be foundational and primary to our understanding of that topic. The first direct mention of "church" in the New Testament is here in Matthew 16, spoken by Jesus. This passage needs careful consideration as we are seeking to understand God's idea of "church."

In Matthew 16:13, we read that Jesus and His disciples traveled to Caesarea Philippi. This region was not a Jewish center, but it was a major site of Gentile religious activity and worship. There were many temples established there for the worship of various gods. There was even a dark and demonic worship site called the Gates of Hades. It was here, in the midst of religions hostile to the God of the Bible, that God chose to reveal the identity of Jesus (*"You are the Messiah, the Son of the living God"* [Matthew 16:16]). It seems Jesus was openly challenging the spiritual forces behind all the temples and religious sites with a bold declaration that He was the Messiah. Jesus then declares that His people, His "church," will have authority and power over the spiritual forces of darkness.

"And I tell you that you are Peter, and on this rock I will build My church, and the gates of Hades will not overcome it. I will give you the keys of the kingdom of heaven; whatever you bind on earth will be bound in heaven, and whatever you loose on earth will be loosed in heaven." (Matthew 16:18-19)

Of everything Jesus could have said about the purposes, practices, and priorities of the Church, the first thing He wants us to know is we are at war. We face an enemy. There is opposition and resistance to Jesus and His Church. That is what He chose to stress in this first mention of "church." We learn it is Jesus's church (it doesn't belong to the pastor or the elders) and He will build it, but it happens in the context of resistance and warfare, in a clash between the spiritual and natural realms. Further, Jesus gives the church resources ("loosing and binding") to be actively engaged in the struggle. And, He says we will be victorious.

WHY THE TERM "EKKLESIA"?

When Jesus says, "I will build My church," the Greek term He uses is "Ekklesia"—"I will build My Ekklesia." His listeners were probably surprised that Jesus chose to use the word "Ekklesia." He didn't say, "I will build My synagogue" or "I will build My Temple," both of which were religious concepts recognizable by His followers at the time. Instead, He chose to use the word "Ekklesia," a common, secular term, not a religious word. In Greek and Roman cities, an ekklesia was an assembly of people with authority to govern and make decisions about the affairs of the city. It was through the ekklesia that Greece and Rome exercised authority and established their rule over that location.

When Jesus said, "I will build My Ekklesia," He was saying Rome may have her Ekklesia representing the authority and interests of the Roman empire, but I also will have My Ekklesia, representing MY Kingdom. It will represent My concerns and bring My authority to bear. It will promote My values and priorities. Jesus was infusing new meaning into the word Ekklesia.

Thus, our understanding of the word "church" needs to be adjusted. The Ekklesia (Church) is not a building nor is it a Sunday morning event. It is the people who gather to represent Jesus and His interests. He gives them authority to establish His will and purposes, and to go forward against all that the gates of Hades represents. Jesus's intent is that we understand the spiritual power He has bestowed on us. Of all Jesus could have said about Church in this first mention in Matthew 16, He chose to emphasize the supernatural spiritual power that His Ekklesia holds over the forces of darkness.

When Jesus speaks of His Church loosing and binding, He wants us to understand we can impact the unseen realm. We are not helpless victims of fate or karma. We are granted authority to change things. Jesus's description of His Ekklesia in Matthew should be reflected in the ministries and priorities of the Church. Intercession, spiritual warfare, bold praying, and supernatural ministry should be the result when a church embraces Jesus's view. And what other view should we adopt? It's His church. He builds it. He's the Head (see Ephesians 4:15).

Our fears and feelings of helplessness should diminish. We are promised victory. Demonic powers fear us. The Antichrist is afraid of us. No matter the assault on our lives and families, no matter the troubles and brokenness we face, we have authority to pray and believe the "gates of Hades" will not prevail against us.

THE BODY OF CHRIST

"For just as each of us has one body with many members, and these members do not all have the same function, so in Christ we, though many, form one body, and each member belongs to all the others. We have different gifts, according to the grace given to each of us." (Romans 12:4-6)

"For we were all baptized by one Spirit so as to form one body—whether Jews or Gentiles, slave or free—and we were all given the one Spirit to drink. Even so the body is not made up of one part but of many...Now you are the body of Christ, and each one of you is a part of it. And God has placed in the

church first of all apostles, second prophets, third teachers, then miracles, then gifts of healing, of helping, of guidance, and of different kinds of tongues." (1 Corinthians 12:13-14, 24-28)

"So Christ Himself gave the apostles, the prophets, the evangelists, the pastors and teachers, to equip His people for works of service, so that the body of Christ may be built up...Instead, speaking the truth in love, we will grow to become in every respect the mature body of him who is the head, that is, Christ. From him the whole body, joined and held together by every supporting ligament, grows and builds itself up in love, as each part does its work." (Ephesians 4:11-12, 15-16)

Another concept that describes the Church is that of a body. Christian believers are members of a body, a living organism. We're not an organization but an organism. As the Scriptures above stress, just as each part of our physical bodies has a specific function that benefits the whole body, so each believer, as a member of the Church body, is to carry out a role that benefits the rest of the Church, contributes to the mission of the Church. Thus each member is connected to the others, and each member is to contribute to the health and mission of the Church.

Read the Scriptures above once again. It's clear that any church that fosters a spectator and consumer attitude among its people, with little expectation, opportunity, or encouragement for members to serve is unbiblical. These verses also show there are to be no solo Christians, but that each of us is to be connected with other believers, serving together.

SPIRITUAL GIFTS AND FOLLOWING THE SPIRIT

Because Scripture regularly ties the concept of the body of Christ to spiritual gifts, we need to consider how the modern American Church has approached the gifts of the Spirit. You can find the gifts listed in 1 Corinthians 12:7-10,28, Romans 12:6-8, and Ephesians 4:11. Over the past 40 years, it has been common for churches to help their members identify their personal spiritual gifting through spiritual gift tests. The Bible says God has given at least one spiritual gift to every believer. Spiritual gift tests are intended to help people identify what spiritual gift or gifts God had given them. The idea is once people identify their gifts, they then can join an appropriate ministry in the church, filling a position that will best use their gift. This will result in members being comfortable and effective in the tasks they take on. I've given these test materials to hundreds of people. But I've stopped using them for several reasons.

First, I don't think the tests, at least the ones I'm familiar with, necessarily identify supernatural spiritual gifts. Their method of identifying gifts doesn't seem to separate true spiritual gifts from natural traits, personality preferences, aptitudes, and skills that people have acquired through training or experience. Of course, when we dedicate our natural skills and strengths to serve God, they are a blessing to the Church. But that doesn't make them a spiritual gift. Spiritual gifts are not something we are naturally born with or acquired through training but rather are imparted to us by the Holy Spirit. The tests I've seen tend to dilute the definition by naming every ability as a spiritual gift.

Second, in practice, these gift tests tend to be used as a church "Zip recruiter" to find people to keep church programs running and thus limiting all God might have intended in bestowing the gifts on an individual. What I'm addressing here is the motivation behind the use of gift tests. The emphasis tends to be on finding volunteers to keep programs running and not on finding God's purpose and destiny for that individual. It makes needs of the church the priority.

I don't mean to be too critical here because I know many people for whom the tests opened a door into a very fulfilling ministry in their churches, and as the verses in this section indicate, everyone should pitch in to help their church. But there is limited imagination when our focus is reduced to how someone can fill an open position in the church programs. These tests should be an exercise in helping envision people for their God-given destiny. It is more kingdom-minded and great commission-focused to consider how gifts can also apply to our marketplace careers and life outside of church. Most tests don't go beyond trying to match people with open slots to keep the church machinery running. Why not focus on how the gifts you've identified in your life can also impact decisions about your career and your current marketplace job, and how you can bring Kingdom solutions into those realms through exercising your supernatural gifting? Why not cast vision for bringing your gifts to bear in your business, office, or classroom? Are there ministries outside the church you should serve in? What civic organizations or clubs should you join? How about what political offices you should run for? Instead of limiting your spiritual gifts to a place at church, expand your focus and pray and dream about how your gift can impact your greater sphere of influence. Daniel brought spiritual gifts of knowledge and prophetic ability to the courts of Babylon and thus impacted kings. God gifted Joseph to administrate the Egyptian kingdom. How can your gift impact the world?

ARE WE LED BY THE SPIRIT OR BY OUR TEST RESULTS?

But my biggest concern with spiritual gifts tests is how we use them to determine where we will serve instead of looking to the Holy Spirit Himself to guide us to the "good works He's prepared in advance for us to do" (see Ephesians 2:10). The premise behind knowing your spiritual gifts is that God wants you effective and confident in serving Him and thus He wants you to serve out of your gifting. So, if you can discover your gift(s), you will discover where the Holy Spirit wants you to serve. Find your gift and you find your call. Well, that's true until it isn't. You will be comfortable, confident, and effective when you are using your gift in service. But what if the Holy Spirit doesn't want you comfortable and confident? What if this is a moment in your life when He isn't so concerned with you being effective as much as being faithful? What if He wants to throw you into an assignment for which you have no experience or personal competence or previous gifting and thus can only depend on Him? The American Church has accepted the notion that the proof of God's assignment for you is the ease and effectiveness in which you carry out a task. But the Bible has its share of stories of people called out to obey and serve God in tasks for which they had no desire or previous gifting or aptitude, assignments in which they were very uncomfortable and stretched. We can't allow our spiritual gift alone to determine our ministry involvement. We must be listening to the Holy Spirit.

Moses' call into "ministry" is noteworthy. It required 34 verses of Scripture to record Moses' resistance to God's call to lead Israel (Exodus Chapters 3 and 4). He had no confidence that he could fill this ministry slot. But God dragged him into it, against his better judgment. He was convinced he was the wrong man for the job. Other people also thought he was the wrong man for the job (see Exodus Chapter 5). It's fairly common in Scripture to find people feeling inadequate when called by God. Gideon, Jeremiah, and Jonah all resisted God's call, feeling no confidence, gifting, or desire for the work God had for them

The apostle Paul is another example. Paul was trained as a Pharisee, meaning he was an expert in Jewish law, traditions, and scriptures. He had been mentored by the best Jewish instructors. All his extensive relationships were in the Jewish community. As a Pharisee he would have avoided relationships with Gentiles. Paul would have made a superb apostle to the Jews. But instead, Jesus made him an apostle to the Gentiles (see Galatians 2:8 and 1 Timothy 2:7). Can you imagine that conversation? "Paul, you are an expert on Jewish history and traditions, you are trained to teach the law, and you move among

Jewish people with ease. You would make a perfect apostle to the Jews. However, that's not where I'm sending you. I'm making you an apostle to the Gentiles. As a Pharisee, you've avoided and despised the Gentiles all your life. You have no experience that you can fall back on. You will have to depend on Me alone."

This is a common way that we grow spiritually. Jesus puts us in situations for which we have no gifting or experience and says, "Trust Me, depend on Me, look to Me."

This forces us to confront fear and unbelief, and we learn to nurture trust and dependence on the Holy Spirit. Let's not say, "Lord, give me the spiritual gift and then I'll go and serve." He says to us, "First say yes to Me and go, then I'll give you the gifting." Don't look to your list of perceived gifts to determine where to serve. Surrender to the Holy Spirit and let Him take you to the place He has chosen. Sometimes the task He assigns to you will line up with your gifts and strengths, but sometimes it won't.

After ten years of ministry in Japan, Harriet and I returned to the States and settled in the Seattle area. I was finishing a ministry graduate degree at Seattle Pacific University and later taught a class as an adjunct professor at Lutheran Bible Institute. We also began attending a church that had financially supported our missionary work. We wanted to volunteer and help out at the church, so we began to pray and look for how we could serve. In Japan I had served in mission leadership, was on teams starting new churches, had experience training new missionaries, and had led a nationwide summer outreach involving 170+ missionaries. So I assumed the Lord would lead us into ministry that could tap into all of that. But soon after arriving in Seattle, we were sitting in a church service, and I was half-listening to a staff person at the podium giving announcements, when she said, "Also we have a big need for someone to teach our first-grade Sunday school class"; right then I heard the Holy Spirit say, "THAT'S what I want you to do." My immediate reaction was,

"You're kidding!" I think I said it out loud. Again I heard: "That's what I want you to do, teach the first-grade class." Now, my reaction wasn't from some notion that teaching six-year-olds was beneath me. But I was surprised because I'd never taught first-graders before, and, besides, I had all this other ministry ability and experience to offer the church. But my next reaction was to laugh and say, "Okay, let's do it!" I leaned over to Harriet and said, "I think God wants us to teach the first-grade class." She looked at me and said, "What do you mean 'us'?" But I said, "If I gotta do it, you gotta do it, too!" So we tracked down the children's pastor and told her we'd take the class. She handed us a stack of curriculum and said, "Good luck."

When we arrived for our first class, we discovered what they hadn't told us: There were seventeen boys and one girl! Thus began a year of teaching Sunday school, though we weren't so much teachers as we were riot control cops. It was actually a lot of fun and also a time to love on kids with bad home situations. I think the call to teach the class was just another opportunity for the Lord to test our responsiveness and obedience to His call. Will we say "Yes, Lord" even when it doesn't make much sense?

If your church home uses spiritual gift tests, by all means take the test. But I encourage you to keep in mind what I've written above.

BROTHERS, SISTERS, AND THE FAMILY OF GOD

Years ago in a ministry I was serving with, we hit difficult financial troubles. As leader I had earlier promoted some ministry expansion which stretched us financially. Then, unfortunately, there came a downturn in the economy which began to impact the ministry's health. We reduced budgets and some of us took pay cuts, but eventually we realized we would have to release some staff. Those were some of the hardest conversations I've ever had, telling people

I loved that they would no longer have a job. I remember sitting after the final meeting was over and the person had left angry, hurt, and in tears. I remember thinking, "I will never do church like this again. I'm not sure what church is supposed to look like but it's not this. Those are my brothers and sisters. How do you fire family?!"

The experience above illustrates the struggle many people have with how the typical American church or ministry is structured with staff that wear dual hats of employee and brother-in-Christ, sister-in-Christ. It's why many of us are moving toward the simplicity of house churches. The most common way the church is described in the Bible is that of a family. Words like "household" and "brothers and sisters" permeate the New Testament. The Greek word translated "household" means belonging to a family, related by blood. We find this throughout the New Testament:

"Therefore, as we have opportunity, let us do good to all people, especially to those who belong to the family of believers." (Galatians 6:10)

"Consequently, you are no longer foreigners and strangers, but fellow citizens with God's people and also members of his household." (Ephesians 2:19)

"if I am delayed, you will know how people ought to conduct themselves in God's household, which is the church of the living God, the pillar and foundation of the truth."
(1 Timothy 3:15)

"Keep on loving one another as brothers and sisters." (Hebrews 13:1)

"Do not rebuke an older man but exhort him as you would a father; treat younger men like brothers, older women like mothers, younger women like sisters, in all purity." (1 Timothy 5:1-2)

The household concept is further reinforced by the fact the early churches met in homes:

"They broke bread in their homes and ate together with glad and sincere hearts." (Acts 2:46)

"Aquila and Priscilla greet you warmly in the Lord, and so does the church that meets at their house." (1 Corinthians 16:19)

"Give my greetings to the brothers and sisters at Laodicea, and to Nympha and the church in her house." (Colossians 4:15)

Understanding the true nature of "Church" will determine your attitude and expectations as you attend a church. Are you coming to a restaurant or to a family potluck?

If I think I'm in a restaurant, I sit at a table, somewhat separated from others, and have little interaction with other diners. As I look at the menu, I might be disappointed because they don't offer some dishes I'd hope for. I order a meal, but it arrives at my table late and isn't as tasty as I'd wanted, and the waiter was slow in acknowledging me and meeting my needs. So I decide to go somewhere else next time. That is a mindset many people have when attending church. That way of thinking about church isn't surprising as church services are structured as an event put on by professionals in front of an audience. The design of worship services tends to illicit a restaurant response.

But if I think I'm going to a family potluck, my expectations are different. I bring a casserole along with everyone else. When I arrive, I gravitate to the kitchen, crowded with relatives and join them in preparing the meal, or maybe I help the uncles set up chairs and tables. I meet cousins I haven't seen for a long time and get introduced to boyfriends of nieces. Later, when driving home do I think, "I am not going back because the ham was cold, and I don't like mandarin oranges in my jello, and it was a little crowded and nobody came to wait on me?" Of course not! You don't bring the same insistence on having personal wishes met when attending a family reunion. The deal is, Church as portrayed in Scripture is to be more like a family potluck than a restaurant.

I used to think that traditional churches at which members addressed each other as brother or sister (Brother Jim or Sister June) were quaint or maybe a little phony. I don't think that way anymore. While we might not actually address each other as brother or sister, we need to nurture the idea that fellow believers are part of my family. When we do, we are thinking biblically.

God intends that His Church is made up of close sibling relationships. Because of this, the New Testament has many admonitions about how we treat each other in the church. These are famously called the "one anothers," as over 50 times the phrase "one another" is used. For example:

"Be devoted to one another in love. Honor one another above yourselves." (Romans 12:10)

"Be completely humble and gentle; be patient, bearing with one another in love." (Ephesians 4:2)

"Finally, all of you, be like-minded, be sympathetic, love one another, be compassionate and humble." (1 Peter 3:8)

"Be kind and compassionate to one another, forgiving each other, just as in Christ God forgave you." (Ephesians 4:32)

"You, my brothers and sisters, were called to be free. But do not use your freedom to indulge the flesh; rather, serve one another humbly in love." (Galatians 5:13)

"All of you, clothe yourselves with humility toward one another, because, God opposes the proud but shows favor to the humble." (1 Peter 5:5)

"And this is His command: to believe in the name of His Son, Jesus Christ, and to love one another as He commanded us." (1 John 3:23)

When believers treat each other according to Scripture, then the safest, most encouraging, most healing, most inclusive relationships in our lives will be found in the Church.

Unfortunately, many of you became disillusioned with church because you encountered judgment, division, and conflict between believers. As a new Christian, I remember casually mentioning to a seasoned believer how I was enjoying a book written by a particular Christian author. She immediately tried to set me straight on how dangerous the book was because she didn't agree with some of the author's Biblical interpretations. She dove in, harshly attacking his character and intelligence. I thought, "Wow, you really hate him, don't you?" She said something like, "I love him in the Lord" but then continued to attack and ridicule his teaching. I guess if you say something like "I love them in the Lord," that frees you to continue despising and belittling them. I remember this incident so clearly because I was a new believer, and I was still assuming all Christians would treat one another with love and kindness.

How we treat Christians with whom we disagree is a really big deal:

"Anyone who claims to be in the light but hates a brother or sister is still in the darkness. Anyone who loves their brother and sister lives in the light, and there is nothing in them to make them stumble. But anyone who hates a brother or sister is in the darkness and walks around in the darkness. They do not know where they are going, because the darkness has blinded them." (1 John 2:9-11)

This passage should give us pause. It tells us a believer can walk in spiritual darkness. What determines whether or not we walk in darkness, is not how well we know doctrine or the Scriptures. It's determined by how well we love fellow believers. You may pride yourself in knowing theology and apologetics, but if you despise your brother or sister, you will make theological mistakes because you are walking in darkness. Of course, believers can have serious theological differences with one another. But these are to be addressed with respectful conversation, listening thoughtfully to each other. Unfortunately, too often, such conversations are replaced with personal attacks and accusations.

There's a story about evangelist D.L. Moody complaining to God about another pastor with whom he disagreed. But in the midst of his complaint, the Lord spoke up, saying, "Watch what you say! That man is the apple of my eye!" This is why a great regular prayer when disagreeing with another person is "Lord, let me see this person through Your eyes; let me see them the way You see them."

SHEPHERDING GOD'S PEOPLE

I'll close out this chapter with some thoughts about leadership in the church. As I write this, the American Church world is experiencing two more high-profile "celebrity" pastors leaving their pulpits because of sin. Many of us are feeling a "the hits just keep on coming" vibe as there has been a continual parade of churches and ministries rocked because of the sinful behavior of top leaders.

It seems God is cleaning house by exposing shepherds who have been harming the sheep. He expressed His anger at abusive shepherds in Ezekiel 34:

"This is what the Sovereign Lord says: Woe to you shepherds of Israel who only take care of yourselves! Should not shepherds take care of the flock?...You have not strengthened the weak or healed the sick or bound up the injured. You have not brought back the strays or searched for the lost. You have ruled them harshly and brutally...This is what the Sovereign Lord says: I am against the

shepherds and will hold them accountable for my flock. I will remove them from tending the flock so that the shepherds can no longer feed themselves. I will rescue my flock from their mouths, and it will no longer be food for them." (Ezekiel 34:2-10)

This passage assures us that God sees the behavior of leaders who abuse the sheep, and He will intervene to remove those shepherds. Contrast the behavior of the abusive, self-indulgent shepherds whom God confronts in Ezekiel with what Peter writes as he describes the kind of people God wants to serve as shepherds:

"Be shepherds of God's flock that is under your care, watching over them— not because you must, but because you are willing, as God wants you to be; not pursuing dishonest gain, but eager to serve; not lording it over those entrusted to you, but being examples to the flock. And when the Chief Shepherd appears, you will receive the crown of glory that will never fade away." (1 Peter 5:1-4)

"Not lording it over them"—Narcissism and abusive leadership style is a common accusation these days against pastors who are being removed from ministry. People smarter than me are saying a big part of the problem is the leadership culture found in many churches today has been adopted from the corporate world. Practices and priorities that create strong CEOs in the corporate world don't necessarily produce godly leaders for the Church. In case after case, churches and ministries have developed leadership systems that allowed narcissistic and abusive people to hold top positions and then protected those individuals from scrutiny.

It seems we should step back and reconsider what God has said about leadership in His Church. What follows are four traits from Scripture that seem foundational for everyone with leadership responsibilities in the Church. These observations might help you assess leadership as you seek a church home.

SERVANT OF ALL

First, Jesus's teaching on leadership was a radical departure from the world's practice:

"Jesus called them together and said, 'You know that those who are regarded as rulers of the Gentiles lord it over them, and their high officials exercise authority over them. Not so with you. Instead, whoever wants to become great among you must be your servant, and whoever wants to be first must be slave of all. For even the Son of Man did not come to be served, but to serve, and to give His life as a ransom for many.'" (Mark 10:42-45)

This is Jesus's primary word about leadership. We are to serve others and put them before ourselves. Jesus had authority and power over all things, but He modeled values of humility and self-sacrifice when He, the Lord of the universe, washed the feet of His disciples in John 13. After drying the last foot, He said:

"You call me Teacher and Lord, and rightly so, for that is what I am. Now that I, your Lord and Teacher, have washed your feet, you also should wash one another's feet." (John 13:13-14)

Jesus insisted that His future leaders hold the same values and practices as He did. Jesus did not use the Church for His personal gain. Instead, He sacrificed Himself for the Church:

"I am the good shepherd. The good shepherd lays down His life for the sheep." (John 10:11)

"Christ loved the church and gave Himself up for her." (Ephesians 5:25)

Humility and sacrificial love—this is Christian leadership 101. And yet, from the number of scandals exposing self-indulgent, abusive, and narcissistic behavior among top leaders in the American Church, it's apparent that even this fundamental, most basic requirement for Christian leadership has been ignored. Self-sacrificial love and humility is what Jesus, the Head of the Church, insists we bring to the table if we are to serve as shepherds and leaders in His Church.

Humility will prevail in our hearts when leaders remain aware of the honor it is to serve God's people. A story from Ronald Reagan's presidency captures this. On a hot summer day, he was seated at the famous Resolute desk in the Oval Office, signing papers and working through a large stack of documents. His chief of staff, noticing Reagan was wearing his tie and suit, and knowing he had hours of paperwork ahead, said, "Mr. President, why don't you take off your suit jacket so you can be more comfortable?" Reagan looked up at him and said, "Not in this office." President Reagan felt the weight of the heritage, the history, and the solemn responsibility of the presidency and felt that the honor of sitting at the desk in the Oval Office demanded his best efforts and his highest respect. He was serving the call; the call was not serving him. Surely if the Oval Office evokes that kind of response, then our call to serve in the footsteps of the great Shepherd demands we bring our best efforts to our responsibilities and we walk in humble gratitude for the privilege to serve His Church.

FATHERS AND MOTHERS, OR CHIEF EXECUTIVE OFFICERS?

A second trait of leaders from Scripture is how they perceive their role. The New Testament speaks of church leadership in terms of fathers and mothers. This is fitting, given the stress on the Church being a family:

"...*Just as a nursing mother cares for her children, so we cared for you. Because we loved you so much, we were delighted to share with you not only the gospel of God but our lives as well. Surely you remember, brothers and sisters, our toil and hardship; we worked night and day in order not to be a burden to anyone while we preached the gospel of God to you. For you*

know that we dealt with each of you as a father deals with his own children,
encouraging, comforting and urging you to live lives worthy of God, who
calls you into his kingdom and glory." (1 Thessalonians 2:7-9, 11-12;
emphasis mine)

Paul saw his leadership role as a parent sacrificing for his family:

"To this very hour we go hungry and thirsty, we are in rags, we are brutally
treated, we are homeless. We work hard with our own hands. When we are
cursed, we bless; when we are persecuted, we endure it; when we are slandered,
we answer kindly. We have become the scum of the earth, the garbage of the
world—right up to this moment. I am writing this not to shame you but to
warn you as my dear children. Even if you had ten thousand guardians in
Christ, you do not have many fathers, for in Christ Jesus I became your father
through the gospel." (1 Corinthians 4:11-15; emphasis mine)

If church leaders see themselves as mothers and fathers, they will
carry a vision for each person in their ministry, just as a loving parent
has hopes and dreams for each of their children. Their desire is to
see all their people walk into the destiny and identity God intends
for them. They will be focused on building people rather than a
ministry.

Furthermore, having a parental heart toward the members in churches
reduces feelings of intimidation when people with strong giftings and
abilities join. Leaders who are nurtured by the values of the corporate
world can feel pressure to be the smartest person in the room, the
most skilled person, the best communicator and so on, because it is
believed that these establish their right to lead. When others who
also have strong gifts and abilities join the church or ministry, the
newcomer can be perceived as a threat.

This is what happened to King Saul when David became popular.
After David killed the giant Goliath (see 1 Samuel 17), King Saul
brought him into the army:

"Whatever mission Saul sent him on, David was so successful that Saul gave him a high rank in the army. This pleased all the troops, and Saul's officers as well. When the men were returning home after David had killed the Philistine, the women came out from all the towns of Israel to meet King Saul with singing and dancing, with joyful songs and with timbrels and lyres. As they danced, they sang: 'Saul has slain his thousands, and David his tens of thousands.' Saul was very angry; this refrain displeased him greatly. 'They have credited David with tens of thousands,' he thought, 'but me with only thousands. What more can he get but the kingdom?' And from that time on Saul kept a close eye on David." (1 Samuel 18:5-9)

The success of David brought out the insecurities and jealousy in King Saul. These grew into open hostility and violence as Saul brought the power of his office against David. The result was diminishing authority for Saul while David grew in strength and favor. However, if Saul had seen himself as a father toward David, it would have been an entirely different story. Fathers and mothers WANT their children to do better. When your children outshine you, it's a delight to your heart, not a threat. You want them to go beyond you and achieve more. You want your ceiling to be their floor.

When we first began Agape School of Supernatural Ministry, I sensed the Lord tell me that if I would not be intimidated, He would bring people to Agape with greater gifts and abilities than my own. He wanted to entrust them to the school so they could grow and so the school could provide them a platform for their personal ministries to flourish. This would require us school leaders to not feel threatened by their gifting. Thus, at Agape, we seek to give people platforms and opportunities to shine. I see my role is to serve them and help "father" them. That approach is actually very liberating because I'm not striving to prove myself or hold onto my position.

WHAT ARE WE PASSING ON?

Consider the verse on discipleship from 2 Timothy 2:2:

"And the things you have heard me say in the presence of many witnesses entrust to reliable people who will also be qualified to teach others." (2 Timothy 2:2)

Notice how this verse traces the discipling process through four groups: Paul to Timothy to reliable people to others. Four generations, with each generation discipling the upcoming one. Do we understand the result of succeeding generations adopting the attitudes and values of the ones who went before them? If Paul felt threatened by the strengths and abilities of others, then he would choose to train disciples whose abilities would remain less than his own and who wouldn't surpass himself. Then those leaders having had that insecurity modeled before them, might do likewise, choosing people to disciple who wouldn't outshine themselves. This would result in a downward spiral in which each succeeding generation would be weaker and less capable, because insecurity and jealousy would be entrenched in the culture, controlling the selection of new leaders. However, if we have the heart of a mother or father, wanting every person to grow and surpass ourselves, and if that value is part of the ministry culture, then each generation can increase in gifting and strength in an upward spiral.

OVEREMPHASIS ON THE GIFT OF LEADERSHIP

A third trait is right sizing the function of leadership in the life of shepherds. The corporate world assumes that a successful organization will have a strong leader who drives the organization to achieve expansion goals. That assumption has been adopted in the church and ministry world. There is a current ad on Facebook directed toward church staffs, listing what are perceived to be the 97 must-read books for today's pastors. At least 90% of the books listed deal with the art of leadership, primarily books originating in the corporate world. However, when we examine Scripture, the emphasis on leadership ability seems to be understood differently. For example, there is a spiritual gift of leadership, but it is mentioned only one time in the Bible:

"We have different gifts, according to the grace given to each of us. If your gift is prophesying, then prophesy in accordance with your faith; if it is serving, then serve; if it is teaching, then teach; if it is to encourage, then give encouragement; if it is giving, then give generously; <u>if it is to lead, do it diligently</u>; if it is to show mercy, do it cheerfully." (Romans 12:6-8, emphasis mine)

This is the only place the gift of leadership is mentioned, and it isn't even clearly defined so we can only speculate what qualities the gift entails. It is curious that possessing the gift of leadership is not included in the criteria for selecting church leaders. It is not found in the lists of criteria in Acts 6, 1 Timothy 3, or Titus 1. A person will need some leadership ability to function as pastor, elder, or deacon. But a New Testament picture of church leadership is focused on other traits. Examine these three passages, which are the main compilations in the Bible, of the qualities and abilities God desires church leaders to have:

"Brothers and sisters, choose seven men from among you who are known to be full of the Spirit and wisdom. We will turn this responsibility over to them." (Acts 6:3)

"Here is a trustworthy saying: Whoever aspires to be an overseer desires a noble task. Now the overseer is to be above reproach, faithful to his wife, temperate, self-controlled, respectable, hospitable, able to teach, not given to drunkenness, not violent but gentle, not quarrelsome, not a lover of money. He must manage his own family well and see that his children obey him, and he must do so in a manner worthy of full respect. (If anyone does not know how to manage his own family, how can he take care of God's church?) He must

not be a recent convert, or he may become conceited and fall under the same judgment as the devil. He must also have a good reputation with outsiders, so that he will not fall into disgrace and into the devil's trap. In the same way, deacons are to be worthy of respect, sincere, not indulging in much wine, and not pursuing dishonest gain. They must keep hold of the deep truths of the faith with a clear conscience. They must first be tested; and then if there is nothing against them, let them serve as deacons." (1 Timothy 3:1-10)

"An elder must be blameless, faithful to his wife, a man whose children believe and are not open to the charge of being wild and disobedient. Since an overseer manages God's household, he must be blameless—not overbearing, not quick-tempered, not given to drunkenness, not violent, not pursuing dishonest gain. Rather, he must be hospitable, one who loves what is good, who is self-controlled, upright, holy and disciplined. He must hold firmly to the trustworthy message as it has been taught, so that he can encourage others by sound doctrine and refute those who oppose it."
(Titus 1:6-9)

From the criteria listed above we can see the Church was to select leaders based on matters such as character traits (such as self-control), on evidence of their personal lives being well managed, on their commitment to the Word, and on their ability to teach it. I think we need to correct the overemphasis on leadership as a function of the pastor and elder roles, and instead, increase emphasis on the Biblical criteria found in the passages above. It seems that if churches and ministries prized the qualities listed above and built leadership teams that insisted on these, then most of the failures currently rocking the church world would have been prevented.

Take, for example, the emphasis on public speaking ability in the American Church today. We find the ability to teach is included among the traits that elders and deacons need to have (see 1 Timothy 3 and Titus 1). However, the ability to speak seems to be elevated in the American Church as a primary way to select point leaders. We are convinced that great leaders are those who speak the best.

Arguably, then, neither Moses (*"I have never been eloquent...I am slow of speech and tongue."* [Exodus 4:10]), nor Paul (*"My message and my preaching were not with wise and persuasive words..."* [1 Corinthians 2:4]) would be selected by screening committees choosing leaders in today's American churches.

I made a list of nine well-known church leaders whose personal sins have recently wrecked their churches and ministries. The one thing they all have in common was their ability to deliver powerful, TED-talk quality messages. I've heard each of the nine at conferences and ministry events over the years—they all had a quick wit and held our attention with creative, inspirational sermons. However, as their dismissals from ministry show, speaking ability is not proof of godly character, and we'd be wise to right-size its importance when selecting leaders.

THE MODESTO MANIFESTO

One leader who never experienced scandal or moral failure was Billy Graham. He and his team of associates stayed together for decades and maintained a consistent reputation for moral and financial integrity. They attributed much of their success to a code of conduct they adopted in 1948 as young men starting in ministry. While conducting an evangelistic crusade in Modesto, California, the team compiled a list of guidelines they would follow in order to avoid scandal in their ministry. The result is what is known as the Modesto Manifesto. The Manifesto addresses four areas of ministry life that tend to most often lead to scandals. In our Agape school ministry, we've adopted this Manifesto as a code of conduct for ourselves, rewriting it to fit our situation:

A. MONEY AND DONATIONS
We will have in place processes and policies that will ensure all money is handled with integrity. There will be accountability in each

step. While not currently a member of ECFA (Evangelical Council for Financial Accountability, to which many of the largest North American ministries belong), we will adopt practices that adhere to their standards of conduct. (1 Timothy 6:10, 17–19; 1 Peter 5:2-3; Daniel 6:4; Psalm 112:5)

B. SEXUAL IMMORALITY

We will avoid any situation that would have even the appearance of compromise or suspicion. If married, we will not travel, meet, or eat alone with a member of the opposite sex other than our spouses. If meeting for purposes of work or ministry, we will do so in settings that are professional and safe, with full awareness of spouses and colleagues. (2 Timothy 2:22; 1 Thessalonians 4:3-4; Ephesians 5:3)

C. RELATIONSHIPS WITH OTHER MINISTRIES AND BELIEVERS

We will love our fellow believers in Jesus Christ and will strive for relationship and cooperation when possible. We will speak highly of local churches and encourage our students to continue serving their home churches. If criticized by fellow believers, we will bless publicly and refuse to take offense, choosing to either ignore criticisms or to contact them privately for discussion. Among ourselves, we will speak of other ministries, even those which oppose us or with whom we disagree, with honor and genuine love. (2 Timothy 2:24; Matthew 5:11-12, 39, 44; Romans 14:1-13)

D. PUBLICITY AND REPORTING

To earn the trust of others, our words must be consistently trustworthy. Therefore, we will show integrity in our publicity and media reports. We will not exaggerate numbers or results but will strive for accuracy in all of which we speak. We will seek to confirm the facts of any testimonies of healing, deliverance, and other reports of God's wonderful power. We will be biased toward conservative estimates. Hype, spin, and exaggeration will be avoided. (2 Corinthians 8:21; Ephesians 5:25; Proverbs 12:22)

I think it is valuable for a ministry to identify a code of behavior that the team agrees to follow, especially in this season of so many church scandals. But a code is only as effective as the willingness to follow it. In some recent high-profile moral failures, the churches had codes of conduct similar to this Manifesto, but they did not hold their point leaders accountable. They allowed a double standard of behavior, and the ministry paid the price. Some have critiqued the restrictions in the Manifesto that prevent men and women meeting alone as limiting opportunities for women to advance in responsibilities and leadership. However, if your ministry strongly values everyone fulfilling their God-ordained destiny, that everyone, men and women, be given platforms and have ceilings removed, then leaders will find ways to provide equal access while maintaining appropriate, healthy relational boundaries.

VALUING THE PRESENCE OF GOD

A fourth trait of scriptural leadership is highly valuing the Presence of God. Ultimately, ministry success in the life of church leaders is not due to personal charisma, seminary training, speaking ability, or other natural strengths. It is dependent on the presence and power of God in the life of the leader.

Jesus, speaking to the future leaders of His church told them, *"I am the vine; you are the branches. If you remain in Me and I in you, you will bear much fruit; apart from Me you can do nothing."* (John 15:5, emphasis mine)

Jesus's words here should prompt a leadership style that radically prioritizes prayer, waiting on God, listening to Him, and seeking Him. Jesus wants the leaders in His church truly dependent on Him. Jesus told these same people not to go out and launch ministry in their own strength, according to their own good ideas. He told them to wait:

"I am going to send you what my Father has promised; but stay in the city until you have been clothed with power from on high." (Luke 24:49)

"...He gave them this command: 'Do not leave Jerusalem, but wait for the gift My Father promised, which you have heard Me speak about. For John baptized with water, but in a few days you will be baptized with the Holy Spirit.'" (Acts 1:4-5)

Jesus told disciples to wait until they were filled with the Presence of the Holy Spirit. Don't we who serve as leaders in churches today need the same dependence on God? Ministry training and instruction is helpful, but these were never intended to take the place of our dependence on the Holy Spirit. Spiritual power is not found in our degrees or our titles; it's found in Him. Unfortunately, especially here in the West, we've developed theologies that quiet the Holy Spirit's voice and have replaced supernatural direction, power, and presence with systems and processes birthed in the corporate world.

Two passages speak of Jesus's Presence with us:

"And surely I am with you always, to the very end of the age." (Matthew 28:20)

"After the Lord Jesus had spoken to them, He was taken up into heaven and He sat at the right hand of God. Then the disciples went out and preached everywhere, and the Lord worked with them and confirmed His word by the signs that accompanied it."
(Mark 16:19-20)

When Jesus says, "I am with you always," He didn't intend that to merely be a comfort in hard times, but He intended church leaders to look to Him for direction and help in all of their ministry, working in partnership with Him. Church leadership in the Bible is marked by an ongoing dependence on God. So, when assessing a church, it is appropriate to ask if the pastors, staff, elders, and leadership team are walking in dependence on God. Are they intimate friends with God, pressing into Him, growing in hearing His voice and making decisions and taking risks that are prompted by Him?

This is a big deal because people will rise to the spiritual temperature of their leaders. Hebrews 13 tells people to look to their leaders as examples: *"Remember your leaders, who spoke the word of God to you. Consider the outcome of their way of life and imitate their faith"* (Hebrews 13:7). May they see leaders who live not only lives that are holy and honorable, but also lives that demonstrate a surrendered dependence on God, listening for His voice, taking risks, and performing exploits in response to the Holy Spirit.

ACTIVATION

If you have not yet found a church home, then pray and ask Jesus to lead you to the people He has for you. If wounds and disappointment from past church experiences are preventing you from moving forward, then address these, perhaps walking through the healing process found in Chapter 7.

Jesus does not want you to live a solo Christian life, but satan will work to keep you isolated and alone. That's how he destroys believers. *"...Your enemy the devil prowls around like a roaring lion looking for someone to devour"* (1 Peter 5:8). Lions kill their prey by first isolating them from the rest of the herd.

Pray and believe Jesus will lead you to a church home. It might be a small group of people meeting in a kitchen, or it might be a typical church that meets on Sunday morning.

Go through the verses in this chapter and identify the traits and qualities of churches that are especially important to you and ask the Lord to lead you to a church home that is manifesting those qualities.

SUGGESTED READING

Ford, Lance. *The Atlas Factor*. Richmond, Virginia: 100 Movements Publishing, 2024.
(Ford challenges how church leadership is perceived and practiced in the American Church. He calls the Church back to a New Testament understanding of leadership.)

Johnson, Bill. *When Heaven Invades Earth*. Shippensburg, Pennsylvania: Destiny Image, 2005. *(I first read this book in 2005 and was profoundly changed by it. Johnson challenges us to church ministry that is Holy Spirit-dependent.)*

Silk, Danny, *Culture of Honor*. Shippensburg, Pennsylvania: Destiny Image, 2009.
(Speaks to how church members should relate to one another. One of our texts at Agape.)

Silvoso, Ed. *Ekklesia*. Bloomington, Minnesota: Chosen Books, 2017.
(Explains in greater detail the meaning of "Ekklesia" and how it changes our understanding of church.)

For those living in the Peoria, Illinois, area, consider enrolling at
AGAPE SCHOOL OF SUPERNATURAL MINISTRY

Empowering Christians to reach their full potential through understanding their new identity and destiny.

Directors Bob See and Ryan Foster

"Agape SSM takes sheep, turns them into lions and gives them a territory."
Pastor Stifan Sanganahalli

Go to *agapessm.com* for information.

If you are interested in bringing an Agape ministry team to minister in healing and evangelism at your church or group, please contact us at *agapessm.com*.

Printed in the United States
by Baker & Taylor Publisher Services